The Six Panics And Other Essays

Hirst, Francis Wrigley, 1873-1953

THE SIX PANICS

THE SIX PANICS

AND OTHER ESSAYS

BY

F. W. HIRST

METHUEN & CO. LTD.
36 ESSEX STREET W.C.
LONDON
1913

First Published in 1913

PREFACE

MY object in writing "The Six Panics' has been not so much to prevent the recurrence of false alarms in the sensational press—for no reasonable man can hope to do that—as to prevent the abominable waste of public money in which a successful panic always ends. It is all-important that the governing classes and the leading statesmen, who are trustees for the nation and for the public funds, should feel ashamed of the hoax which has now been practised upon them so often. If this little book serves to supply them with a defensive armour against the arrows of future panic-mongers, I shall be very well satisfied. In some of the shorter essays I have touched upon other matters which have interested me in the last few years.

Certain portions have already appeared in the *Economist* or elsewhere, but I thought it worth while to take this opportunity of revising and collecting them.

F. W. HIRST

London, *July* 1913

CONTENTS

THE SIX PANICS

ON PANICS IN GENERAL

DR. JOHNSON defines "panick" as a sudden fright without cause. The ancient Greeks attributed such alarms to the action of the God Pan, calling them Pan's frights, or simply Panics, whence our early scholars transplanted the word to English soil. Phidippides on his famous run from Athens to Sparta met Pan, who complained (so Herodotus tells us) that his worship was neglected by the Athenians, though he had often done them a good turn, and would gladly do them another in the future. The hint was taken, and according to another legend the god made good his word at Marathon by causing a panic among the Persians.

In a city, or in an army, panic may grow out of a mere rumour. It is part of the psychology of crowds that their emotions and fears can easily be aroused and quickly wrought upon. But a nation is not a crowd. To evoke a national panic in a modern state is a very difficult operation. An army may fling down its arms and run away *en masse*. A false cry of fire in a crowded meeting or theatre may cause a general rush to the doors. But a whole nation cannot be fooled by a false report. You cannot imagine all the towns and villages of England, Ireland, Scotland, and Wales reduced to a state of terror by a stage whisper, even though it ran through the whole of the newspaper press. If Gladstone and Bright and General Booth had combined with Stead and the Jingoes in 1884, something worthy of Pan might have ensued. But under less favourable circumstances the semblance of a panic may be created even in an educated country like ours—enough, let us say, to increase the sale of newspapers, guns and stores, battleships or flying machines. What the newspapers can do, and what they cannot do, in this field is worth ascertaining and describing. The modern newspaper panic is a phenomenon of which every intelligent reader must be more or less conscious. Men still alive can remember the last of the French Invasion panics, and so are able to compare the impressions made on the public mind and public policy in the early sixties with those produced by the German Invasion panics which have flourished since the Boer War. One thing not generally noticed certainly deserves attention. The fuss and fury of of our yellow press, though it thrill smart society in London, though it may sway the minds and policy of Ministers, produces no proportionate effect on the individual citizen. Blood-curdling reports and rumours, backed by the gloomiest forecasts of veteran soldiers and sailors, do not destroy our national composure. On the Continent during the Morocco crisis and again during the Balkan War, when Austria and Russia stood for weeks at daggers-drawn, thousands of quiet and sensible people in France, Germany, and Austria drew their deposits out of the banks and hoarded gold. Traders reduced their commitments, and people near the frontier made preparations to remove their households and belongings into the interior. But in this little island, even at times when —to judge from speeches and pamphlets and leading articles—invasion, starvation, and utter destruction were imminent, the Englishman remained in his home perfectly calm and inactive. The panic swept in large headlines across his breakfast-table ; but he went in to business as if no calamity were impending. The idea of drawing out his deposits or preparing to bolt from the coast to the interior never entered his mind. He persisted in buying and selling and speculating as if the French or German menace were negligible. He never thought of suspending business relations with the countries whose armies and navies were about to be launched in deadly earnest against the British Empire. In short, his actions proved that he did not believe all that he was told. This is worth remembering; for we are always over-apt to confuse the minds and opinions of our people with the nonsense they have to read. Perhaps the foundation of English panics like those I am to describe is laid in the love of excitement and in the natural pugnacity of our countrymen rather than in any propensity to unreasoning fear; for no race, I believe, is more plentifully endowed than ours with courage and common sense.

Judged by this test of individual action the last real panic in England came in 1866 after the fall of Overend & Co. The popular instinct of self-preservation took the form of a run on the banks. Every failure increased the desire for cash and weakened credit. Bagehot watched the symptoms of the malady and prescribed the remedy. "A panic," he said, "is a species of neuralgia, and according to the rules of science you must not starve it." Therefore when the public "goes for gold" those who hold the cash reserves must advance freely on good securities. The armour-plate interests would say by false analogy that the way to cure a naval panic is to advance Dreadnoughts freely on credit.

But America is the classical home of commercial and financial panics. Since 1907 Americans have come to regard a collapse of credit with a suspension of cash payments by the banks as an inseparable sequel to every great outburst of prosperity and speculation. "In Wall Street," writes Mr. Van Antwerp, a lettered and ingenious member of the New York Stock Exchange, "the question is ever in mind as to the next panic. The last one left its sting; we are interested now in knowing about the future. Have we learned how to avoid these difficulties? May we hope to diminish their force and mitigate their terrors? May we rely upon the superior organisation of business and the greater quantity and quality of capital to soften the effect of the next shock? We may lull ourselves into a coma of fancied security as we reflect upon experience and its expensive lessons, but we deceive ourselves if we think that we shall finally arrive at a point where these convulsions shall cease." Our author consoles himself and his countrymen with the flattering paradox of a Frenchman: "the riches of nations can be measured by the violence of the crises they experience." A people with a healthy, vigorous, mobile life, we are told, is bound to be impatient. From time to time it must advance too fast. Over-confidence leads to over-speculation. At last credit topples over, and society rushes into the banks for national bank-notes, greenbacks, silver certificates, or cash of any description. Seen through Wall Street spectacles, "a panic is a state of mind. It cannot be regulated by statute law nor preached down by press or pulpit. At such times suspicion, apprehension and alarm take possession ; reflection and sobriety are crowded out ; men do and say irrational and unreasoning things ; incidents trifling in themselves are exaggerated into undue proportions ; all kinds of difficulties are conjured into the imagination." One might pause to criticise this theory. American finance is a tempting theme. But I must not digress any further. I will merely express my own conviction that Bagehot would have prescribed even for an American panic ; for I cannot think that a civilised country, however prosperous, need tolerate or regard as inevitable periodic suspensions of cash payments by its banks or Trust Companies.

The Six Panics of which this essay treats covered a period of sixty-six years ; but there was a long interval of twenty-three years between the Third and the Fourth, which must be attributed in large part to Cobden's scathing exposure of the first three, with the restraining influence exerted over public opinion and government after his death by Gladstone and Bright, as well as by the moderate and genuinely conservative views of Lord Salisbury. Why their successors have pandered to the guilty passion for naval and military extravagance is one of the political puzzles of our time. If men of light and leading and resolution can find the answer in these pages

they will be on the road to a remedy. For the
modern problem of armaments, most perplexing and
menacing of all the evils which humanity imposes
on itself, we can offer no simple or single-handed
solution. But no one who labours to reveal the
hidden interests, the secret motives, the unseen causes,
the invisible wires and all the stage machinery of
what has well been called " The Great Illusion,"
need fear that his labour will go unrewarded. He
is the happiest of all courtiers—the courtier of
Truth, a sovereign who requires no servility and
dispenses no patronage.

THE FIRST PANIC, 1847–1848

THIS panic was begun late in the year 1847 by
the unauthorised publication in the *Times* of a
letter from the aged Duke of Wellington. It was
addressed to a brother officer, and afforded " painful
evidence of enfeebled powers." Two years previously
Lord Palmerston, after declaring (falsely) that the
French fleet was equal to ours, had gone on to say that
the Channel is no longer a barrier : " Steam navigation
has rendered that which was before impassable by a
military force nothing more than a river passable by
a steam bridge." The Duke improved on this in his
letter as follows : " I am accustomed to the consideration of these questions, and have examined and
reconnoitred over and over again, the whole coast
from the North Foreland, by Dover, Folkestone
Beachy Head, Brighton, Arundel to Selsey Bill, near
Portsmouth ; and I say that excepting immediately
under the fire of Dover Castle, there is not a spot
on the coast, from the North Foreland to Selsey
Bill, on which infantry might not be thrown on

8

shore at any time of tide with any wind and in any weather."

These categorical statements were accepted as gospel by people who had no means of knowing the truth, though from the pen of any other person than the great Duke they would have provoked contemptuous incredulity. In December and January the Duke of Wellington's alarm was echoed widely in the newspapers, not always by wholly disinterested parties. "At the end of 1847," said Cobden in the House of Commons (February 26, 1849), "we had a panic among us, and we were then persuaded by Mr. Pigou the gunpowder maker that the French were actually coming to attack us." The Panic ended dramatically. Lord John Russell was Chancellor of the Exchequer, and the Budget he produced on February 18, 1848, raised the Income Tax from sevenpence to a shilling in the pound, in order to increase armaments and to reorganise the militia in accordance with the Duke of Wellington's advice. When this stiff addition to taxation came into view, in association with preparations against the danger of invasion, the danger seemed to diminish and the panic abated. Public meetings of protest were called. Men of all parties joined to denounce the proposal, and to demand instead a reduction of public expenditure. Petitions poured in, until on February 28th Lord John Russell withdrew his Budget and left the

Income Tax at sevenpence. A touch of burlesque, as Cobden remarks, was imparted to the closing scene of the first invasion panic by the abdication and flight from France of Louis Philippe, the dread Monarch who was to have invaded and conquered England. A Committee of the House of Commons was appointed to recommend reductions in military and naval expenditure, and the Queen's Speech of 1849 (ignoring the revolutionary tumults and wars which convulsed the Continent) contained a gratifying announcement : " the present aspect of affairs has enabled me to make large reductions on the estimates of last year."

THE SECOND PANIC, 1851–1853

THE reductions thus dramatically begun continued till 1852. "During this time," wrote
Cobden, "with the exception of the usual letters from
Admiral Napier [1] in the *Times* on the state of the
Navy and a volume published at the close of 1850 by
Sir Francis Head on 'The Defenceless State of the
Nation,' which was calculated to throw ridicule on
the subject by its exaggerations, little was said about
a French invasion. Even the Great Duke's letter
was for a time forgotten. But only for a time : the
occasion alone was wanting to revive the panic with
increased violence. The country had been rapidly
advancing to that state of prosperity in which its
timidity and pugnacity seem equally susceptible of
excitement." The *coup d'état* of December 2, 1851,
and the re-election of Louis Napoleon as President
of the Republic, furnished the occasion. It was now
discovered that Louis Philippe, the ogre of the first
panic, had been a peaceful quietist, a complete con-

[1] The Lord Charles Beresford of those days.

trast to Napoleon, around whose terrifying personality the new alarms gathered. Throughout December and January in preparation for the meeting of Parliament on February 3rd the London newspapers teemed with invectives against the French President and the French people. The cries of invasion were renewed, with declarations of our defenceless condition. " At the same time there was the usual eruption of pamphlets, written chiefly by military and naval officers, containing projects for every variety of defensive armament." In the debate on the Address (February 3, 1852) the Earl of Derby remarked on the madness of accusing a neighbouring nation of hostile intentions, vituperating the head of their executive, and at the same time declaring publicly how easily an invasion could be carried out. Simultaneously the Prime Minister, Lord John Russell, remarked in the House of Commons : " Really, to hear or read some of the letters, some of the language used by some portion of the press, one would imagine that these two great nations, so wealthy, so similar in enlightenment, were going to butcher one another, merely to try what would be the effect of percussion caps and needle guns." Nevertheless—although in the three previous years French naval strength whether measured by men, by ships in commission, or by expenditure, had been less than in any three previous years since 1840—

both Derby and Russell spoke of increased preparation with a view to make invasion impossible. On
February 16th Russell introduced a Bill for the
enlargement of the militia, but was defeated on an
amendment moved by Palmerston to enlarge its
scope. Derby then came into power, and after
asserting that "our naval forces were never in a
better or more effective condition," proceeded to
introduce a Militia Bill which received Palmerston's
approval. To carry such a Bill it was necessary to
spread belief in a sudden surprise attack on a large
scale. Accordingly Palmerston once more assured
the House of Commons that steam had bridged the
Channel, and that fifty or sixty thousand men could
be transported without notice from Cherbourg to our
shores in a single night. This absurd hypothesis, as
Cobden remarks, was indispensable to afford standing
ground for the Second Panic. A leading general
pointed out that "the sudden arrival of a French
army in this metropolis was simply an impossibility."
A leading admiral reminded the House that Palmerston had not told them how this army was to be
transported across the Channel in face of a superior
navy: "It would take fifty or sixty vessels to
embark those men he spoke of as being ready for
action at Cherbourg, and it would take as many
more vessels to protect them in the Channel. With
a fleet of thirty steamers in the Channel he (Admiral

Berkeley) would defy any enemy to attempt a surprise, and should like to see them attempt to disembark on our shores in the face of such a force."[1] But Palmerston with characteristic effrontery persisted that "the very ship despatched to convey to this country intelligence of the threatened armament would probably not reach our shores much sooner than the hostile expedition." At that time (when steam had bridged the Channel!) our superiority in merchant steamers over France was as twenty to one, our superiority in sailing vessels being only five to one. But in spite of the plain facts there was enough panic in the air of London to float Palmerston's theory of a nocturnal invasion; and the Militia Bill (unaccompanied this time by additions to the Income Tax) passed through all its stages. The Militia Bill, indeed, was unpopular. Eight hundred petitions were presented against it and not one in its favour. It was opposed by most of the members representing the great centres of industry. The panic was a newspaper panic, which worked on the House of Commons and the Ministry through London Society —one of the first but by no means the last of its kind. Old Joseph Hume, the veteran economist, remarked in one of the debates: "Our present panics are not due as in times past to the old women, but to our having too many clubs about London, containing

---

[1] Hansard, vol. 120, pp. 1136–7.

so many half-pay officers, who have nothing to do but to look about for themselves and their friends. These are the people who write to the newspapers anxious to bring grist to the mill somehow or other."

After the passing of the Militia Bill Parliament was dissolved (July 1, 1852), and before the new Parliament assembled there occurred two imposing events, the death of the Duke of Wellington in September, and in November the *plébiscite* by which Prince Louis Napoleon was chosen Emperor of the French. The former filled the public mind with recollections of the glories and horrors of the old wars. By the latter, says Cobden, "the traditional terror connected with the name of Bonaparte was revived; people began again to talk of invasion, and before Christmas the alarmists had more complete possession of the field than at any previous time."[1]

At the beginning of December, 1852, Napoleon accepted the title of Emperor. In announcing this in the Lords, Lord Malmesbury made a most sensible and pacific speech, but the Government proposed at the same time in the Commons an addition of 5,000 seamen and 1,500 marines to the navy in order to "man the Channel with a larger force." The Secretary of the Admiralty asked for the money as a

[1] The *Times* Annual Summary for 1852 describes with equal eloquence the unscrupulous ambition of Napoleon, the restoration of our defences and the final explosion of the dogma of Protection.

vote of confidence in the Executive, pretending that his Government was "in the possession of secret and important intelligence." On this use of the confidence trick Cobden remarks that it involved a double fallacy: (1) That there was or could be any such secret and important intelligence ; and (2) That if there were the mischief of referring to it was less than the mischief of disclosing it. The proposed increase was carried without a division, but when Disraeli, the Chancellor of the Exchequer, went from expenditure to taxation, his Budget was defeated and the Peelite administration of Lord Aberdeen came into office. The panic, which had begun, as we have seen, in 1851, lasted into the summer of 1853, unallayed either by our own increase of armaments or by the failure of the French Government to respond. There was a large output of pamphlets with such titles as "The Peril of Portsmouth," and the newspaper press was busy in a fashion very familiar to us now. In Cobden's words :—

"The alarm was constantly stimulated by startling paragraphs in the newspapers. One day the French army at Rome was reported to be chafing and dissatisfied, because it could not share in the invasion of England and the sack of London : the next, there were whispered revelations of a secret plan, divulged by General Changarnier, for invading England and seizing the metropolis (which he publicly contradicted) : then we were told of a plot for securing a naval station in the West Indies : next, the French Government had sent an order for steam frigates to Messrs. Napier, of Glasgow (which was contradicted on the authority of those gentlemen) : there was a cry of alarm at the apparition of a French ship-of-war at Dover, which, it afterwards turned out, had been driven in by stress of weather : then there were small French vessels of war seen moving about the Isle of Wight, to the surprise of some of our authorities, who should have known that the French Government are bound by convention to send cruisers into the Channel, to see that the fisheries regulations are observed by their fishermen ; and then came the old story of French vessels being seen taking soundings in our waters, though, as everybody knows, the most perfect charts of the Channel, published under the authority of the Admiralty, may be purchased for a few shillings."

As a matter of fact the French army had been reduced by 50,000 men, and French naval expenditure had been unusually low—less than $3\frac{1}{2}$ millions sterling—for three years running—1850–1852.   In only one of the previous sixteen years had France so few ships in commission as in the year 1851, when this second panic commenced. The *Times*, then at the zenith of its glory, and far more powerful than all the other London papers put together, took a prominent part in misleading the public; but at length its virulent attacks on Napoleon produced uneasiness among the merchants and bankers of the City, who convened a meeting " to express their deep concern at witnessing the endeavours continually made to create and perpetuate feelings of mistrust, ill-will and hostility between the inhabitants of the two great nations of England and France."   They even despatched a deputation of leading citizens to carry a friendly address to the French Emperor.

A dramatic turn of events converted the whole fashionable world of England from a French Panic to a French Alliance. Those who, in the spring of 1853, most furiously denounced the French Emperor, began to court him in the autumn, and clamorously urged that the fleet and army, which had been preparing to resist a French invasion of England, should join in an Anglo-French invasion of Russia. To mark the monstrous inconsistency of public feeling and the levity of those who manufactured it, Cobden supposed an invalid to have been ordered for the benefit of his health to make the voyage to Australia and back :—

"He left England in the month of February or March. The Militia was preparing for duty; the coasts and dock-yards were being fortified ; the navy, army, and artillery were all in course of augmentation ; inspectors of artillery and cavalry were reported to be busy on the southern coasts ; deputations from railway companies, it was said, had been waiting on the Admiralty and Ordnance, to explain how rapidly the commissariat and military stores could be transported from the Tower to Dover or Portsmouth; and the latest paragraph of news from the Continent was that our neighbours, on the other side of the Channel, were practising the embarkation and disembarkation of troops by night. He left home amidst all these alarms and preparations for a French invasion. After an absence of four or five months, during which time he had no opportunity of hearing more recent news from Europe, he steps on shore at Liverpool, and the first newspaper he sees informs him that the English and French fleets are lying side by side in Besika Bay. An impending naval engagement between the two powers is naturally the idea that first occurs to him ; but, glancing at the leading article of the journal, he learns that England and France have entered into an alliance, and that they are on the eve of commencing a sanguinary war against Russia !"

So ended the Second Panic.

THE THIRD PANIC, 1859–1861

IT has been seen how quickly the directors of military and naval sentiment in England diverted fashion from France to Russia, and how readily a noisy and unthinking section of the public, which they are accustomed to dupe, embraced the French invader as a brother in arms. Those who exist for war, and those who thrive by war, always insist on having some formidable enemy who is on the point of attacking us in time of peace. The function of the Foreign Office on their view is to maintain friction with a suitable Power; but if an opportunity offers, as it did in 1853–4, they are ready in a moment to surrender the potential enemy for the sake of a real war, with a tacit understanding that old animosities may be resumed for armament purposes on the conclusion of peace. In the spring of 1856, at the end of the Crimean War, a grand naval review was held at Spithead. On May 8, 1856, Lord Palmerston and the Earl of Derby boasted that no country had ever possessed so mighty an armament. " We had," said Palmerston, "at the beginning of the war a total force of 212 ships, and at the end of the war we have 590." The increase was chiefly in gunboats and mortar-vessels, which were described by the First Lord of the Admiralty as not only useful in attack but "a valuable and effective armament for protecting our shores from assault." For the moment large ships were out of fashion. We commenced the Crimean War, as Captain Scobell observed, with large ships; "and it was only after two years' experience that we discovered the gunboat tribe. If some time ago"— referring to Admiral Napier's fiasco—"we had had this magnificent fleet of gunboats, something would have been done in the Baltic which would have been remembered for centuries."[1] The Russian fleet in the Black Sea which had been used to justify naval expenditure in 1852, was now sunk. Nevertheless the First Lord, on May 18, 1857, introduced navy estimates higher than ever before in time of peace, justifying them by reference to the French navy, which he said was nearly equal to ours in line-of-battle ships and frigates. They had of the first built and building 40 to our 42, and of the second 37 to our 42. The First Lord disparaged the gunboats, etc., of which he had made so much a year before, and omitted 9 screw block-ships which were among the most effective of our large vessels. The

[1] See Hansard, vol. 142, pp. 1423 and 1425.

French official list of battleships was 31, as furnished by the Minister of Marine. Sir Charles Napier, undaunted by his failure before Cronstadt, accepted the Admiralty figures, ignored block-ships and gunboats, and renewed the old scare. "France is equal to us in ships, but superior in the means of manning them. She has an army of 300,000 or 400,000 men, and we have but 20,000 in Great Britain. What would the consequence be if war were to spring up? Why, there would be an invasion immediately." And he declared a little later that we were "no longer the first naval nation in the world."[1] In view of the extent to which the writings and popular speeches of Admiral Sir Charles Napier contributed to the creation of invasion panics Cobden makes the following remarks, which, with a little change, might be applied to some of our contemporary heroes :—

"On his return to the House of Commons, after being superseded in the command of the Baltic fleet, during the Crimean War, he became possessed by a morbid apprehension, amounting almost to a state of monomania, respecting the threatening attitude of France and our insufficient means of defence. It was not peculiar to his case, for it is common to all who share his delusion about the danger of an invasion, that he always lost sight of all that was already done, and called for something else as the sole means of security. Thus, he demanded more line-of-battle ships, and ignored the existence of the new force of small vessels; then he called for a Channel fleet, whilst he threw contempt on the

[1] Hansard, vol. 145, pp. 434 and 770.

block-ships ; when the Channel fleet was completed, he declared that the crews were in mutiny from mismanagement ; when the number of line-of-battle ships was so great as to extort from him expressions of satisfaction, he asked what was the use of ships without seamen ; when the number of seamen voted for our royal navy exceeded that of the entire sea-going population of France, he called aloud for a reserve ; and when he had been triumphant in all his demands, he reverted to the opinion, which he had been one of the first to proclaim, that the whole navy must be reconstructed, for that 'a broadside from the modern shell guns would tear holes in the sides of our wooden ships through which it would be easy to drive a wheel-barrow.'"

According to Napier, France was always preparing to invade us and was always increasing her armaments enormously. To those who sat near him in the House he would almost predict the very month when the French might be expected in England :—

"Cherbourg had been always described by him as the chief source of our danger, until the great public visit to that port dispelled the phantom-ships with which he had been haunted ; but still he would expatiate on the facilities which its enormous docks and basins offered for embarking an army ; declaring on one occasion that 'the troops could walk on board ; *cavalry, mounted on their horses, could ride on board ;* and artillery could easily be shipped, for thirty sail-of-the-line could lie alongside of the wharves alone.' Notwithstanding that he drew on himself occasionally the censure of his brother officers for disparaging our naval strength, and was more than once rebuked for encouraging insubordination among the seamen, he still persevered ; and such is the force of reiteration, that he was at last justified in the boast that, although 'he had been called an alarmist, and laughed at for many years on that account, he had lived to see his views adopted.'"[1]

The fact seems to be that "his nerves were completely gone." This was the official explanation given for Napier's removal from the chief command in the Baltic, and this explains his obsession about a French invasion when in other respects his intellectual and rhetorical powers remained unimpaired. Cobden observes that old age is often accompanied by decrepitude in one particular quality such as nerve or courage. "The very faculty for which a man is most distinguished may, by an excessive and continued strain, be the first to give way." The moral for statesmen and publicists is clear: it should teach charity in weighing the motives of veteran panic-mongers and at the same time warn us against accepting from the timidity of age counsels of extravagance which would be ridiculed if they were offered by the rash inexperience of youth. It happened however that in 1857 and 1858 the statesmen in power were not disposed to launch out on panicky preparations. The Manchester School, under the leadership of Cobden and Bright, exercised a strong influence, and its doctrines of public economy were widely held. At the commencement of the session in 1857, Disraeli, who led the Tory party in the Commons, moved resolutions aiming at a

[1] See Cobden's "Third Panic" and Hansard, vol. 156, p. 989.

reduction in the scale of expenditure. " I cannot but believe," he said, " that if these resolutions are carried we shall witness some beneficial changes in the financial system of this country. I think we shall give a great impulse to salutary economy, and shall in a most significant manner express our opinion that it is not advisable that England should become what is called a great military nation. I am not afraid to express the old fashioned opinion that a standing army is dangerous to the liberties of this country. I know that we must have troops. We have had an army of which every man has reason to be proud, and I wish to see that army maintained in its spirit and efficiency. What we want are scientific officers, and that the machinery of our militia shall be nurtured and maintained in efficiency. For the rest we may trust to the resources of the country, which will increase in proportion as we reduce its taxation. . . . I hope that the glory of the late war and the, if possible, greater glories of wars to come will not induce the people of this country to sanction extravagant military establishments. I will express my opinion that with due economy and with able administration the more you reduce the burdens of the people the greater will be your strength when the hour of danger comes." [1]

Cobden, Gladstone and Lord John Russell sup-

[1] See Hansard, vol. 144, pp. 106–35.

ported these views, the last-named statesman putting
the case against war expenditure in time of peace
with great earnestness and power. He argued that
the English system, endorsed by Pitt, of keeping
low establishments in time of peace had proved a
source not only of wealth but of military and naval
strength to the country :—

"We have thus been enabled to secure a surplus revenue,
to reduce taxes and abolish customs duties which pressed
upon the energies and checked the industry of the people ;
we have enabled our population to grow rich ; and we have
seen in the last [the Crimean] war what that wealth was
able to effect ; for when our enemy was exhausted, and our
Ally was so far weakened in its finances that its war spirit
flagged, the Government of this country found that, owing to
our wealth, we had more than sufficient to pay for the large
expenditure of the war ; and the spirit of our people, if terms
of peace had not been accepted, was such that for five, six,
or ten years longer, if necessary, we might have made the
exertions necessary for war. Now these are the things which
produce good terminations of wars, and not large and expensive establishments, with generals and admirals growing so
old that they are unfit for their duties when war comes.
It is by moderate establishments, by rendering such establishments good and efficient, by attending to everything which
cannot easily be originated or replaced ; it is by such a system,
and by relying on the greatness of the country and on the
spirit of our people, that you will be most formidable in
war, and not by any new fangled system of increased estimates during a time of peace."

This powerful and combined attack had its effect,
and even the most virulent panic-mongers in parlia-

ment and the press were deterred from stirring up mischief in Europe by the great mutiny which threatened us with the loss of India. It is true that this catastrophe and the China War provided Napoleon the Third with an ideal opportunity for executing the design with which our alarmists credited him. But the Emperor, instead of conquering England, offered a passage through France to the troops we sent out to suppress the mutiny. Early in 1858 Lord Palmerston's Government fell, and that of Lord Derby succeeded. In spite of Sir Charles Napier's efforts—the House of Commons only laughed at his picture of a Russian fleet coming up the Channel [1]—the Navy Estimates went through quietly. The chief feature was Lord Clarence Paget's shrewd warning against wooden three-deckers and the pig-headed determination of the Admiralty, influenced perhaps by the vested interests, to continue expending money on the construction of a type which was already superseded by the invention of iron armour.

In 1859 peace being restored the panic-mongers renewed their activity in the press by describing naval preparations in France. But they produced little effect, says Cobden, on the public mind. Unlike its predecessors, the Third Panic "had its

[1] June 11, 1858, "What would become of the Funds God only knew," cried the gallant sailor.

origin chiefly in elevated and official circles." What motives were at work cannot easily be guessed. "Viewed in the light of facts," writes Cobden, the tone of excitement and alarm which pervaded the First Lord's statement (February 25, 1859) "becomes simply incomprehensible." The French Panic of 1859 is indeed only comparable in size of superstructure and absence of foundation with the German Panic of 1909, which I shall try to describe later on.

What were the facts?

In 1858 the total expenditure on the British Navy was £10,029,000, on the French £5,337,000. The expenditure on wages in dockyards was £991,000 against £640,000. The seamen of our navy numbered 55,883 against 29,602 in the French Navy. An official report in the hands of the Government (but not published till a year later) showed that since 1852 British ships in commission had risen from 203 to 267 and that over 11,000 men had been added to the fleet, whereas the French ships in commission had fallen from 175 to 152, and only 768 men had been added to the establishment.

Such being the state of the case what did the First Lord of the Admiralty, Sir John Pakington, ask and say?

He asked for an addition of £1,200,000 to the

shipbuilding vote and proposed to raise the *personnel* to 62,400—the largest number ever maintained during peace. He declared that on succeeding to office he did not find the navy " in a proper and adequate state for the defence of our coasts and the protection of our commerce," added that its strength did not exceed that of a neighbouring power, and invited the House of Commons to "aid him in his attempt to restore the naval supremacy of England." This mendacity was accompanied not for the last time by prophecy. He predicted that at the end of 1859 France would have 40 line-of-battle ships against our 36. Two years later, after the forecast had served its purpose, a Secretary of the Admiralty admitted in the House of Commons that France even then had only 37 line-of-battle ships *built and building*.[1] Such however was the impression produced by Sir John Pakington's statements and forecasts, enhanced by an appropriate air of mystery, that the House of Commons offered no opposition to his proposal to add 26 men of war to the navy in one year.[2] Those who wish to study the two fleets in detail will turn to Cobden's analysis and Busk's useful work on *The Navies of the World*. Cobden came to the conclusion that the superiority of the British over the French Navy, great as it was, would have

[1] See Hansard for April 11, 1861.
[2] Hansard, vol. 152, p. 942.

been considerably greater but for the bad financial management of our Admiralty and "the waste of money, which is always going on in this country upon unnecessary and useless constructions." Possibly an apprehension that popular criticism might be directed against itself induced the British Admiralty on this occasion to work up feeling against the French Government and to make it appear that the French Admiralty had been spending secretly enormous sums on shipbuilding. The fact is that the period from 1852 to 1858 was one of transition from sailing ships to steam vessels, as the following period was one of transition from wooden ships to ironclads. The French had been spending their money in converting old sailing ships into steamers, while we had spent ours mostly on new construction. According to the Official Report previously referred to "the cost of converting a line-of-battle ship of 90 guns is estimated at £25,000, and the cost of building the same at £105,000; but the latter will of course be a far more efficient and durable vessel." The results were as follows: In 1852 Britain had 94 line-of-battle ships, of which 21 were steam and 73 sailing; France, 6 steam and 45 sailing. In 1858 Britain had 35 sailing to 10 French, and 59 steam to French 40. In the same year we had 464 steam vessels of all sizes to 264 French. But considering that materials, machinery, etc., were 30 per cent.

cheaper in France than England, the comparison of results proved " an enormous amount of misapplied capital and labour in our dockyards." [1]

The debates on the Navy Estimates of 1857 to 1859 are used by Cobden to illustrate the dramatic transformation of opinion which sometimes follows removal from office to opposition and vice versa :—

" On the 18th May, 1857, Sir Charles Wood, the First Lord, in bringing forward the Navy Estimates, stated that France had forty and England forty-two screw-liners. On the 12th April, 1858, Sir John Pakington who had just succeeded to the office of First Lord, alluding to this statement of his predecessor, said—' it was not fair to exclude the block-ships, as you must do when you say that you have only two line-of-battle ships more than the French.' On the 25th February, 1859, Sir John Pakington, in moving his Navy Estimates, stated that France had twenty-nine, and England had also twenty-nine screw line-of-battle ships, totally omitting the block-ships. On the 6th of April following, Sir Charles Wood, then in opposition, reminded the First Lord of this omission, and contended that the block-ships were good and efficient for the defence of the coast."

---

[1] In a debate on the Navy Estimates of 1859, Mr. Bentinck said he had asked many of the most eminent owners of private yards in Great Britain, " Supposing you were to carry on your yards upon the system on which Her Majesty's dockyards are conducted, what would be the result?" The invariable answer was : " If we were to approach that system with the Bank of England at our back we should be ruined in six months." The whole debate raised by Lord Clarence Paget's motion on dockyard expenditure deserves perusal. See Hansard, vol. 153, p. 39 *sqq.*

Meanwhile the French Emperor's hands were full enough with the war against Austria. In this war aristocratic sentiment in England favoured the Austrians, while the popular sympathies were naturally on the side of Italian nationality. The outbreak of this war made the theory of French aggression against England doubly and trebly absurd. Yet it was used by the panic-mongers as an argument for a great increase of military and naval preparations which eventually resulted in immense waste of public money. Lord Derby's Government appealed to the country in April and Parliament reassembled on May 31st. There was a large Whig majority, and in June Lord Palmerston returned to power with Mr. Gladstone as Chancellor of the Exchequer. In the following month the Third French Invasion Panic boiled over in both Houses of Parliament. The debate in the House of Lords on July 1, 1859, teemed with the finest flowers of panic oratory. Lord Ellenborough called for 70 battleships and forts galore. He said that for "six months in the year an enemy may land 60,000 to 80,000 men on any beach on the south coast of England." Lord Howden, who lived in France, turned up in the Lords to assert that the whole French population longed to invade England in order to rob and humiliate their old enemy; and then "the French eagles might stream from every steeple from Acton to Ealing, and from Ealing to Harrow. . . . There was not a single widow in France who would not give her last son, or a single beggar who would not give his last penny to carry out such a project." These gross absurdities were contradicted by Lord Brougham (then 81 years of age), who, however, also called for more armaments. A few days later Lord Lyndhurst, then 87, let off a fiery piece of rhetoric, which (we are told) fluttered the fashionable world and agitated the clubs for a fortnight. It was a trumpet call to arms, in which the aged orator contrasted his memories of Camperdown, the Nile, Trafalgar, and other glories of the last war with the humiliating dangers of the present, when steam had converted the Channel into a river, which a large French army might cross in a single night. "I know," he added, to prove the imminence of the danger, "from information which I have received, and the accuracy of which I do not doubt, that the French are at the present moment building steamers for the purpose of transporting troops, each of which is constructed to carry 2,500 men, with all the necessary stores." This fiction was repeated in the form of a question in the Commons, and on July 29th Mr. Horsman made what Cobden calls "the great panic speech of the session, unexceptionable as a rhetorical performance," demanding a loan for national defence, and "absolutely destitute

D

of one fact or figure to prove the danger against
which we were called upon to arm." If Horsman
had been a commercial traveller in armaments, his
eloquence could hardly have gone more directly and
visibly to the point than in the following sentences :—
" Every public or private yard should be put into full
work ; every artificer and extra hand should work
extra hours, as if the war were to begin next week.
As gunboats could be built more rapidly than men-
of-war, gunboats should be multiplied as fast as
possible ; as volunteers could be enrolled faster than
the line, they should at once be raised ; as rifles could
not be made fast enough in England, we should
renew that order in Belgium, even though they
should cost sixpence a piece more than the Horse
Guards' regulation ; and night and day the process
of manufacturing, constructing, arming, drilling
should go on till the country was made safe, and
then we might desist from preparations, and return
to our peace expenditure, with the certainty that
these humiliating, lowering and degrading panic-
cries of invasion would never disturb our country or
our Government again." Cobden reminds us that
when Horsman called for the multiplication of gunboats to resist French preparations we had 162
against the 28 possessed by France, and that the
tonnage under construction at our dockyards had
been more than doubled. As for " the iron cased

vessels" of France which existed in Horsman's speech, *La Gloire*, the first, did not make her trial trip till a year later. After closely comparing the actual facts and figures with this panic rhetoric, the great critic of extravagance observes : " The alarm on this occasion, as in the case of the previous panic of 1851, was excited at the very time when it happened to have the least foundation ; which might appear strange did we not know that panic is not a product of reason but of passion, and that it is quite as likely to occur under one state of circumstances as another."

The Panic of 1859 gave a stimulus to the Volunteer or Rifle Corps movement, and fiery meetings were held all over the country at which militant patriots let off steam against the French. Towards the end of the session Lord Palmerston said they could count on about 200,000 men including 60,000 regulars and 100,000 militia to resist an invasion. But during the recess the public caught the infection as it spread downwards from the upper circles of society. Even men of steady nerves and ordinary sense were alarmed ; for they asked with reason : Was it likely that the Government, unless it had proofs of danger, would have imposed such unnecessary expense on the country ? When responsible statesmen act extravagantly an indulgent and credulous public will generally listen to those who say : " the

Prime Minister is acting on secret information which it would be dangerous to disclose." In 1860 and 1861 the first fruits of the panic were gathered, and the harvest of wasteful expenditure would have been much larger but for the heroic efforts of Mr. Gladstone as Chancellor of the Exchequer and the brilliant success of Cobden in negotiating the famous commercial treaty with France. The Navy Estimates of 1860 reached a grand total of £12,800,000, and Lord Clarence Paget, the Secretary of the Admiralty, was readily exonerated by the Opposition for this practical reversal of the views he had put forward in opposition. Lord Clarence Paget's argument reflects no credit on his character. Cobden writes :—

"To reconcile the country to this enormous expenditure, it was necessary that the French navy should be made to assume very alarming proportions. But how was this to be accomplished by any ordinary mode of comparison? If the expenditure in the dockyards had been compared, ours would have been shown to be double that of France; if it had been a comparison of seamen, the number voted, together with the reserve, would have been found nearly three times as great in England as in France ; had the ships in commission, or the ships afloat in the two navies, been compared, the effect would have been the reverse of what was desired. A very ingenious and perfectly original mode of comparison was adopted. The number of ships in *commission* in England was compared with the number *afloat* in France : they chanced to be 244 in each case, and this equality was, perhaps, the temptation to adopt the new method. Had the numbers afloat in both cases been given, they would have been, as afterwards incidentally appears in the statement, 244 French and 456 English." [1]

It must be added that the shipbuilding programme announced by Lord Clarence Paget (large wooden steamships) was diametrically opposed to the opinions and criticisms he had expressed in opposition. It was already obvious from experiments that these ships would be mere slaughter-houses, and that the future lay with armoured vessels. Such exhibitions as this may provoke the question whether in the public interest some casuist ought not to define the limit of consistency beyond which Ministers of the Crown should not be allowed to wander. The limits have not yet been defined ; and later records of the Admiralty have revealed even more wonderful instances of elasticity in political ethics.

On May 1, 1860, Lord Lyndhurst revived the panic in the Lords, and called upon the Government to report progress in its war preparations. He sniffed at the treaty of commerce which had just been concluded, and proceeded to draw very cleverly a false comparison of the British and French navies, a comparison which " did not contain one fact that would bear the test of fair examination." But it was unfashionable and even unpatriotic to criticise fictions favourable to the theory of a French invasion, and the

[1] See Cobden's *Third Panic* and Hansard, vol. 156, pp. 966-9.

facts stated in reply by the Duke of Somerset and Lord Clarence Paget failed to restore to reason "that vast body of excited opinion in the country, of which," as we read in Morley's *Life of Gladstone*, "Lord Palmerston was the cheerful mouthpiece." Under the Duke of Somerset, indeed, common sense soon began to prevail over the naval fever. But at the War Office Sidney Herbert suffered from a severe attack of the cerebral disorder. Already in November, 1859, his informants had persuaded him that France was about to declare war on England. It was fortunate indeed for the country that Gladstone was at the Exchequer. How he wrestled with Palmerston and Herbert, battling against the huge loan for fortifications, how he was beaten at first and forced to submit to a considerable measure of waste, but at length by contesting every inch of ground with the invaluable support of Cobden and Bright, succeeded in restoring sanity and economy, is told in a splendid chapter of Gladstone's life. In 1862 the threat of a tenth penny on the income tax "proved to be a strong physic," and the Cabinet ordered £750,000 reductions in the Army Estimates. The publication of Cobden's *Three Panics* made all reasonable men ashamed of the scare. Lord Eversley is no doubt right in holding that to Cobden's scathing exposure of these senseless frights and of the fabrications ac- accompanying them, we may trace the fact that from

1862 to 1884 there was no recurrence of panics, and
no expansion of armaments.   In spite of the loan for
fortifications economy triumphed during Mr. Gladstone's second reign at the Exchequer.   He could not
prevent the naval and military estimates rising from
26 millions in 1859 to 28 millions in 1862, but they
were gradually reduced to 24 millions in 1866 and an
enormous load of taxation was removed ; for the trade
and revenues of the country were advancing by leaps
and bounds.   Gladstone and Cobden, it should be
remembered, were just as determined as Lord Palmerston to maintain an ample margin of security.   But
they hated ostentatious, extravagant, and provocative
preparation for war.   "We have no adequate idea,"
wrote Gladstone, "of the predisposing power which
an immense series of measures of preparation for war
has in actually begetting war."   To substitute concert
for conflict, and proportional reductions for proportional increases, was the aim and object of their
endeavours, when they sought so successfully to
improve our relations with France, at that time the
second Naval Power.   The principle of reciprocity in
adjusting naval forces was Cobden's substitute for
that insane competition in armaments which threatens
civilisation with bankruptcy, and piles up debts and
taxes, for the sole benefit of the manufacturers of
war material.   There is still, alas! "a vacant niche
in the Temple of Fame for the ruler or minister who

shall be the first to grapple with the monster evil of the day." But there is encouragement in looking back upon the heroic efforts which prevailed over the Third Panic ; for they provided our governing classes with such a grounding of common sense as assured the nation more than twenty years of comparatively peaceful progress.

THE FOURTH PANIC, 1884

THE efficacy of Cobden's medicine is proved by the long respite which Cabinets, parliaments and all sections of the British public enjoyed from armament panics after the subsidence of the third French Invasion panic in 1861 and the publication of the *Three Panics* in the following year. The natural cravings of professional soldiers or sailors and the commercial instincts of contractors were kept in check. Cardwell's famous reforms promoted economy and efficiency in the army, and the Franco-German war made a French invasion more than ever ridiculous without suggesting thoughts of a German peril. At last in the autumn of 1884—when the Naval Expenditure of Great Britain was about 11 millions against £7,653,000 for France, and upwards of 3½ millions for Russia—Mr. W. T. Stead, a clever journalist who indulged an unfortunate talent for sensations, restarted the old business of Naval Panic-monger in the *Pall Mall Gazette*. How far Mr. Gladstone's Second Administration, weakened by disturbances in Ireland, by troubles in South Africa, by an Afghan boundary dispute with Russia and by the Egyptian entanglement, yielded against its better judgement to the cries for more naval expenditure which Mr. Stead evoked from various quarters I shall proceed to show. Of popular panic there was no trace; but Mr. Stead and his fellow-conspirators managed to produce a feeling of nervous disquietude in high society, and although the results were small in comparison with later performances the year 1884 deserves attention as the beginning of a most disastrous expansion in naval armaments, in which the provocative impulse has too often been furnished by Great Britain.

It must not be supposed that between the Third and what I venture to call the Fourth Panic there had been no agitation for additions to Naval Expenditure. The so-called armour-plate interest is never asleep. But the official policy of successive Governments was strong enough to resist these demands. What that policy was has been very well described by Lord Eversley, who was himself a member of the Board of Admiralty under the Duke of Somerset :—

The number of seamen and marines, and the number of ships in commission were maintained at about the same rate. The tonnage of new ships constructed in the dockyards or by private contract was added to, and the increase of about one million in the Navy Estimates during this period was mainly devoted to this purpose. Careful watch was kept on what was being done in this respect by other countries, and especially by France. It was held that if the battleships of England were maintained in the proportion of three to two to those of France . . . the position of this country was perfectly safe. During this period demands were not unfrequently made for large increases of the Navy, and especially in respect of the building of more ironclads and cruisers. But these efforts were resisted by the successive heads of the Admiralty; and ex-Ministers generally supported those in power in opposing extravagant schemes in this direction. The arguments used for this purpose were to the effect, that it would be very unwise and impolitic, by large and spasmodic efforts, to increase the Navy, as it would only induce other Powers, and especially France, to follow our example, with the result that in the end we should find 'ourselves in no better position, relatively to others, than before such increases; and, further, that any great increase in shipbuilding would, in the rapidly advancing development of naval science, result in multiplying types of vessels, which in a very short time would become obsolete and useless.[1]

The wisdom of this safe and cautious policy is proved by the fact that it provoked no rivalry in naval armaments. Other powers were content to rest upon their oars so long as Great Britain was satisfied with its normal superiority. In those days First Lords and other official exponents of naval policy were comparatively quiet in their utterances and comparatively businesslike in their performances. These great positions of trust were not used for

[1] *The Burden of Armaments*, p. 67.

purposes of self-advertisement, or for the issue of boastful challenges to possible rivals.   Neither Mr. Disraeli nor Mr. Gladstone encouraged naval hysterics or military fireworks.   In those years we had adequate security at a reasonable price ; and Ministers forewent the pleasures of declamation.   It would be possible to quote opinions of Front Bench men like Mr. W. H. Smith[1] and Sir H. Campbell-Bannerman[2] on either side to show how much good sense, how much forethought, how much responsible self-restraint were exercised in the particular interests of Great Britain and in the general interests of the world.   Unfortunately in the autumn of 1884, when unemployment was rife in the shipbuilding trade, Mr. Stead, actuated probably by no worse motive

[1] See Hansard, 1880, vol. 251, p. 602.

[2] "We have been invited by writers of great authority in the public Press," said Sir H. Campbell-Bannerman, "to take another course, to open up a new era of great Naval Expenditure, and to launch forth upon a sea of new projects and unknown expense in shipbuilding. . . . We are not disposed to follow that advice.   In the first place, we believe that we are quietly and steadily making and preparing such additions to the Navy as fully to maintain our position.   In the second place, I would ask the Committee what would be the effect in Europe if England were suddenly to embark on a new career of Naval Expenditure, and possibly set the example of a fresh international rivalry on the sea, which could in the end but add to the miseries which the system of portentous military establishments already inflicts on the world ? "—See Hansard, 1883, vol. 277, p. 603.

than an irresistible desire to be the centre of a journalistic sensation, flung himself against this sober policy, using as editor of the *Pall Mall Gazette* the influence of a newspaper whose reputation had been built up on very different foundations by Mr. John Morley, his predecessor and former chief.

According to an old official of the Admiralty this first success of "the advanced school of naval thought" was won "most unexpectedly" and owed its origin to the merest accident. Lord Salisbury, the Conservative leader, on a visit to Portsmouth in the summer of 1884 had heard discontent expressed about the state of the Navy by some of the officials there, and referred to the matter in a speech, which seemed to express a doubt as to whether the navy was strong enough to ensure the national safety. A few days afterwards, on June 9th, Lord Northbrook, the First Lord of the Admiralty, defended the Admiralty from these criticisms in the House of Lords. He "set forth in glowing and exaggerated language the very efficient state of the Navy,"[1] and overwhelmed Lord Salisbury with comparative statistics, showing that the Liberal Government had done more than its predecessors, and that the French navy was far behind our own. But he also rashly remarked that he would be at loss to spend

[1] See *Naval Administrations*, by Sir John Henry Briggs, for some time Chief Clerk of the Admiralty. London, 1897.

the money if the House of Commons put three millions into his hand. This statement of course put the naval experts and all the armour-plate agents, great and small, on their mettle. Every professional and commercial instinct was piqued by this appalling example of public lethargy.

When they perused Lord Northbrook's speech, writes Sir J. H. Briggs in the volume just quoted, "the heads of the Naval profession were thoroughly astonished and taken aback ; and a famous controversy was the immediate result, which led to the publication of a series of articles in the *Pall Mall Gazette.*" In this controversy, he adds, "the most distinguished Admirals and Naval experts soon took a part, and in their numerous contributions to the Press gave ample proof of the great ability and skill with which they were able to defend their cause and uphold the vital interests of the country." And so Lord Northbrook, on his return from Egypt at the beginning of the autumn session "discovered," in the words of a *Times* chronicler, "that public opinion had been aroused, and that the facts disclosed in speeches and letters, not only by *independent* persons like Sir Edward Reed, but by officials like Sir Thomas Brassey, were being debated with much warmth."[1]

The panic—it was really not much more than a

---

[1] See Annual Summaries reprinted from *The Times.* Vol. ii. p. 243. London, 1893. The italics are mine.

professional agitation for taxpayers' money which
died down as soon as something was forthcoming—
was heralded by a speech of Lord Henry Lennox to
a Conservative Working Men's Club in the dockyard
constituency of Portsmouth on September 12th.   By
that time politicians were beginning to return from
the Grouse Moors, and Mr. Stead launched his bolt
on September 15th with a clever leader entitled
" What is the Truth about the Navy ? "   It was in
the too familiar style which now palls on the public
palate.   But then perhaps it seemed strong ; for the
mixture of Burke, the Penny-a-Liner, and the Penny
Dreadful was comparatively new.   " Can we or can
we not demonstrate beyond all gainsaying our irresistible superiority in armour, guns, speed and coal-
carrying capacity over any combination of fleets
which it is reasonable to believe could be brought
against us ? " was the question propounded in order
to invite the desired negative—a negative which was
supplied on the very next day in a formidable article
of five pages bristling with blood-curdling figures and
technical horrors of all sizes and shapes.   It was
signed with the initials A. F., and entitled " The
Truth About the Navy by One Who Knows the
Facts."   This Monster was accompanied by a
smaller one dressed in Mr. Stead's best style—a
well assumed pose of stupefied astonishment and
horror on learning so suddenly that his beloved

fatherland lay prostrate at the mercy of foreign powers. Speaking of "the Truth" as it appeared to "A. F." Mr. Stead wrote :—

"So startling were his disclosures, so alarming the net effect of his exposé of the weakness of our defensive position, that we hesitated in making it public before submitting his statements to the examination of some of the most competent and careful authorities in the service in both its branches, administrative and naval." The picture of a sensational journalist hesitating to publish a startling and alarming disclosure is worthy of the pencil of Max Beerbohm. As all the facts collected by Mr. Arnold Forster (A. F.) were provided (unless I am much mistaken) by a naval officer, who afterwards rose to confer far greater services on the Armour-plate ring, it is clear that the standard of loyalty to the Board of Admiralty was not very high at the time. "He sets forth," proceeded the editor with evident relish, "one of the most gloomy pictures of the condition of our navy that has probably ever been published in an English newspaper, and one which, unless its substantial accuracy can be promptly disproved, must arouse the nation to energetic and immediate action." Mr. Stead then incautiously launched into a statistical argument : "No amount of special pleading can get over the fact that whereas 15 years ago we spent as much on our Navy as was spent on the combined navies of France, Italy, Germany and Russia, we are now spending eleven millions against their fifteen." Thus selecting a particular year when Italy and Germany were spending practically nothing the editor of the *Pall Mall Gazette* suggested that our Naval estimates ought always to be the equivalent of the aggregate spent by these four strangely chosen bedfellows who could not on any conceivable hypothesis have united in war against us ; and from these absurd premises he jumped to the required conclusion : "Unless we are prepared to live on sufferance—and such States are seldom long suffered to live at all—we must make up our minds to face an immediate and very considerable addition to our naval expenditure."

From this characteristic effusion of the panic-monger, which has been reproduced *mutatis mutandis* hundreds of times in the last ten years by papers of the *Daily Mail* stamp, one turns to "the facts" to learn from "A. F." that France had outbuilt us in ironclads, and yet that we had sacrificed repairs to construction, that our guns were inferior to those of France and Italy ; that in case of sudden war the French could defeat us in the China seas and the Chilians in the Pacific, while "the new ironclad of Brazil would sweep our South American squadron off the sea." As to commerce protection—the Admiralty by the way insisted upon "capture" as

E

our most valuable weapon—"we have nineteen
thousand merchantmen scattered over the world to
protect and only twenty-four unarmoured ships of a
speed exceeding fourteen knots for their protection."
The writer then demanded huge sums for the construction of naval docks and the fortification of
coaling stations in all parts of the world, observing
that one hostile cruiser "could with almost entire
impunity destroy to-morrow the coaling stations of
Hong Kong, Singapore, Bombay, the Cape, Ascension,
St. Helena, Mauritius, St. George's Sound, Fiji, and
Vancouver's Island." As to the home ports, only two
harbours were "adequately protected." The fleet
was also eight thousand men short, and lastly "to
bring us into line with our rivals one hundred torpedo
boats should be laid down at once." In a word we
were, as usual during panics, hopelessly inferior in
every branch of the service. For years we had been
spending far more than our rivals and getting much
less for our money. But of course the naval officers
and Admiralty officials, who provided the *Pall Mall
Gazette* with its "facts," like the journalists who
declaimed upon them, carefully obscured the obvious
moral which should immediately have been drawn
from "the Truth," if it had been true, "about the
Navy." That moral was, and is, that if our Board
of Admiralty, manufacturing and contracting in a
country where ships and materials of all kinds are

far cheaper than elsewhere, could not provide a superior navy, its Board should have resigned and the men responsible should have been summarily ejected to make room for competent officials who could give the nation good value for its money. But of course no such demand was made. The writers were ingeniously maintaining a thesis for the sole purpose of extracting more money from the pockets of the people, and of enlarging the patronage of a great spending department. No public office will ever admit that economy will yield the funds required to satisfy new demands. No contractor will ever complain that contracts with the Admiralty and War Office are too lucrative. Prodigality and inefficiency always go hand in hand.

Like a good journalist, Mr. Stead had arranged that his own cries of horror and astonishment should be well echoed, and there immediately appeared letters from Admiral This and Vice-Admiral That, couched in the most gloomy phraseology. On September 20th, two days only after "the Truth" had leaked out, the *Pall Mall* was able to inform its readers that "the unanimity of assent is bewildering and appalling. We had hoped, etc., etc." More letters from Admirals followed. On September 22nd the *Observer* observed quite seriously: "The plain truth is that the English Navy has no longer command of the sea," and the provincial press (with one or two creditable exceptions) followed, though less extravagantly, in a similar vein. But in spite of newspaper hysteria the panic did not go very deep. The Conservative opposition had not at that time adopted the modern fashion of pressing unlimited expansion of armaments upon their opponents in office. Mr. W. H. Smith sent a moderately cautious letter to the *Times* suggesting the appointment of a commission of inquiry. But the *Pall Mall Gazette* went on clamouring that the public had been " thoroughly aroused," and this iteration impressed the ministerial mind. The *Daily Telegraph* heard " a cry of patriotic anxiety rising in the country to which no Ministry could close its ears." Mr. Childers, the Chancellor of the Exchequer, wrote on September 26th to Sir John Adye : " The *Pall Mall Gazette's* furious demand for more naval expenditure has been received with considerable approval."

Among the letters printed in the *Pall Mall Gazette* was one from Admiral Sir T. Symonds, who " felt sure " that war was about to break out and that history would repeat itself : " After the most mature and deliberate consideration I deem it my bounden though most painful duty to state that I consider the Navy so starved, so weak in numbers, armament, structure, personnel, etc., that if a war broke out to-morrow with France I do not see how we could possibly avoid the most awful disasters." And yet

about the same time during a debate in the French
Chamber it was authoritatively said, no doubt with
good reason, that "in speaking of foreign powers we
must set aside the English navy, with which our fleet
cannot enter into comparison for the number of
first-class ironclads, cruisers, or torpedo boats." So
perhaps there was some excuse for "the shortsighted
economists and inveterate grumblers" [1] not yet
extinct in England, who continued to criticise naval
expenditure and objected to the increase of debts and
taxes at a time when agriculture was depressed
and trade bad. The sequel may now be related in a
very few sentences. Mr. Gladstone's Government,
harassed as it then was by difficulties at home and
abroad, resorted to an increase of taxation and
debt. To meet the cost of extra expenditure for war
a supplementary budget raising the income-tax from
fivepence to sixpence was introduced on November
17th, and on December 2nd Lord Northbrook
announced in the House of Lords a programme of
extraordinary expenditure on the Navy—a sum of
$5\frac{1}{2}$ millions sterling for shipbuilding, naval ordnance,
and coaling stations to be spread over the next five
years. It was but a small concession to the clamour
raised by the *Pall Mall Gazette* for a minimum
addition of four millions sterling to our annual
outlay on the Navy. "In nearly all quarters,"

[1] See *Times* leader, November 13, 1884.

remarks the *Annual Register,* "the Government's answer to the popular demand was pronounced inadequate. Nevertheless there arose a few anti-alarmists or sceptics who declared that the outcry in the newspapers was chiefly, if not wholly, the work of the professional advisers of the Admiralty, assisted in a great measure by the large shipbuilders, whose yards were empty and whose trade was temporarily at a standstill." The Fourth Panic, however, was now at an end. But little was heard of the miserable state of the Navy in 1885, journalists and politicians of all parties having other fish to fry. It may be doubted whether many of those who contributed to it had ever worried much over the condition of the Navy, or slept any better when more ships were built and more stations fortified.

.   .   .   .   .

Before passing to the Fifth Panic it will be convenient to review very briefly the next twenty years of naval armaments, the second decade of which was marked by an appalling outburst of naval extravagance. The years of the Boer War were a golden age for contractors of all kinds, but the gold was furnished at the expense of the funds and the taxes.

From 1885 to 1892 our military and naval expenditure moved slowly but irregularly upwards. With Mr. Gladstone in Opposition and Lord Salisbury

in office, the atmosphere was not suited to a provocative or sensational expansion in armaments. In
the autumn of 1887 a scheme of retrenchment was
contemplated, and Lord Randolph Churchill resigned
his office as Chancellor of the Exchequer because
the reductions were insufficient for his purpose. The
incident is well described in Lord Randolph's
Life, and throws some light upon naval finance,
as well as upon the ways of experts. Lord George
Hamilton, the First Lord, himself admitted, or
boasted, in defending a reduction of £700,000 on
the Navy Estimates of 1887, that the saving had
been associated with an increase in the effective
strength of the Navy. In 1888 Lord George continued to speak and act as an economist; but in
1889 he turned right-about-face on the plea that
his advisers had scented an addition to French naval
expenditure on battleships. As a matter of fact,
the French naval expenditure was under eight
millions in every year from 1884 to 1889, except
1887, when it rose to £8,452,000 ; and even in
1890 it was only £8,060,000, against a British
expenditure of £17,529,000. On this trivial
pretext, however, Lord George Hamilton introduced and passed the Naval Defence Act of
1889, which provided for an expenditure of
£21,500,000 in the next five years upon 70 new
vessels. Of the total cost, 10 millions was to be

defrayed by loans whose repayment was spread over
seven years. Not content with inaugurating this
vicious policy of borrowing for ships—which was in
effect a raiding of the Sinking Fund in order to avoid
new taxation—Lord George Hamilton also propounded a dangerous and mischievous novelty in the
shape of a two-Power standard. The Naval Defence
Act was immediately answered by the French Government with a supplementary estimate. As usual the
armament firms profited, and the attempt to increase an already long lead merely led to an all-
round increase. It was the omen of a far more
calamitous and costly rivalry. But, at first, there
was a pause. For the next three or four years our
naval expenditure remained at something over 15
millions. But in the month of December, 1893, Lord
George Hamilton, Mr. Balfour, and Mr. Chamberlain
attacked Mr. Gladstone's Government with a motion
demanding another large increase. It was a weak
Government, and most of its members were inclined
to follow Lord Rosebery's bigger navy policy, for-
getting that a particular increase leads to a general
one, in which every nation loses. Mr. Gladstone
resigned rather than acquiesce, and the naval
expenditure was raised in 1894–5 to over 17 millions, and in 1895–6 by the succeeding Government
of Lord Salisbury to over 19½ millions. Mr. Gladstone admitted that (as Chancellor of the Exchequer

and Prime Minister) he had made "limited con-
cessions" to scares in 1860 and 1884, but in 1894
he could find no justification.   Apparently the love
of power and patronage and display grew with every
fresh concession which the Board of Admiralty
wrested from a reluctant but ever-weakening
Treasury.   Liberal Imperialists and Tory Chau-
vinists played into one another's hands.   And
behind them, behind or below the fashionable society
and finance in which they moved, whether in office
or opposition, was the insidious, incessantly growing
power of the great armament firms, with their light
skirmishing parties of smooth-tongued ambassadors,
who acted sometimes as representatives at the
Admiralty, sometimes as commercial agents in
Turkey, Brazil, China, Japan, or any other poverty-
stricken Power which could be persuaded to entertain naval ambitions, sometimes, again, as "our naval
expert" upon one of the associated newspapers.
This was a period of quiet but rapid development,
during which a great armour-plate ring managed
to suck from the taxpayer larger and more lucrative
contracts year after year.   It is only too easy to
see from the figures by whom in the critical period
of 1893 to 1897 the pace was forced.   In 1893
we spent on the Navy roughly 15¾ millions, France
10, and Russia 5½.   In 1897 we spent 22 millions,
France 10½, Russia 6¼.   In 1899 our naval expendi-

ture had risen to $27\frac{3}{4}$ millions, against 12 millions for France, and $8\frac{1}{2}$ millions for Russia, while Germany's naval outlay had grown to $6\frac{1}{2}$ millions. Under cover of the vast borrowing for the Boer War, our Admiralty did not neglect its opportunities. In 1904 British naval expenditure was $42\frac{1}{2}$ millions, French $12\frac{1}{2}$, German nearly 12, Russian $11\frac{1}{2}$. It is a most disgraceful chapter in the history of British policy; and the principal blame must rest upon the politicians, the Press, the society and finance of London. An appalling laxity about public money, beginning before and continuing after the Boer War, was accompanied by a luxurious style of living, which sapped the vigour and independence of Parliament. At length a lowering of the national credit, an increase in the burden of taxation, and a period of bad trade and unemployment led to a great popular reaction against the whole degenerate system of Government over which Mr. Balfour then presided. Tariff Reform failed to revive his party. After effecting a considerable measure of naval retrenchment in order to avoid another unpopular addition to taxation, the Unionist Government fell, and suffered an unexampled defeat at the General Election of January 1906.

THE FIFTH OR DREADNOUGHT PANIC

IN the political crash of 1906 Lord Rosebery
vanished and Imperialism went out of action
for a time. A new spirit, embodying new ideals
of social reform in association with the retrenchment of unproductive expenditure, was fitly represented by a new Premier in the person of Sir H.
Campbell - Bannerman, a man of broad, popular
sympathies and shrewd common sense. He was
a sincere lover of peace. Detested now, as he
had before been despised and insulted by smart
society, he was yet so popular with the rank and
file on his own side, that he was able in two
brief years to give important expression to a new
spirit, both in finance and in Colonial politics. Unfortunately, he was heavily handicapped, first by
the so-called invention of the Dreadnought, secondly
by the persistent Chauvinism of the leaders of the
Opposition, and, thirdly, by the successful resistance
of the Admiralty and Foreign Office to the reform
of naval warfare. I deal with this third problem in

a later essay. "Capture" and Prize-Money are cardinal features in the great armour-plate policy. They are a double stimulus to naval expenditure, which is thus able to represent itself in every country as a necessity of commercial defence.

But to return to the Dreadnought. By what means the armament people managed to induce Mr. Balfour's Government to build the first Dreadnought, and to advertise it as a ship which had made all previous battleships obsolete, is a mystery not likely to be cleared up during the lifetime of the individuals chiefly concerned. How happy a hit it was for the contractors, and how disastrous to the taxpayers, will be seen from the following points :—

1. Since that time the fashion has been to build every new battleship bigger than the last, with more armour plate, larger guns, and everything in proportion, so that one super-Dreadnought now costs double as much as a monster battleship of ten years ago. The continuance of this folly is explained by the plaudits which the advertisement of each fresh monstrosity evokes from half the Press.

2. This augmentation in size was not accompanied by a reduction in the ships laid down. On the contrary, in a very short time, as we shall see, by playing on the theory that the Dreadnought made other ships obsolete, other Powers were in-

duced by the international armour-plate Press to build similar ships, and to make special efforts so that they might thus be able, with unexpected ease and celerity, to challenge Britain's naval supremacy. The secret of the Dreadnought (such as it was) was carefully explained in the British Press at an early stage in its construction, and in a short time British armament firms were merrily building these ships for foreign countries, and so helping to produce the statistics which the Admiralty required to force larger and larger programmes upon Parliament.

3. One further advantage from the contractor's point of view must not be omitted. The Dreadnought was built just large enough not to go into most of our docks and harbours. Consequently, an enormous expenditure on docks requiring another set of lucrative contracts was called for speedily and urgently. Thus the Dreadnoughts cost far more than they appeared to do. Even if they had not been imitated, they would have been an economic and naval blunder of the first magnitude. The Dreadnought will be marked down by the recording angel as a double offence against the British nation and against the human race. But for this " invention " most of the slums in our great towns could have been cleared away without any addition to rates or taxes.

These criticisms have been offered over and over

again; but no attempt has ever been made to answer them (so far as I know) either by Mr. Balfour, or the late Lord Cawdor, or by Sir John Fisher (now Lord Fisher), who won such credit and renown as the father of the first Dreadnought, or by Sir Philip Watts, the actual designer, who went from Armstrong's to the Admiralty. Personally, I am certain that the whole theory of the superiority of the big ship is a fallacy, whether applied to the Merchant Service or to the Navy. Economy and efficiency—to say nothing of the torpedo and submarine—point to a return to a smaller type. But enough has been said here to show the appalling magnitude of this blunder. Its consequences are written large in the Fifth or Dreadnought Panic.

I have said that in 1904 British naval expenditure had risen to 42 millions, 20 millions in excess of that of France and Russia combined, and more than 32 millions in excess of that of Germany. Yet in the following year the new Imperial Defence Committee discussed the possibility of an invasion of England, and Lord Roberts was so deeply impressed by the defenceless state of the nation, that he thought proper about this time to retire from the Defence Committee in order to prosecute a missionary campaign on behalf of compulsory service for the Army. Meantime, the party exigencies already mentioned had caused, in the spring of 1905, a rather severe retrenchment in the Navy Estimates, and it may be convenient here to set forth the total naval expenditure in votes (leaving out the expenditure on works from borrowed money) in the periods between the ending of the Boer War and the Panic of 1909 :—

NAVAL EXPENDITURE AFTER THE WAR, 1903-8.

Year.	Numbers.	Ship-building Contracts. £	Total Expenditure from Votes. £
1903–4	125,948	10,832,371	35,709,477
1904–5	130,490	10,071,514	36,859,681
1905–6	127,667	7,781,483	33,151,841
1906–7	127,431	8,388,514	31,472,087
1907–8	127,228	7,452,262	31,251,156
1908–9	126,935	7,147,464	32,181,309

Public sentiment (outside Fleet Street) in 1904 and 1905 was so much exasperated by the contrast between a general trade depression and the thriving condition of armament manufacturers that Mr. Balfour actually boasted before he left office of his great naval economies, and especially of "the courageous stroke of the pen" by which the Admiralty had withdrawn 160 ships from the fighting line. Credit was also taken for the abandonment of many foreign and colonial stations, which had been fortified at vast expense, and for a concentration of the fleet in the home seas. No doubt had this, or anything like it, been proposed by a Liberal Government, they would have been denounced as traitors to the country and to the Empire. However, the reductions were made, and in February, 1906, Mr. Edmund Robertson, the Secretary of the Admiralty, in introducing the first Naval Estimates of Sir H. Campbell Bannerman's administration, showed that the actual expenditure (including expenditure on naval works out of loans) was 36 millions, as against 42 millions two years before. He gave the whole credit of this reduction to Mr. Balfour's Government. In July, after reviewing the new programme, he announced that the Board of Admiralty had unanimously decided to reduce it from four to three Dreadnoughts, and also to knock off three destroyers and four submarines—a prospective saving of about $2\frac{1}{2}$ millions. In order, he added, to encourage an international arrangement for the reduction of armaments at the Hague Conference of 1908, next year's programme would be reduced to two battleships, a third to be added if the Hague Conference did nothing in this direction. Mr. Balfour denounced his successors for these further economies; but the Prime Minister observed that until 1909 we would be the only Power with a Dreadnought, and, of course, our preponderance over either France or Germany was overwhelming. In March, 1907, Mr. Robertson was able to show a reduction of £450,000 in the Navy Estimates, to £31,419,000, and went on to argue that he had made an actual reduction of nearly $2\frac{1}{2}$ millions, taking into account the stoppage of borrowing for works, etc. On the same reckoning, our Naval Expenditure had been reduced to $33\frac{1}{2}$ millions, against $41\frac{1}{2}$ three years before, but more than double the expenditure of 1892. In these debates Mr. Balfour declared that the Navy ought to be equal to that of the two next strongest Powers " with a margin of safety." In the next year (1908) the Navy Estimates showed an increase of nearly a million; but Mr. Balfour and the Opposition again complained that the expenditure was inadequate, and "inconsistent with national safety and honour." By this time the destruction of the Russian navy by Japan and the refusal of France to join in the naval race, had forced the Admiralty and Foreign Office to look about for another enemy. They found one in Germany, where Krupp's influence was powerfully assisted by our diplomacy, and by the sly threat of commerce destruction supplied by our representatives at the Hague. The death of Sir Henry Campbell Bannerman also paved the way for the events of 1909. Already in 1908 our naval experts were beginning to work up statistical forecasts of the future, and on March 9th Mr. Balfour gave figures derived, one must suppose, from naval officials or armament firms, to show that in the autumn of 1911 Germany would have thirteen

F

Dreadnoughts against our twelve. He excluded the *Lord Nelson* and the *Agamemnon*. Mr. Balfour's theory seemed to derive a certain plausibility from its vagueness and obscurity as well as from his insistence on the fact, however irrelevant, that the German shipbuilding programme began in June and the British in December. In July and August two leading Socialists, Mr. Blatchford and Mr. Hyndman, began to write up a German invasion scare in *The Clarion*, and a year later Mr. Blatchford contributed a set of scare articles to the *Daily Mail*.[1]

The Times and other newspapers set to work in the autumn, when the Naval Estimates were being prepared. Finding that the United States and Germany were then spending 45 millions, *The Times* proclaimed that our formula should be to keep ahead of these two next strongest naval Powers. Everything now depended upon Mr. Asquith and Mr. McKenna. Mr. McKenna, who had been in opposition, and afterwards, at the Treasury, a champion of naval economy, was now at the Board of Admiralty. Mr. John Morley at the Indian Office, Mr. Lloyd George as Chancellor of the Exchequer, and Mr. Churchill at the

[1] For the value attached by the Armour Plate people to Mr. Blatchford's work, see a Diary of Events furnished by Mr. Mulliner to *The Times* of January 3, 1910.

Board of Trade, were supposed to be out and out
opponents of naval expansion.   The Panic, however,
was soon in full swing.   The Unionist newspapers
were reinforced by the theatre.   On January 28,
1909, "The Englishman's Home" was produced at
Wyndham's.   It represented an invasion of England,
in which the Territorials played a ridiculous part.
It was patronized by the Court, and the Censor
refused to allow it to be parodied!   In February
it leaked out that Mr. McKenna had put forward
demands for a great increase of naval expenditure.
It was broadly hinted in the press that otherwise
his Naval Board would have mutinied, and it was
reported in reliable quarters that dissensions had
broken out in the Cabinet.   The main question was
whether four Dreadnoughts or more should be provided.   It also became known that Mr. McKenna had
come back from a trip in the Admiralty yacht, " converted," as the "Annual Register" puts it, "by Sir
John Fisher to the principle of a strong navy."   The
Navy Estimates issued on March 13th showed an
increase of £2,823,000.   A large sum was to be
spent on a naval station and harbour at Rosyth,
which marked at once the acceptance of the Dreadnought theory and of the German Invasion theory.
Only four monster battleships were provided for ;
but this victory of the economists was to prove illusory, for "the Government also asked for power, if

necessary, to prepare for the rapid completion of four more armoured ships, beginning on April 1, 1910, to be completed by March, 1912." There was also a large programme of cruisers—pure waste, for in this arm the German Navy was hopelessly behindhand. The most obvious sign of panic lay in the announcement that the contract for Rosyth (after great sums had been spent in buying out the local landowners) was to be accompanied by a bonus of £800 a week for each week *saved* on the time. The contractors were bribed to hurry! All this extravagance was subservient to the monster shipbuilding policy. It seemed to be thought necessary to exaggerate the value of the Dreadnoughts, and to go on increasing their size in order to maintain the reputation of the individuals responsible for the original blunder. A dirigible airship was also to be constructed.[1]

Practically the whole Liberal Press was up in arms against these Estimates as provocative and unnecessary. It was felt that the Imperialist wing of the Cabinet, reinforced by Mr. McKenna, was leading the party along a false path. On the other hand, the Tory Press, delighted with the situation, was eager to

[1] This I suppose was the *Mayfly*, which fell to pieces at Barrow while it was being launched, and just after it had been approved by the Government inspectors. There was an inquiry, but somehow the affair was hushed up, and as far as I can make out the taxpayer footed the bill.

improve it, and clamoured for more. A crowded House and an excited public therefore awaited Mr. McKenna's speech introducing his first Estimates on March 16th. He began by admitting that the Estimates were of "exceptional gravity," that they would involve still higher ones next year, and that they required strong justification from a Liberal Ministry and a Liberal Minister pledged to retrenchment in armaments. "During the last few weeks a number of friends of the Government have reminded me—anticipating, I suppose, the increase of the vote next year, that the policy of the present Government had been declared to be one of Peace, Retrenchment, and Reform. I agree most cordially with that policy, and I can well understand that any addition to the naval expenditure may be viewed with the greatest alarm by many persons whose political convictions I share, and whose good opinion I greatly value. . . . No one can suppose that the present Government have made themselves responsible for Estimates on such a scale with a light heart. If I may speak of myself for a moment it would be to say that there is no man in this House who is more earnestly desirous of retrenchment in expenditure on armaments than I am, or more reluctant to have forced upon him by the circumstances of the time so burdensome a programme. My first experience of official life was at the Treasury. In that admirable department I learned the practice and the theory of economy. If I find myself in a situation which is above my pretensions, I recognize, I believe, that I owe it to the fact that I am known to adhere to the principles which I learned in my first office." This seems to mean that Mr. Asquith had appointed the First Lord for the special purpose of introducing into the Admiralty those principles of economy and retrenchment which Mr. McKenna had preached to it in his missives from the Treasury a year or two before. "But," as he added, "there are occasions when even the most determined economist is willing to make a sacrifice"; and this was one. Indeed, Mr. McKenna almost as well as Mr. Winston Churchill may stand to prove that in up-to-date politics the deepest convictions may have to be sacrificed when a real opportunity arrives of carrying them into official life. Mr. McKenna therefore set himself to show that these exceptionally grave and financially burdensome proposals were justified and required by "the safety of the Empire."[1] This justification was to be found in the rapid progress of foreign Powers, and especially Germany, which he selected "for arithmetical purposes" as "the standard by which to measure our own requirements." This was an unlucky phrase in view of the arithmetic that followed.

[1] "The safety of the Empire stands above all other considerations. No matter what the cost, the safety of the country must be assured." But why should this platitude have carried more weight in 1909 than in 1907 or 1905?

In order to produce the panic required to float his
Estimates through the House and overcome the
reluctance of the Liberal rank and file, Mr. McKenna
began by excluding the ordinary battleships, in which
we had, of course, an overwhelming superiority—
both of numbers and quality—as compared with
Germany. The next step was to produce a fleet
of German Dreadnoughts in some future year large
enough to bolster up a panic programme. Confining
himself, therefore, to Dreadnought battleships and
Dreadnought cruisers, he gave the following figures.
In 1911 we expected to have 16 against Germany's 13. But if the German construction were
accelerated, as he declared it had been, Germany
might have 17 in April 1912 against our 16, and
in any case would have 17 in the autumn of 1912
without acceleration. To maintain our superiority
in Dreadnoughts the Admiralty must therefore be
authorised to have four more ships by March 1912
in which case we should possess 20 Dreadnoughts
against the German 17.

In the course of this official exposition, which
sounded far more formidable than my brief abstract,
Mr. McKenna cleverly paused to do homage to
the wonderful expansion which would make these
miracles certain :—

I think we may stop here to pay a tribute to the extraordinary growth in the power of constructing ships of the

largest size in Germany. Two years ago, I believe, there were in that country, with the possible exception of one or two slips in private yards, no slips capable of carrying a Dreadnought. To-day they have no fewer than fourteen of such slips, and three more are under construction. What is true of the ships is true also of the guns, armour, and mountings. Two years ago any one familiar with the capacity of Krupp's and other great German firms would have ridiculed the possibility of their undertaking to supply the component parts of eight battleships in one year. To-day this productive power is a realized fact.[1] It will tax the resources of our own great firms if we are to retain supremacy in rapidity and volume of construction.

One of the most ingenious methods adopted by the international armament firms, of which in April, 1913, Krupp has furnished the classical example, has been to spread false information as to what armament firms in other countries are doing or preparing to do. Just as an armament tout gets an order for one battleship at Buenos Ayres, and then uses this to procure an order for two at Rio, so do the rival Admiralties and co-operating armament companies of Western Europe laud the efficiency and magnify the power of the potential

[1] Is there any one now who can bring himself to believe that this and the preceding sentences were within any reasonable distance of the truth? But they sounded awful. The sentence which follows is the key to the whole panic. In this connection one of the most interesting figures is that of Mr. Mulliner, for whose appearances students of the Panic may refer to a series of articles in the *Daily News* (May 1913), entitled " Armaments and Patriotism."

enemy in order to divert an ever larger stream of taxes into their own purse. From this point of view the invention of the Dreadnought has been a perfect godsend, and I often think that those who started, and advertised, and perpetuated the delusion, with all its fashionable follies and puerile panics, have received very inadequate recognition. They ought to be crowned every year by the Armour Plate ring.[1]

If the secret information furnished for trade purposes by members of the Armour Plate ring, usually to the Press, or the War Office, or Admiralty, but on special occasions to prominent politicians also (who swallow greedily anything of this kind), could be revealed, a good deal of light might be thrown upon this debate. It is also to be remembered, in contemplating the tissue of false forecasts upon which this whole panic and panic expenditure were built up, that our Admiralty and War Office were at this time letting loose quite a swarm of spies, who served the double purpose of supplying false information to subserve expansion of armaments, and of increasing the ill-feeling which had been already worked up between England and Germany.

[1] There is a delightfully naïve passage in this speech of Mr. McKenna's explaining how "the advent of this new and improved machine [the Dreadnought] has materially curtailed the profitable life of our previously existing fleet."

So much for the forecasts with which, aided by the Intelligence Department of the Admiralty, Mr. McKenna had been able to provide the House of Commons. They were the basis on which he built up his Estimates. But there was a further prize to be gained. There were the contingent Dreadnoughts. Give the House of Commons and the public a still more alarming set of statistics, and the jingo catch—

> "We want eight,
> We won't wait,"

might be set to official music.

And so Mr. McKenna was followed by Mr. Balfour, who, as ex-Prime Minister, and originator of the Defence Committee, spoke with peculiar authority, and played with more than his usual skill on the nerves of the simpler sort. Of course, he had "never risen on any occasion" with a greater sense of responsibility or a greater sense of "the immense effect on national destiny which may result," etc. After a few preliminaries of this kind, the great debater suddenly declared that the question was not whether we were maintaining a two-Power standard, but whether we were maintaining a one-Power standard. His speech and that of the Prime Minister afterwards almost suggested that the safety of the Empire had been provided for by a preliminary consultation between the leaders of

Peace and Retrenchment and the leaders of naval and military expansion. Mr. Balfour mocked at the Hague Conference. While we were trying to encourage an imaginary and illusory reduction of armaments the German Government "logically and naturally occupied all the time that we expended in nursing these empty hopes, these vain expectations, in not only building ships and laying down ships, but what is of far more importance, making those enormous preparations, that immense expenditure upon plant, machinery, slips, and docks which have put them, as the right hon. gentleman himself admitted, in a position, compared with us, which no nation up to the present time has ever yet been."

After complaining that the Government had laid down only three Dreadnoughts a year instead of four, which was the number his own Government had proposed in a memorandum, Mr. Balfour enlarged and descanted on "the immense development of German potential output,"[1] and "the extraordinary state of peril we are likely to be in in 1911," which he had himself foreseen in 1908 and now regarded as certain. He insisted that Germany could now build as fast or faster than England. He declared that the Germans had already advanced their pro-

[1] For Mr. Mulliner's share in these illusions, see extracts given in the articles in the *Daily News*, referred to previously.

gramme "by four or five months." Mr. Balfour then proceeded as follows :—

On the two years' basis of building we shall in December 1910 as I calculate have ten, and only ten Dreadnoughts. But the Germans at that date, as I calculate, will have thirteen. That assumes of course that I am right in stating —and I do not think I shall be contradicted—that the Germans anticipated their programme by four months. If you work that out, and assume that the German ships begun last November, in anticipation by five months of the ordinary date are completed in two years, then you will find I am not wrong in saying that in December 1910 we shall only have ten Dreadnoughts and the Germans will have thirteen."

This "danger period," he added, extended from December 1910 to March 1911. Then from April 1st to July the Germans would have thirteen Dreadnoughts to our twelve. After July our number would rise to fourteen, but in the meanwhile the Germans would have seventeen. This was too much for the Prime Minister, who ejaculated, " In July 1911?" Then came the following dialogue:—

Mr. Balfour. Yes. Of course, that depends on what they lay down this year. It is admitted on all hands that they will have thirteen in 1911.

Mr. Churchill. No, no.

Mr. Balfour. Yes, that is right. There is no doubt they will have thirteen on April 1st, 1911.

Mr. McKenna. My own opinion is that they will have

thirteen completed in August 1911.[1] They will not have thirteen completed in April 1911.

Mr. Balfour. That is because the right hon. gentleman makes them build in more than two years, and if you do that I think you must equally make us build in more than two years. Experience of the past has shown us that in the last few years we have not built in twenty-four months, and those causes may affect us in the future, as they may affect Germany, but assuming the same standard of shipbuilding, then I say, according to my calculation, the Germans will have thirteen on April 1st, and if they lay down four ships this year before July they will add to those thirteen four in 1911, and they will then have seventeen—again, of course, on the two years' basis.

Mr. McKenna. I should like to explain to the right hon. gentleman that the four ships for the next German financial year are the ships in respect of which I am informed that materials and armaments have already been begun. Those are the four ships which were to be laid down—technically laid down—on April 1st. The right hon. gentleman is supposing that another four ships will be laid down. The four ships of the 1909–10 programme will be laid down technically on April 1st, 1909, but the right hon. gentleman must not suppose that another four ships will be laid down on April 1st.

Mr. Balfour. That is exactly what I do suggest. I am very grateful to my right hon. friend for having interrupted me, because there is really no dispute as to the facts, except that he seems perfectly confident that the four ships of the what I call German anticipated ships were not laid down. My anticipation was, and is, that they were laid down.

Mr. McKenna. I would not like to express any decided opinion as to whether any of them have or have not been laid

---

[1] As a matter of fact, on March 31, 1912, Germany had 9 Dreadnoughts in commission and Great Britain 15.

down, but that they will be declared officially laid down on April 1st.

Mr. Balfour. The information I have given me was, rightly or wrongly, that those ships were laid down last year. The right hon. gentleman is not prepared either to assent or to contradict that proposition. He says, what is, to me, I admit, very immaterial, that they will be officially announced as laid down on April 1st next. What we want to know is whether they were, and, still more, whether those ships, which, no doubt, were in the programme for 1909 year, if they were laid down in November, as I believe they were, that means that the Germans laid down eight Dreadnoughts last year. They may lay down no Dreadnoughts this year. They may say, and the Government apparently think they are going to say, "We anticipated the four ships for 1909-10 by laying them down in November. Therefore we have no ships this financial year." But there are two other things they may do. Having laid down eight ships last year, they may lay down four ships this year, or they may do this year what they did last, and add eight ships. Of the capacity of their yards, and of their great engineering shops nobody now doubts. It has been practically admitted by the right hon. gentleman.

Therefore I say I was right in my original estimate that we have to count on the possibility of there being seventeen Dreadnoughts to our fourteen in July, 1911, and that even when the two ships laid down next November are built, we shall then be only sixteen Dreadnoughts to the Germans seventeen. And then, if the Germans go on at the rate, which is more than possible, the probability is that they will have on April 1, 1912, twenty-one Dreadnoughts to our twenty. The hypotheses are these—I want to make it perfectly clear to the Government and to the House—eight Dreadnoughts laid down in 1908 by Germany ; and if four are laid down in 1909 there will be seventeen on April 1, 1912. If eight are laid down this year, as eight have been laid down last year, there will be twenty-one on April 1, 1912, to our twenty. And if the Germans imitate the policy of the present Government and lay down not only their eight in the financial year, but, as well, demand a new group of four when the Government propose to begin their new group of four—namely, on April 1st—they will then have twenty-five.

Mr. McKenna. No—— (the rest of the statement was inaudible).

Mr. Balfour. I think not. What the right hon. gentleman said across the table to me was that while that might be possible on paper it was beyond the constructive power of the German shops and the German yards—in other words, that they cannot lay down eight this year and four at the beginning of the next financial year. Well, sir, that is not the information which has reached me. He may have, and has, access to better information. Yes; but observe it is not so very easy to know what the Germans know. When did the Government discover they were laying down their four ships in November? When did the Government discover that the Germans deserved the warm eulogy passed upon them by the First Lord of the Admiralty with regard to the immense unprecedented development of their powers of turning out those great battleships, and (what is almost more important) the turrets and guns without which the great battleships are useless?

Mr. Balfour then improved on the awfulness of the situation by hinting that the Admiralty did not know the worst about Germany's secret preparations in its docks and shipyards. Mr. McKenna had admitted it to be possible for Germany to have twenty-one Dreadnoughts on April 1, 1912. He believed she might have twenty-five.[1] He had done his "very

---

[1] When the date arrived Germany had nine!

best to check the figures." He had not proposed the problem " in an alarmed spirit. " He had been forced to it most reluctantly against all the traditions of British statesmanship. And why?

Now for the first time in modern history we are face to face with a novel situation, so new, so dangerous, that it is very difficult for us thoroughly to realise all that it imports. For the first time there is bordering upon the North Sea, upon our own waters, the waters that bathe our own shores, a great Power that has got the capacity, and looks as if it had the will, to compete with us in point of actual numbers in respect of those great battleships. I am afraid nothing can be done; it is too late to do anything with regard to the years that precede November 1911. What has been done has been done with regard to that. I look at even that period with the greatest anxiety, but we can do nothing now to remedy it. No activity on the part of our dockyards, no generosity on the part of our taxpayers, can make good that deficiency, if that deficiency does indeed exist. Let us without recriminations turn to that period of the future with regard to which we can do something. That portion of the future is that which lies within what I may call the scope and reach of the building programme with which this House has now got to deal.

Thus Mr. Balfour at the end of this consummately clever and successful speech was getting to business. More money for the Navy. An addition of nearly three millions to the Estimates and the programme presented were " utterly insufficient." He complained that Mr. McKenna had spoken of the cost with alarm. "I thought," he said, "that the financial alarm would be far overshadowed by that greater and more dominating alarm which for the first time has come home to me with regard to the actual command of the sea in our own waters." But he welcomed the "security no matter at what cost" part of the First Lord's statement and called upon the Government to live up to it, however much it might embarrass their budget. It would be unfair after all this to withhold from the student of the Fifth Panic Mr. Balfour's peroration :—

I therefore do most earnestly beg the Government and the Committee to consider not indeed in any spirit of panic, but with a full recognition of the absolutely novel and, as I think, alarming circumstance in which this country finds itself, whether they cannot do something with the enormous resources which we have at our disposal in the way of the building of ships, guns, turrets, and our power of finding the necessary funds for dealing with the question of national defence. I ask them not to hesitate, not to delay, but to use to the utmost and as quickly as possible, without paltering, every possible machine which they have at their disposal for restoring to this country what I greatly fear we have temporarily lost—not that two-Power standard, which is far beyond question in this debate, but the one-Power standard in the matter of ships of first-class power, which for the first time in our history seems to be slipping from our grasp.

The House will see that I have dealt with the fundamental and vital aspect of the subject of national defence, and I hope the Prime Minister will see that this discussion can go no further, that we cannot touch on other details of the

G

Navy Estimates, however important, until we are satisfied that everything is being done which national honour and national safety require.

The Prime Minister's very first sentence showed that the words of the Leader of the Opposition had not fallen on stony ground :—" I do not in the least complain of either the tone or the substance of the right honourable gentleman's speech." It was not, he said, a party issue, but a question of the Empire's safety. A Government which sacrificed Empire to expediency or tactics " would be well deserving of the condemnation which history always pronounces upon those who are false to a great public trust." He would therefore deal with these grave matters in " a detached and certainly not a party spirit." First of all the whole strength of the fleet had to be considered, not the mere strength of Dreadnoughts. By enlarging on this, the Premier might have dispelled the panic atmosphere ; but unfortunately he passed at once to the German Peril. He spoke of our " friendly and open " diplomatic intercourse with Germany, but added that the naval expenditure of the German Government was governed solely by reference to their own needs. Of this " we have been assured more than once, and in the most formal manner." . . . " It is perfectly clear that there is no room for a mutual arrangement for reduction. I regret it very much, but I do not complain. The Germans, like

every other nation, are the best judges of their own
national requirements. It is no business of ours to
offer either criticism or advice, but to accept the facts
as they state them ; and we must adapt our programme to our national requirements." He went on
to declare that the Government was not setting the
pace, but was most anxious to slacken it, and further
that they were not animated by any unfriendly intentions to Germany. They were acting to preserve
supremacy at sea "solely according to the elementary
instinct of self - preservation." Mr. Balfour had
attacked Sir H. Campbell-Bannerman's Administration for not building more Dreadnoughts. Mr.
Asquith defended his predecessor on the ground that
"nothing is worse than to over-build yourselves in
great ships." Particular types so soon become obsolete that those who control the money of taxpayers
should hold their hand, and not exceed the requisite
margin of superiority. In the last three years they
had kept up the requisite margin of strength. Then
as to Dreadnoughts or "capital ships" (though he
did not much like the phrase), Mr. Asquith read out a
table of Dreadnought dates supplied to him by the
Admiralty. He called it the Admiralty computation;
and as it was upon these figures, authenticated by
Mr. McKenna, that the Prime Minister persuaded
his reluctant followers to pass the Estimates, and
subsequently (in spite of an official denial from

Germany) to authorize the programme of contingent Dreadnoughts, they must be here set out :—

THE DREADNOUGHT TABLE.

		Great Britain		Germany
December, 1910.		10.		5.
March,	1911.	,, ,,	12.	,,	9 (5).
May,	,,	,, ,,	12.	,,	11.
August,	,,	,, ,,	14.	,,	11.
November,	,,	,, ,,	16.	,,	13.
March,	1912.	,, ,,	16 or 20. ,,	13 or 17 (9).

(The figures in brackets are the true figures which the mighty expansion of the German yards actually produced.)

Mr. Asquith then proceeded at some length to explain the novel provision in the Estimates. We have taken power, he said, to lay down on April 1, 1910, four more Dreadnoughts "if the necessity should arise, that is, if the acceleration of the German programme goes on. . . . Supposing that power we have taken becomes exercisable we shall have 20 ships [in April, 1912]. . . . The Germans by that time may have 17." If by additional acceleration they were likely to attain Mr. Balfour's figure of 21, there would be plenty of time to make further provision to advance beyond 20. "But I must say— and it is fair and right to the German Government that I should say it—that we have had a most distinct declaration from them that it is not their intention to accelerate their programme." He believed most implicitly in the good faith of this declaration, though it was not a pledge or agreement, and though there would be no bad faith if they altered their intention, and laid down 8 ships in one financial year as Mr. Balfour had suggested.[1] Then in answer to an interjection from Mr. Balfour the Prime Minister added: "I said 17 was a possibility—13 is a certainty. It is because 17 is a possibility that we are taking this power;[2] otherwise we should not take it at all."

The Prime Minister went on to say that his previous estimates of German construction had not "been verified by subsequent experience," though he "spoke of course on instruction," and "got his information from the best possible sources." He agreed with Mr. Balfour that his estimates had been falsified because he had assumed (1) that the paper programme of Germany would not be exceeded, and (2) that the German rate of shipbuilding would not be more than thirty months per ship. He was sorry to say that subsequent experience had falsified both assumptions. The Germans had accelerated both their programme and their rate of shipbuilding. As to the speed of construction :—"This is a fatal and

---

[1] A few minutes before Mr. Balfour had intervened to say : "I quite believe that the Germans would only have four or five [Dreadnoughts] in March, 1910, but in December, 1910, they will have 13." As a matter of fact Germany had only 5 in commission on March 31, 1911 !

[2] "To lay down if need be four ships on 1st April next year."

most serious fact. We have both these sets of considerations. Both of them, I agree, invalidate the hypotheses which only a year ago I addressed to the House when speaking on this topic. I think that hon. members on this side of the House should think twice or thrice before they refuse to the Government the power which we are asking the House to give." They asked it in the supreme interest of national security. There was no set of men more anxious than ministers "to save money for the purposes of social reform or to get rid of this horrible, devastating, and sterilising expenditure."

Some suspected, but no one could prove, that the Prime Minister had been hoaxed. He spoke with official authority, and as all his forecasts were capped by the Opposition they naturally produced a prodigious effect. Hitherto the reading public had discounted the panic-mongering of the Tory press because almost every Liberal newspaper had ridiculed the scare, and had shown by official figures that British naval preponderance over Germany was overwhelming in every branch of the fleet. But now how could the man in the street believe critics who declared that the Admiralty had found a German mare's nest? The Admiralty experts, in close association as it would seem with the armour-plate interests, had managed after a long controversy to impose a very heavy additional programme on the Cabinet.

When the decision was once taken, and the Prime Minister had adopted the false official forecasts, he had to encounter hostility in the party ranks. He knew that this sudden and sensational addition to naval expenditure, following immediately upon his succession to the Premiership, was regarded with deep suspicion and dislike by Radicals and Labour men, as well as by the Liberals of the Manchester school. He was therefore led to paint a gloomy picture of impending danger. In order to induce his party to swallow the Estimates he had to represent them as an indispensable provision for securing the safety of the country two or three years later. He persuaded himself that what the spies and intelligence men and experts told him was true, and he persuaded the House also. From this point of view it was a masterly and successful performance. But his very success in the House of Commons produced for the first time something in the nature of a general panic, or at least a real uneasiness among the outside public. The Tories of course were delighted, the Liberals felt depressed and humiliated; for the scare they had ridiculed had been treated by their leader as a grave reality. He had given the whole weight of his authority to the forecasts by which it was supported. He had burnt what they had adored and adored what they had burnt. " It was the speech of the Prime Minister," as Mr. Balfour remarked complacently a few days later,[1] "which, I think, has caused this anxious feeling throughout the country." It is much easier to produce an impression of this kind than to dissipate it; but on March 18th, when the House went into Committee on Vote A of the Navy Estimates, Mr. Asquith—in response to a wild anti-German speech by Mr. Wyndham pressing for more expenditure in all directions, and to a plea for caution and moderation from Sir Charles Dilke— poured cold water and ridicule upon the panic-mongers with a cheerful vigour which seemed to show that he at any rate had not suffered in health or spirits from contemplating the gravity of the national peril.[2] He began by expressing general agreement with Sir Charles Dilke, whom he thanked for bringing out points ignored in the extraordinary and "very artificial" agitation which was "going on outside." As between the British and German Governments he was glad to think "there is on this matter not only no friction, no unfriendliness, or suspicion," but a common feeling that each must act independently as regards national defence, and that neither could complain of the other's naval programme. He went on to say that, in spite of the

[1] "The debate in this House has alarmed the country," said another member. "It is impossible to open a newspaper without seeing nearly a page devoted to the alarm felt throughout the country" (Mr. Bellairs).—Hansard, March 18th, 1909.

[2] The Estimates, of course, were by this time secure.

figures he had disclosed and the speeches he and the First Lord of the Admiralty had made and the new state of things which had come into existence since last year, " there was no occasion for anything in the nature, I will not say of panic, but of alarm or even disquiet." What, then, was his object in addressing the House a second time ?

" It is to dissipate as far as I can—and I think I shall be able to do so completely—the absurd and mischievous legends to which currency is being given at this moment as to the supposed naval unpreparedness of this country. A more unpatriotic, a more unscrupulous misrepresentation of the actual situation than that which is now being presented in some quarters I have never experienced." The Prime Minister then proceeded to make the speech which might have come on this occasion from a leader of the Opposition like Disraeli, if he had been minded to put the taxpayers' case against a further expansion of naval armaments. First of all he said they would have at the end of the year in commission nine Dreadnoughts to Germany's two. " There is nothing very alarming in that. If I may say so, the old women of both sexes, whose slumbers are at present being disturbed by fantastic visions of flotillas of German Dreadnoughts sufficient to land an invading army on our shores, may dream without any apprehension for another twelve months." But far

more important was the comparative list of pre-Dread-
nought battleships. A full-length survey followed.
In 1912 (the Danger Year!), he said, we should have
40 first-class battleships apart from Dreadnoughts
displacing 585,000 tons, many of them, like the
Lord Nelson and *Agamemnon*, in the first bloom of
youth, and all in full fighting effective strength.
Against these Germany would have twenty displacing 241,000 tons. The British 40 were not only
bigger but carried more and bigger guns—152 twelve-
inch guns against 40 eleven-inch guns on the German
ships. " It is ridiculous to pretend that we shall be
in a position of inferiority as compared with Germany
or any other power' in the world in 1912." Passing
from battleships to armoured cruisers, Great Britain
in 1912 would have 35 of 416,000 tons displacement
to Germany's eight of 78,500 tons displacement,
carrying 68 nine-inch guns to their six! He might
have added that of submarine craft we were expected
in 1912 to possess 84 to Germany's 16.[1] Mr. Balfour
who followed did not attempt to question the correct-
ness of these figures,[2] and their significance was driven

---

[1] See *Navy League Annual* for 1910, p. 239.

[2] Yet on March 29th Mr. Balfour moved a vote of censure
on the Government. In this speech he referred to an inter-
view he had had with " a great contractor," and complained
that the Government had not given instructions to the great
armament contractors to prepare for large orders until his
vote of censure was on the table.

home by Mr. Winston Churchill (then President of
the Board of Trade) in a letter to his new constituents at Dundee, which earned him much abuse
from the Yellow Press. He ridiculed "the Dreadnought fear-all school" and added : "It is lucky the
sailors don't believe them." All battleships, great
and small, new and old, "are equally a prey to the
submarine, to the torpedo boat, and the floating
mine." The British navy had double as many sailors
and they were picked twelve-years service men
against three-year conscripts. Our whole naval
strength was more nearly thrice than twice that of
Germany. The German invasion scare was "a false,
lying panic started in the party interests of the Conservatives." In the following month at Manchester he
denounced "a braggart and sensational expenditure
on armaments" and described his personal antipathy
to it as an inherited peculiarity.[1] "We live in a
period of superficial alarms," he told the Edinburgh
people, "when it is thought patriotic and statesman-
like, far-seeing, clever, and Bismarckian to predict
hideous and direful wars as imminent." He could
see no real antagonism of interests between England
and Germany. The Government, he promised his
constituents, would not be driven by the "windy
agitation of ignorant, interested, and excited hot-

[1] " I have always been against that, as my father was before
me."

heads into wasting the public money upon armaments upon a scale clearly not designed merely for
purposes of material defence, but being a part of
a showy, sensational, aggressive, and Jingo policy,
which is supposed to gain popularity from certain
unthinking sections of the community. We take
our stand against that."

But the most effective of the purple, anti-panic
patches with which Mr. Churchill adorned his social
and economic rhetoric remains to be quoted :—

In my judgment a Liberal is a man who ought to stand as
a restraining force against an extravagant policy. He is a
man who ought to keep cool in the presence of Jingo clamour.
He is a man who believes that confidence between nations
begets confidence, and that the spirit of peace and goodwill
makes the safety it seeks. And above all, I think, a Liberal is
a man who should keep a sour look for scaremongers of every
kind and every size, however distinguished, however ridiculous
—and sometimes the most distinguished are the most ridiculous
—a cold, chilling, sour look for all of them, whether that panic
comes from the sea, or from the air, or from the earth, or from
the waters under the earth. [1]

Meanwhile the panic raged furiously on every Tory
platform and in every Tory newspaper. Lord Roths-
child presided over a Mansion House meeting which

[1] This and most of the previous quotations are from
"Liberalism and the Social Problem," a volume of Mr.
Churchill's speeches carefully revised by himself, with a pre-
face in which he pressed his opinions and arguments
"earnestly and insistently on the public."

called upon the Government at all costs to build the eight Dreadnoughts at once. The scare certainly damaged the Liberal candidate in the Croydon by-election at the end of March, when bands of youths paraded the streets singing, "We want eight; we won't wait." But about the same time the approach of the Budget began to exercise a sobering influence which was also reflected by Sir Edward Grey. He said, speaking of naval and military expenditure in Europe: "You may call it national insurance. That is perfectly true; but it is equally true that half the national revenue of the great countries in Europe is being spent on what are, after all, preparations to kill each other. Surely the extent to which this expenditure has grown really becomes a satire and a reflection on civilisation. Not in our generation perhaps; but if it goes on at the rate at which it has recently increased sooner or later, I believe it will submerge that civilisation." The burden, he added, "if it goes on at this rate must lead to national bankruptcy." About this time a very friendly speech was made by Prince Bülow, the German Chancellor, who stated definitely that Germany would have only 13 Dreadnoughts in 1912; and on April 21st a debate was initiated in the House of Commons on the policy of prize money and capture at sea when a number of enlightened and independent members of both parties (among them Messrs. F. E. Smith, J. A. Simon, and

J. M. Robertson) advanced strong arguments for abandoning a policy which clearly contributes to the insecurity of commerce and to the rivalry in naval armaments. A few days later came the tremendous budget; and in the political convulsion it produced the fear of a German invasion fell into the background. A prospective deficit of nearly 14 millions, due mainly to Old Age Pensions and the Expansion of Armaments, was met partly by additional taxes on tobacco, spirits, and motoring; partly by graduating the death duties and income-tax. The super-tax on high incomes was invented to pay for the super-Dreadnought. It has proved to be, as I once called it, the greatest armour-plate budget of modern times. It was a prompt, bold, startling, and decisive interpretation of a new scale of expenditure in terms of a new scale of taxation. As a revenue producer it has been marvellously successful. From a Conservative standpoint it was the greatest misfortune which has befallen the country since 1832, for in an effort to destroy it the House of Lords came to grief. Two General Elections were won by Mr. Asquith. The Parliament Act was placed upon the Statute Book, and a Home Rule Bill was passed for the first time through the House of Commons. All this long train of woe may be traced by any intelligent Tory to the fact that his leaders surrendered to the pressure of tariff reformers and scaremongers. But for these two surrenders "the people's budget" would have been unnecessary, and the swing of the pendulum would almost certainly have restored the Conservative party to power in 1910 or 1911.

Thus in its political and financial consequences the Panic of 1909 proved of far greater import than any of its four predecessors. The absurdity of the scare was of course pointed out at the time. On March 22, 1909, Sir Charles Dilke, who never opposed naval expenditure, remarked in the House of Commons:—"Surely we can do without alarm at this time, for in regard to ships of every kind we have a much greater naval preponderance than we ever had." Mr. Massingham's courageous anti-panic articles in *The Nation* were echoed in many quarters. I find that I wrote on February 6th in *The Economist*:—"As some people in the City appear to be almost as much frightened as *The Standard*, which talks of a hundred million loan, and suggests that our naval expenditure should be 82 millions, we may perhaps usefully mention two or three sets of facts and figures. In the last ten years Great Britain has spent some 300 millions on her navy; Germany some 108 millions on hers. Our expenditure is now about 34 millions, that of Germany 17 or 18 millions. The tonnage of our effective warships is about 1,852,000, that of Germany's about 628,000 tons." Though I had then no adequate

notion of the underground influences in the armament business it seemed to me highly probable in
view of these figures that the scare had been
" worked up by interested parties."

But it is time to return from the fictions to the
facts, and I will prove to the satisfaction of every
reader that the Panic was a bogus panic, that the
Government and the Opposition leaders deceived
themselves and the House with bogus figures—in
short, that the whole thing was an imposture from
beginning to end, of which a self-respecting country
ought to be thoroughly ashamed.

In the first place the responsibility for the tables
rests with Mr. McKenna. They were supplied by
his own department—whether by means of spies
(of whom there was a perfect plague at this time)
or by Krupp, or by British armament firms, or by
the imagination of the Naval Intelligence Department, neither the public nor the House of
Commons has ever been informed. After their
appearance they were authoritatively denied by
the German Government; but in spite of Mr.
Asquith's expression of most implicit belief in
the German Government's good faith, and in spite
of his declaration that power to build the contingent Dreadnoughts was only taken in case the
German Government changed its intention so as to
have 17 Dreadnoughts in March 1912, neverthe-

less the contingent Dreadnoughts were laid down and the exercisable power was exercised. A year passed. The table of the Navy League Annual, published in 1910, showed that in spite of Mr. Balfour's denials "speed in construction is still in our favour," the average time for constructing a British Dreadnought being 26 months as against 34 months for a German. Nevertheless on March 14, 1910, Mr. McKenna, who had another heavy addition to the Estimates on his hands, was still outwardly confident about the truth of his naval forecasts, and he thus reinformed the House or Commons :—" As regards the statement which I made last year I have nothing to withdraw. And our programme this year is framed now upon our actual knowledge of what is complete or in the course of being completed." But "the danger period," when the forecasts would be overtaken by the facts, was drawing near, and it must have been clear to almost everybody in the Admiralty by the autumn of 1910, that the Panic figures were all wrong. At last on February 8, 1911, Mr. Robert Harcourt dragged the truth out of Mr. McKenna by a series of well-directed interrogatories. If the reader will look back he will see that Germany was to have 12 Dreadnoughts ready in March 1911, and 16 in November. It was now February 1911, and Mr. McKenna informed Mr. Harcourt that she

H

had only 5 and further stated that she could not
possibly have ready more than 9 by the end of
the year—9 at most instead of 16! As to the
year 1912, the Admiralty which had seen so clearly
in 1909 and 1910 was now in a fog. The Admiralty,
said Mr. McKenna, had no information as to whether
4 German Dreadnoughts has yet been either
ordered or commenced, but " it is expected they
will be delivered from the shipyards in the spring
of 1913." Mr. McKenna added :—" I do not expect
21 German Dreadnoughts to have been delivered
from the shipyards in the calendar year 1913." That
was a mild statement. According to the last *Navy
League Annual*, Germany is only to have 19 ready
in March 1914.

"What is to be done?" asked a puzzled critic.
" These false statements were used to extract from
the House of Commons the monstrously swollen
estimates of 1909 and 1910, to secure the laying
down of eight Dreadnoughts in 1909 and five Dreadnoughts in 1910, and to terrify the colonies into the
panic-stricken provision of two additional Dreadnoughts. Surely this colossal blundering constituted
an offence against the House of Commons, against
the taxpayer, against the colonies, and against
Germany." *The Nation* thought that " Mr. McKenna
must realise that his personal position is a serious
one." How could the House of Commons accept his

statements in the future? How could it put any confidence in his judgment? Patriotic people may and do differ about standards of naval strength; but there can be no question among us as to what standard of truth and accuracy is required of Ministers. There may be mistakes made in good faith; but mistakes publicly made in good faith should be publicly corrected and repaired the moment they are found out; and prompt economies should have been effected the moment it was discovered that the forecasts on which the extraordinary programmes of 1909 and 1910 were based had proved so utterly wide of the mark. But the Government never even apologised. Mr. McKenna—who was transferred to the Home Office later in the year to make way for Mr. Churchill—never told Parliament at what time he discovered these mountainous errors, though he quoted a statement which reads like a partial withdrawal made on March 26, 1909, of the forecast he had made on March 16th. He argued indeed that certain facts justified his original presumptions, but he did not explain when or why the facts and presumptions went by the board, or why he did not immediately come to the House of Commons, retail the good news, and revise his estimates in the interests of honesty and the taxpayer. There is a department called the Naval Intelligence Department at the Admiralty, from which, possibly, Mr. McKenna may have drawn the German statistics on which he based his increase of three and a half millions in 1909, and five and a half millions in 1910. To this department the House of Commons voted in 1910 the sum of £16,185.

And what is to be said of the fanciful and fictitious forecasts contributed to the Panic by Mr. Balfour? Beside his statements the exaggerations of the Admiralty look almost modest. He has lost no credit in official circles as prophet or strategist. In fact, in the spring of 1913 he was invited to join the new unparliamentary cabinet, which goes by the name of the Committee of Imperial Defence. And yet it was Mr. Balfour who at the Navy League Meeting in the Guildhall on March 31, 1909, had demanded "eight Dreadnoughts this year and eight next."

Thus the forecasts on which the German Invasion Panic was based were overtaken by facts, and as the fears and suspicions died away the efforts to improve Anglo-German relations gradually bore fruit. In the autumn of 1912 the National Liberal Federation asked the Government to conclude an understanding with Germany similar to that which existed with France, and in the difficult Balkan negotiations of that winter and the following spring a peaceful solution as between the Great Powers was achieved by Anglo-German co-operation.

Let me conclude this account with a few figures to illustrate the financial *sequelæ* and statistical environment of the Dreadnought or German Panic. Here is the total naval expenditure of Great Britain, Germany, and Austria from 1901 to 1912, in pounds sterling :—

Great Britain   ...   .   456 millions
Germany   179   ,,
Austria   38   ,,

The results of the Panic may be set out in a comparison of British and German naval expenditure between 1907 and 1912 :—

	Naval Expenditure for the Year 1907–8.	Naval Expenditure for the Year 1912–13.	Total Increase.
	£	£	£
Great Britain...	32,735,767	45,616,540	12,880,773
Germany ...	14,225,000	22,609,540	8,384,540

This increased charge of nearly 13 millions—which seems certain to grow under Mr. Churchill's management—represents in round figures the interest on a capital of 400 millions sterling, say, two-thirds of the national debt. Its meaning in terms of social welfare may be got at by comparing the amount now raised

by the taxation of certain foods. These taxes worked
out as follows in 1911 :—

		£
Cocoa, Coffee, and Chicory		602,695
Currants, Raisins, and Dried Fruits ...		475,239
Sugar		3,059,455
Tea		6,159,070
		£10,296,459

All these duties, paid mainly by weekly wage-earners,
might be swept away for less than the sum which,
through panic and Anglo-German suspicions, has
gone into the building of extra warships, a sum which,
compelling other powers to increase their expenditure at a like rate, does not leave us one bit more
"safe" in proportion than we were five years ago.

THE SIXTH OR AIRSHIP PANIC

M R. CHURCHILL'S language after he became
First Lord of the Admiralty quickly reas-
sured those who had feared that he might prove " an
economist as my father was before me." The
pledge of substantial retrenchments in our navy
estimates, given by the Chancellor of the Exchequer
in 1911, was broken, and the economists were again
disappointed, despite a large reduction in Germany's
naval programme. Towards the end of February
1913, after Mr. Churchill's proposal for a 1·6 ratio
(eight Dreadnoughts English to five German) had
been accepted by Admiral Tirpitz, the Panic-mongers
decided that the naval situation was too unpromising,
and fell back upon the Air. Hasty and rather crude
arrangements were made for staging a new performance. Circumstantial reports suddenly began to
appear in the *Daily Mail, Standard,* and other newspapers of airships hovering in the dead of night with
searchlights at various points along the East Coast.
The *Daily Mail* took up Airships and Aeroplanes
with as much enthusiasm as if they had been old

flour mills, and pressed for Government expenditure upon these craft with the same disinterested zeal for public security which it had exhibited for public health when it was promoting the purchase of *Daily Mail* bread. The reporters of the *Daily Mail* furnished material for the *Daily Mail* which convinced the editor as easily as the Admiralty's intelligence men had convinced Mr. McKenna. In a few days the *Daily Mail* was able to announce : " It is now established beyond all question that the airships of some foreign Power, presumably German, are making regular and systematic flights over this country." For sceptical readers more exact and topographical statements were prepared. Thus " Airship over the East Coast. Many Witnesses," was one of the headlines in the *Daily Mail* of February 24th. The news began with a couple of introductory paragraphs :—

Evidence of the presence of a mysterious airship over Selby, in the West Riding of Yorkshire, on Friday night [February 21st], was given on Saturday by a number of responsible persons. No one saw the body of the aircraft, but lights were seen and the noise of the engines was heard. Selby is about forty-five miles inland from Grimsby, and is a busy industrial town and market centre on the Ouse. Near the town is Barlby Arsenal, where there is stored a great quantity of army ammunition.

Under the new Aerial Navigation Act which is now in force foreign airships are liable to be shot at, unless they come to earth on a prescribed signal being given.

Then came the evidence. A solicitor of Selby said he had seen two lights in the sky from Doncaster Road, Selby, at 9.15 p.m. They were hovering, and were too big and bright to be stars. They were like the head-light and the tail-light of a motor-car. Next came an insurance superintendent, who was more positive. He stated that about ten o'clock on Friday night he was on the station platform at Church Fenton with a party of Selby business men when they observed " an airship with a strong search-light playing on the railway lines." It was at first very high, then it came down so low that it seemed that it would strike the roofs of the houses. After about twenty minutes in the neighbourhood it left at a high speed. and then they observed a red and green light on either side. Mr. J. Creasor, of Riccall, in the East Riding, stated that an airship with a power-ful searchlight was near that place about eight o'clock, and the whirr of the engine could be heard. Mr. Beckerdyke, a commercial traveller, states that between ten and eleven on Friday night, while driving near Ellerton, his horse was startled by a very bright light " from an airship or something of the kind " which went over the road in front of him. It was going at a rapid rate in the direction of Bridlington.

" That the airship did pass over Selby Abbey on Friday night, making its way for the East Coast, is undoubted." What could be clearer? First, the lights were seen. Then the "noise of the engine" was heard. Then they saw the body of the ship—it had three wheels, one on each side and one in front, and "a faint throbbing noise" came from it. A caustic commentator observed that, but for a game-keeper, who found the corpse of the fire balloon on a moor, somebody in the *Mail* would have reported hearing men "conversing in deep guttural tones" in the clouds before the end of the week. It is on the basis of hoaxes like this, he added, that demands for £1,000,000 for new airships (such had begun to appear in the Press) are solemnly produced.[1]

On February 25th the *Daily Mail* came to business with a leading article entitled "Unwelcome Visitors," beginning :—"Whether or not we accept the circumstantial reports that a strange airship was seen hovering over British territory on Friday and Saturday, it must be taken as certain that this country has recently been visited by foreign air-craft." And the writer proceeded : "What is required is a large provision for dirigibles in the coming Estimates, to erect garages and give orders on a large scale for airships to British makers. We cannot buy these craft abroad."

Previously, on February 20th, this business side of the agitation came to the surface in a news column

[1] *The Star*, February 28, 1913.

(headed "Aeroplane Purchases—Machines for the British Army and Navy") which ran as follows :—

Exhibitors at the Aero Exhibition at Olympia express themselves satisfied with the sales of aeroplanes which have so far taken place. Among the purchases made for the British Government up to the present are :—

One 80-h.p. Sopwith tractor biplane. Sold to the Admiralty.
One 50-h.p. Avro biplane. Sold to the Admiralty.
Two Farman biplanes. Sold by the Aircraft Manufacturing
    Company to the War Office.

This firm delivered a Maurice Farman biplane to the War Office at Farnborough in a forty miles an hour wind yesterday morning.

Other orders have been placed with prominent aeroplane manufacturers, but the official notification has not yet been received.

Representatives of the following firms state that their current orders include :—
    18 Borel military monoplanes for the French War Office.
    50 Caudron monoplanes for the Chinese Government.
    A number of Bristol aeroplanes for the Spanish Government.

An appetite for Government orders can never be glutted, and although "the exhibitors expressed themselves satisfied," their champions in the Press were clamouring for more. The Government indeed was spending freely. From a reply given about this time by Colonel Seely, Secretary of War, to a question in the House of Commons it appears that the War Office alone had twenty airship contractors on its list; but he declined to disclose their names.

As a rule, the newspapers in the provinces were less credulous than those of London. But the *Whitby Gazette* outdid the *Daily Mail*, both in what it saw and what it felt. At the end of February one of its articles was head-lined as follows :—

WANTED, AN AIR-MINISTER.

ENGLAND AT GERMANY'S MERCY.

NORTH-EAST COAST SURVEYED NIGHTLY BY DIRIGIBLES.

FURTHER APPEARANCES OF AIRSHIP AT WHITBY.

The editorial views of this organ (which exerts as much influence in Whitby as the *Daily Mail* in Peckham) deserve to be reproduced.

The marvellous command of the air—and with it the sea and the land—achieved by the lighter-than-air vessels of Germany is being repeatedly demonstrated to Englishmen by night, especially to those dwelling about the north-east coast ; and, whilst many people are sceptical regarding these nocturnal visits, others, realizing them as facts, recognize their immense significance. We are among the latter, and, since the first established fact of the first appearance of an airship over the district, it has, as the Frenchman says, "given us furiously to think."

After this introduction it became desirable to produce local evidence by way of confirming "the flights, on Friday night, over the important naval and military centres of Scarborough and Selby (the former place having a big 'wireless' station, and the latter a huge storage of ammunition)." The first witness was a star-gazer in Skinner Street, Whitby, who, looking out from his bedroom window, had seen a light move slowly across the sky northwards. It was duller than some of the stars and less bright than a shooting star; but after it had been under observation for a minute or two it disappeared behind some buildings. "I am presuming," added this observer, that "I saw *the* airship." The next witness was Mr. William Prentice, junior, whose description of the flight of the aerial vessel over the neighbourhood of Sleights and Aislaby is the gem of the 1913 collection :—

"I was walking round by Larpool on Tuesday night," he told the *Whitby Gazette* representative, "when I saw a light in the sky, approaching from the direction of Aislaby. This was at a quarter to eight o'clock. I watched the light, and saw that it was an airship; and I could hear the working of the engines. It seemed as if it was going over towards Eskdaleside, and was travelling at a great speed; but it turned round, and descended some little distance towards the earth. The machine was showing a red light at the front, a smaller one in the middle, and what seemed to be a greenish light at the stern. I continued to watch, and saw that the machine came to a standstill, when the middle light, which seemed to be a searchlight, was shown. It then lifted a little, shut off its lights, and began hovering round and round. I went towards Ruswarp, and up Ruswarp Lane, and I could see the machine in the air all the time. At about twenty minutes past eight o'clock the airship proceeded in the direction of Pickering, or York, travelling at sixty or seventy miles an hour, I should think, and being out of sight in five minutes. There were several other people who saw it, and some of them seemed to be a bit frightened. The airship appeared to be about a mile above the land, and when the searchlight was put on the land could be plainly seen below. The night was dark, but starlight, and the machine could be plainly seen. When it slackened speed, and manœuvred about, it seemed to be over Briggswath. It came in sight from over The Woodlands when I first saw it. It was a cigar-shaped vessel, with a platform beneath. I could not distinguish any men or any further details." Mr. Prentice, in further conversation with the reporter, referred to the peculiar shape of the airship. At Doncaster, on the previous Friday, he had seen three British Army aeroplanes pass over the town on their way to York. "These were of the monoplane and Cody type, and quite different from the one which he saw on Tuesday."

A few weeks afterwards I was fortunate enough to hear from a friend at Whitby an explanation of Mr. Prentice's vision which had afforded a good deal of innocent amusement in the little town. " It turns out to have been merely a farmer working at night in a field on the hilltop, taking manure about in a creaky wheelbarrow, with a light swung on the top of a broomstick attached to it."

The same airship was seen by a young man employed in the post office at Bedale. A communication from him to the *Whitby Gazette* stated that on Tuesday night his attention was called by a fellow-clerk, who said there was an airship outside. He went out immediately, "and," he says, "there was no doubt that it was an airship." The postmaster and a dozen others saw the "bright star-like light" hovering at an ever-increasing height of probably 5,000 or more feet above the earth. It made its course due north, as if making for the coast, but altered its course for a more westerly direction. It disappeared by about 8.20 p.m. The last witness was a Whitby sea captain who "about the same hour was attracted by a very bright light in the west, a little to the northward of the planet Venus, but, when he had secured his telescope, it had become enshrouded in a haze."

After exhibiting these convincing proofs and ocular demonstrations the local editor pointed out that "the purpose of these airships is obviously to survey strategical positions and obtain practical knowledge of the working of an airship at a great distance from its base, for they can work within a radius of 1,550 miles. They do not belong to a country which is on terms of established friendship with us, like France; otherwise they would come at day time, and have nothing to fear. They can do their work better at night time than by day, because they can concentrate their searchlight upon particular spots, and have more leisure for the purpose; and their occupants can familiarise themselves with the topography of the country generally."

To the sceptics who suggested that if German army airmen wanted to visit England they would come in the day time, this Wise Man of the East Coast replied with editorial scorn :—

"One might as well expect them to bring their whole fleet of twenty-three Zeppelins some fine day, just to show how up to date they are. No, they send their single airships across to take observations just in the same way as they send their odd warships to survey our home waters in a nice, quiet way; so that, if ever it should happen that they wanted to find their way about our tight little island, their individual representatives would be as well equipped for the purpose as they were in the Franco-German war, when every German soldier carried a map of France in his pocket, and was able to show their enemies the way. In plain truth, the Kentish man and the Cornishman would be more at sea on the Yorkshire wolds than would Hans with a German guide-map in his knapsack."

"We have no patience," added the *Whitby Gazette*, "with the newspapers which are pooh-poohing these 'hallucinations,' as they call them; and such conduct is not creditable to them. . . . As we have before stated, Britain is at Germany's mercy now, and it is only the fear of the violation of all international etiquette which keeps her from taking advantage of her superiority."

The phantom airships were not seen only in Yorkshire. On its arrival at Kirkwall from the north isles of Orkney on Thursday, February 27th, the steamer *Orcadia* brought reports of an airship having been sighted in broad daylight off the Island of Sanday on the previous Monday. But—to quote the *Dundee Advertiser*—"it was a considerable distance off, and some of those who observed it thought it was a flock of birds proceeding rapidly southwards." An expert commenting on the news declared that the airships must have been geese, "which fly at a great height and adopt regular formations." He added that "geese breed within the Arctic circle, and if the season is encouraging they push northwards very early so as to get a good start with the great business of life." But if the geese were coming back in large flocks it would mean severe weather in the North, and severe weather in the Arctic circles in February tends to spread southwards and spoil the spring. But these poor shivering geese were duly converted into airships manned by Germans who had crossed the North Sea in order to spy out the promised land.

I

By the end of February the authors of the hoax began to feel nervous. Apparently mischievous persons were reporting apparitions too rapidly for the public digestion. "From all over the country," wrote the *Daily Mail* on February 27th, " reports are reaching London nightly of mysterious lights seen in the sky, and the observers are firmly convinced that they belong to airships. These reports have come largely from Yorkshire and also from the south coast (including Portsmouth), and last night they began to arrive from Liverpool. *The very multiplicity of these reports discredits them.*" The italics are my own. When Liverpool went into the manufacturing business the chief consumer seems to have refused to give any further orders. Nevertheless a long list was offered of lights seen in the sky at various places, and on the same day the Admiralty supplied a *Daily Mail* representative with a story sent in by the Hornsea coastguard who had been watching the movements of a "dirigible carrying lights."

But right on to March 8th visions of airships still haunted the imaginations of nervous persons, although the hoax had been exposed over and over again. On that evening, wrote a correspondent of the *South Wales Daily News*, "there was again a good deal of excitement in some parts of South Wales regarding a strange light near the horizon in the western heavens which was believed to be an airship.

" Shortly after 9 o'clock, while cultivating my fire-side, I received a hurried call from a neighbour to come and see a remarkable light that was supposed to be the airship. It was 9.15 when, in company with half a dozen neighbours, I got a sight of the object. My first impression was of what appeared like a small luminous cloud some 10 or 15 degrees above the horizon. It appeared to be moving slowly. Then suddenly from one end a ray of light shot forth, and a moment later it completely altered in shape, and the nebulous appearance gave place to a concentration of the light, which became dazzlingly bright. ' Look,' said my neighbour, ' now you see it has changed its course. It's turned half round, and now you see the light "head on." ' For some minutes we watched it and it appeared to sway gently, and the rays shot out first on one side and then on another. It subsequently again assumed an oblong nebulous shape, and later again became clear and brilliant. It certainly was most puzzling.

" Returning home a few minutes later, I examined the alleged airship through a pair of powerful field-glasses, and still dissatisfied with my conclusions I watched it through a large telescope with a $2\frac{1}{2}$-inch object-glass, an instrument powerful enough to enable me to detect Jupiter's moons and Saturn's ring. A few minutes' observation sufficed to convince me that the airship was none other than our old friend the planet Venus. At that time it was getting near the horizon, and in the vicinity were a number of small clouds. It was the presence of one of these covering the planet that no doubt accounted for the strange nebulous appearance at times, and also for the fact that the rays were visible sometimes on one side and sometimes on the other."

But although the craze for seeing airships spread with the newspapers, the east coast of Yorkshire which had been the place first chosen remained during the few days of scare the main centre of disturbance. It seems that, to soften this usually hard-headed county, some fire balloons were sent up. It was the discovery of one of these on a moor that gave the panic its *coup de grâce* and made any further reporting of German airships futile. Elsewhere the only physical accompaniments and aids to the imagination were the stars and planets.

. Meanwhile the German Government, anxious lest this new bogey could impede the resumption of cordial relations with our Foreign Office, issued an official record of its airships' movements in order to reassure the British public. On Saturday, March 1st, after it had been conclusively proved that not one of the five or six German surviving Zeppelins had even attempted this hazardous passage across the North Sea, a Berlin correspondent wrote to one of our newspapers :—[1]

[1] The *Sunday Times.*

All the week the German Press has been laughing at John Bull's panicky nerves. The story of the phantom airship, the "flying German," as they call it here, flashing red and green lights over the inviolate coasts of Britain, is naturally a source of unmixed joy to the German editor. The official world takes the matter more seriously, and protests against the suggestion that German airships are sent out on nightly spying trips to England as calumnious. Some surprise is expressed that the British Government has not taken steps to allay the alarm in the country. The view to which Germans in general are gradually coming round is that the English fomenters of the fable are not insane, appearances to the contrary notwithstanding, but that the whole scare is a cleverly rigged manœuvre to force the Government to come forward with a big air-fleet bill. Wonderful as are the feats of the latest Zeppelins, they have their limitations. They are delicate as egg-shell china, cost £50,000 apiece to build, and have a weight-lifting capacity far below what many English people seem to believe. Germany has not got twenty airships that can fly to England and back. She has six (all Zeppelins) which might, if necessary, attempt such a flight. Any of these might reasonably expect to reach our coast, but the German experts all agree that it would be doubtful if it could get back. The return voyage with the benzine running low, and the capacity of the ship and crew approaching exhaustion, would probably end in disaster if the wind were contrary. The idea that these ships can drop from two to five tons of explosives on our heads at any time is absurd. None of them could carry such weights, and on a thousand mile trip so much lifting power would be wanted for benzine that there would be practically none left for bombs. So precious is benzine to the air-shipper that he grudges himself light—which he can only generate by depleting his benzine store—so that if any reader is startled by the sight of red and green lights overhead some dark night, he may be sure that they are not carried by German airships.

On March 18th the finest of the remaining Zeppelins, which had cost £100,000, was completely wrecked by a gust of wind at Carlsruhe, and shortly afterwards another one was forced to come to ground at Nancy, where she was examined by French experts.

The Zeppelins may be the best airships in existence, but their value for offensive purposes is practically *nil*, and their value as observation vessels is much disputed even by German experts, who point out that the great disadvantage of the rigid system is the complete dependence of the ship upon its shed, to which it must return at the end of every trip. A forced landing, on anything except the most suitable ground, means certain disaster owing to the rigidity and delicacy of the aluminium frame. Yet, at a very dull and listless Mansion House meeting in May, which was convened by the *Daily Mail* and the Navy League in order to stimulate public expenditure on airships, an Admiral of the Fleet declared that Great Britain, in consequence of these inventions, had ceased to be an island !

With this meeting, at which Mr. Balfour, Lord Rosebery, and other stars who had been announced, were conspicuous by their absence, my account of the Six Panics may fitly conclude.

PRIZE MONEY AND CAPTURE IN NAVAL WARFARE

IN May 1912, over a well-known signature, there appeared in one of our London newspapers a prescription for putting "new heart in the Royal Navy." The casual reader might have expected to find something enlivening or uplifting—more music perhaps and songs, or more chaplains and prayers. But what the writer proposed was more prize money. The hope of gain according to this new pattern of chivalry is the main cause of gallantry at sea; and so he would like our Government to announce that the enemy's ships and commerce will form a fund for the benefit of our seamen in the next war. "The sea-borne commerce of any maritime Power likely to attack us is a potential prize fund in war time, which might raise to affluence many of the best and bravest of the British nation who follow the sea as a profession." A definition of courage and gallantry, so framed as to glorify the armed brigand or pirate who, at no risk to himself and for the purpose of filling his own purse, plunders an unarmed trader, is surely a little bit out of place at the beginning of the twentieth century. We should indeed be in a bad way if the courage that defends the country were venal, and if our prospects of success in a sea fight depended upon plunder. I seem to remember reading a complaint of Nelson about certain captains who preferred privateering to fighting. The *military* value of the right to plunder was criticised and denied by General Napier, the brave and brilliant historian of the war in the Spanish Peninsula. "It is a common, but shallow and mischievous notion," he wrote, "that a villain makes never the worse soldier for an assault, because the appetite for plunder supplies the place of honour, as if the compatibility of vice and bravery rendered the union of virtue and courage unnecessary in war-like matters. In all the host which stormed San Sebastian there was not a man who, being sane, would for plunder only have encountered the danger of that assault, yet under the spell of discipline all rushed eagerly to meet it." Discipline, he adds, has its root in patriotism, and upon this noble stock moderation and respect for property should be grafted by military law. What Napier advised has now been carried out in all civilised armies, and it is recognised that military success, no less than public policy, requires the suppression of those natural cravings for lust and plunder, inherent in the common soldier, which bad commanders under a looser code used to gratify or condone.

However, our naval expert's remedy for the imaginary disease of declining courage (which he imputes by implication to our bluejackets) will serve a purpose; for this frank avowal lays bare the sinister motives underlying our whole system of prize money. It is the relic of a bygone age. Nor is prize money granted by the naval law of Germany or of the United States. In fact the practices of sea warfare are in the last stage of transition from the age of piracy, when every man's hand was against his fellow, to modern usages, under which armed forces are forbidden to plunder private property:—

Non cauponantes bellum sed belligerantes.

Reformers may find comfort in a retrospect. Bad as are the present laws and customs of the sea, they were far worse in the sixteenth, the seventeenth, and the eighteenth centuries. I will take an illustration from the records of the Star Chamber. In the month of July, 1526, a pirate from Boulogne, under "Frenchmen, pirates, and sea thieves," captured a German ship called the *Jesus*, of Danzig, as she lay at anchor in the Humber. The cargo, a general one, belonged to Norwich merchants, by whom the *Jesus*

had been chartered.   It comprised twenty lasts of
rye, thirty lasts and nine barrels of meal, three half-
packs of flax, six hundred oars, six lasts of pitch,
four lasts of tar, one last of osmonds (iron blooms),
two rolls of wax, and half a last of bow-staves.
The bow-staves would have been contraband of war
and the first two items might have been on any list
of contraband in a modern war.   But piracy was
then one of the regular risks in overseas commerce,
and indeed it was regarded like the slave trade
as a legitimate enterprise by most shipowners.
Here then is a really startling difference between
past and present.   Human nature may not be
intrinsically better.   Such barbarities as those
revealed in the Congo and in the Putumayo have
never been surpassed.   Things have been done at
the sight of which Alva or Judge Jeffreys might
have recoiled in horror.   There is plenty of cruelty
but less opportunity.   There are plenty of thieves
and would-be pirates.   But there is no piracy in
time of peace, because there is no means of selling
prizes, thanks to the marvellous mechanical inventions which have almost abolished space and time.
Those French pirates were not troubled by telegraph
or railway lines.   They took their German ship and
their Norwich goods a few miles up the coast to
the flourishing port of Whitby, which, with its well-
to-do merchants and rich monastery, offered a good

market; and they actually sold the whole of their prize, both ship and cargo, at Whitby. It was a popular sale, well patronised by laity and Church, for the Abbot of Whitby joined with five local men in buying part of the foodstuffs. Afterwards, indeed, they got into trouble before the Star Chamber, for they were sued by the German owner of the *Jesus* and the Norwich owners of the cargo. History does not tell the result; perhaps the buyers of the stolen goods bought off the Court also.

Pessimists who despair of Government may find comfort in this glimpse of the past—when a French pirate could seize a German merchantman, full of Norwich goods in the Humber and sell both ship and cargo in the Whitby market. There is little fear of a return to this unblushing piracy. In time of peace the sober aud skilful mariner has little to fear but the weather. But in time of war there is still scope for privateering in substance, though not in name. In spite of the Declaration of Paris, which formally abolished privateering and formally protected neutral trade with belligerents, a shipowner has no protection against an enemy, and even those who fly a neutral flag are liable to almost unlimited molestation and loss, thanks to the right of search and the law of contraband. How perilous are present practices to merchant shipping and commerce may be judged from the Declaration of London, which is

a compromise between what Continental and British
Admiralties want to be allowed to do. It reduces
everything to black and white, and makes the laws of
naval warfare in some respects a little better, in other
respects a little worse, than they appear in the average
text-book. It was drafted with sublime indifference
to the interests of shipowners and merchants by
diplomats and bureaucrats who knew nothing of
trade, and cared less. It has been thrown out by
the House of Lords, and condemned by many
chambers of commerce. It is dead, I suppose;
but it may be useful as a jumping-off ground for
real reforms, which will come when commercial men
have the wit to see their own interests and the spirit
to enforce them.

The history of warfare, by land and sea, is the
history of a gradual restriction of fighting and destruction to the armed forces on either side. The
indiscriminate murder, brutality and theft of barbarous warfare, have gradually been supplanted by
a series of rules, regulations and customs. Civilised
armies are now bound to respect white flags and
ambulances. Peaceful inhabitants and non-combatants are protected from lust and spoliation. At
sea piracy is prohibited; and even privateering is
supposed to have been abolished by the Declaration of Paris. But for some reason or other Great
Britain has obstinately opposed the liberation of

oversea commerce from depredations in time of war, and the present complicated system, not to say chaos, of laws regulating naval warfare—a system admitted by all to be highly unsatisfactory—is mainly due to the attitude of our Government.

The law in its main outlines was described by Earl Loreburn in 1905 a month or two before he took up the seals of office as Lord Chancellor : " At present international law allows a belligerent, as is well known, to capture and confiscate all the merchant ships of the enemy nation and any enemy goods they may contain. Innocent neutral goods in an enemy ship must be released, but are of necessity liable to damage and depreciation in value ; for it takes time to convey the prize to port and obtain adjudication, and the neutral goods will have then to be transhipped or sold in the belligerent port for what they will fetch. In case of perishable goods the loss may be enormous. Enemy goods in a neutral ship, unless contraband, are covered by the neutral flag, so far as those nations are concerned which have adhered to the Declaration of Paris (1856)." In a series of cogent letters to the provincial press, written since he quitted office, the eminent lawyer and statesman has shown in sufficient detail the mischiefs of the existing law and the remedies that should be applied." [1]

[1] The letters have been reprinted by Messrs. Methuen under the title " Capture at Sea."

The net result of this system of naval warfare is clear. It is lawful for sea soldiers to plunder peaceful traders and to seize merchant ships belonging to a private citizen of the enemy, or of a company registered in the enemy's territory. They may plunder a floating shop or a floating warehouse, though they may no longer plunder or destroy a shop or warehouse on the coast. Thus, if the Governments of Great Britain and Germany managed to wrangle themselves into the most stupid of all imaginable wars—for each nation is a great customer of the other, and they have nothing at all to fight about—our cruisers would have to try to capture the *Imperator* and theirs to capture the *Olympic*. The *Olympic* is partly owned and controlled by American capital, but she and the other ships of the White Star Line would be fair and lawful prizes to be divided up among the enterprising crew of any small third-class cruiser that could catch her. If the prize policy is to be upheld, encouraged and developed every sailor in time of war will want to be on a piratical cruiser, that is to say, on a swift ship which has been allowed the privilege of hunting for prizes instead of fighting the armed forces of the enemy.

The favourite plea for naval expansion both at home and abroad is the necessity of protecting merchantmen from capture or destruction. In the debate on the Navy Estimates for 1913 Mr. Winston Churchill practically threw up the sponge so far as the protection of our merchant fleet is concerned. He explained that, as we cannot possibly build enough cruisers to protect a mercantile marine which traverses every navigable sea, the Admiralty is encouraging shipowners to mount guns on their vessels so that in time of war they can take a hand in the game. A pretty comment this on the policy of capture and the abolition of privateering! The Admiralty maintains the right of its captains to plunder the private merchantmen of a foreign enemy, while it admits not only the liability of British merchantmen to be plundered by foreign captains but also its own inability to protect them.

How obsolete and absurd is this law, to which our naval pundits cling so obstinately, must be patent to any one acquainted with the elementary facts of modern commerce. Not only are ships insured against all the risks and hazards of peace and war, but the system of marine insurance is concentrated in this country, and is so complicated by reinsurance that whatever captures and destruction of floating property occur in war are almost bound to injure British interests. Even in the wars of the eighteenth century London insurers often had to pay for the successes of British as well as of foreign privateers.

Another great change that has occurred in the

last fifty years is this. Owing to the joint-stock principle, most of the valuable ships are owned by companies, whose shares may be, and often are, very widely distributed. Hence a naval robber never knows whose property he is looting! And no one suggests that in case of war with Germany our Government should confiscate shares and securities held by Germans in British shipping or other companies, or even that interest on British securities should be withheld from the subjects of a Power with which we are at war. If we went to war with France we should not confiscate English property and English shares held by French subjects, nor would the French Government disturb wealthy Englishmen in the possession of their pleasant villas in France. If neither morality nor common sense can distinguish between a yacht and a villa, between a ship and a shop, why should international law regard one as lawful plunder and the other as sacred property?

Apparently the only argument of our Admiralty and Foreign Office for maintaining the practice of cruising for prizes—they defeated reform at the last Hague Conference—is that so long as we can afford to keep a larger Navy than other Powers, this threat of ours to plunder or destroy their peaceful sea-going commerce in time of war is of value as a preventive, and also as an actual weapon of offence in case war broke out. The reply is that the threat is not very terrible ; and the weapon is either blunt or two-edged. The injury we could do in this way to any possible enemy would be trifling in comparison with the cost of the war. We might compel our adversaries either to lay up their ships during the war, or to sell them to neutrals. In either case the loss would be but a tiny fraction of the whole loss caused by a great war. What could an enemy hope to do to us? Obviously the possibilities of damage would be in proportion to the magnitude of our shipping ; and it happens that half the world's mercantile marine sails under the British flag.

A fleet of small swift cruisers could be built by any Power at the cost of a single " Dreadnought," and such a fleet might play havoc with our merchantmen before it could be hunted down and captured. What destruction could be wrought in this way, or by converted liners, the example of the *Alabama* sufficiently proves. There has been a great fuss lately about the danger to Great Britain of allowing a nation which is at war to convert swift merchantmen into cruisers. As armour-plate is but a poor protection against modern guns or torpedoes, these converted cruisers would be almost as effective as cruisers specially built for preying upon commerce. It is impossible for the law to make a distinction between one kind of cruiser and another,

K

In short, the abolition of privateering by the Declaration of Paris may turn out to be illusory.

Another very strong reason for a reform of the law is this. The policy of "capture" is the chief popular argument which reconciles other nations to naval expansion, and it is clearly responsible for whole squadrons of costly cruisers, built to capture merchantmen or to protect them from capture. A great part of our naval expenditure, one must remember, is not on "capital" ships—so called, I suppose, because they destroy so much capital—but on cruisers, of which we have upwards of 130 in commission. A very large part of our huge expenditure and of our heavy taxation is due to this suicidal policy of commerce destruction. And let our wealthier citizens take warning that if they allow British Governments to pursue unchecked a policy of continual expansion in armaments, they must expect ere long to pay, as they already pay in Japan, an income-tax graduated up to four or five shillings in the pound.

An international treaty exempting all peaceful shipping and merchandise from capture or destruction in naval warfare would certainly mitigate the competition in Naval armaments. If one nation threatens to destroy the commerce of its rivals, its rivals are certain to make great sacrifices to protect their own shipping, and to retaliate in case of need.

"If I were a German," said Mr. F. E. Smith, in the House of Commons on April 21, 1909, "I would never be content, so long as the right to destroy private commerce exists, until my nation had a Navy which would make it impossible for that power of destruction to be exercised. If we could go to Germany and say we had abandoned this practice which jeopardises the commerce that she, as a strong nation, is entitled to protect, and if in spite of the removal of that risk she still continued to build 'Dreadnoughts,' the position of this country would be a very different one. If we had withdrawn from the right to destroy the commerce of our rivals, and in face of that Germany continued to expand her Navy (which, on that hypothesis, could only be for purposes of aggression), I should not shrink from any sacrifice. Until we have made that offer and given that guarantee of our good faith, we are not entitled even to feel surprised that Germany should feel as justified in protecting her Mercantile Marine as we in protecting ours."

At the last Hague Conference the German delegates supported the abolition of capture, and the British delegates opposed it. On the other hand, the British delegates favoured the prohibition of floating mines, and the German delegates opposed it. Why should not each Government withdraw

its opposition, and conclude a convention with the
United States, introducing these two improvements
into the naval warfare of the future? I, for my
part, do not at all despair of seeing such a change
of policy ; for it is demanded by the spirit of modern
commerce, as it is furthered by the growing strength
and complexity of international trade. Brougham,
an old Radical, Sir Henry Maine, an old Tory, and
Cobden were strong supporters of this reform, which
has been accepted and endorsed over and over again
by important Chambers of Commerce. The late
Marquis of Salisbury and Lord Avebury were of the
same opinion ; Earl Loreburn, Lord Morley, Mr.
F. E. Smith and Sir John Simon (the Solicitor-
General) are with us, and Professor Brentano, one
of the ablest advocates in Germany of a friendly
understanding with England, regards this international guarantee of private property at sea not
only as a good thing in itself, but also as a most
excellent way to quell the suspicions of his own
countrymen, great numbers of whom have undoubtedly entertained the feeling attributed to them
by Mr. F. E. Smith, and have therefore acquiesced
reluctantly in the financial sacrifices demanded of
them by the German Admiralty.

THE BALKAN WAR[1]

ERASMUS once wrote a little book called the "Plaint of Peace," which depicted in lively colours the distracted condition of Europe in the 16th century. And Peace to-day is still complaining. She needs all the aid that Commerce, Humanity, and Religion can afford. At this moment the armies of Austria and Russia are still mobilised in readiness for a giant struggle. French newspapers are full of the Revanche. The German Emperor has proposed a levy of fifty millions sterling on German fortunes. We in sea-girt Britain, fenced off by Neptune from the march of conscript armies, have a special mission to Europe—a mission not (as some conceive) to dispatch an expeditionary force to fight in other men's quarrels, but a mission to stop the carnage in the Balkans, to compose the differences of our neighbours, and bring about, if we can, a general and proportionate reduction in the oppressive burden of armaments.

[1] Written in February, 1913.

War needs to be studied like crime or disease not merely in the abstract but in its actual environment whenever and wherever it occurs. The ancient Greeks used to contrast war, as a malady, with peace as a state of health. In peace, they said, the sick recover; in war the healthy fall sick, are wounded, or die. *In peace the old are buried by the young; in war the young are buried by the old.*

A war has been raging since autumn in the Balkans. It is lauded by our military experts as a singularly triumphant and successful war, and the victors are held up to us for envy, admiration, and imitation. "The Bulgarians had conscription, and so beat the Turks. Therefore we should adopt compulsory service in these islands." Of course the Turks also had conscription, and if they had won exactly the same lessons would have been drawn. But let that pass. I want to offer one small contribution to the study of war by writing down what the victors themselves say about the economic and social effects of their still unfinished triumph.

There came recently from Sofia to the office of *The Economist* (which naturally receives financial and official information of this sort) a printed document in French. It was issued by the Commissioners of the National Debt of Bulgaria, and is, in fact, an official statement, or *exposé*, on behalf of the Bulgarian Government. The full title is, "Exposé sur la question d'indemnité de guerre qui doit être imposée à la Turquie." It recites some of the consequences of the campaign, in order to induce Europe to recognise the claim of the allies for an indemnity from Turkey. Thus we learn about the sufferings of Macedonia and Bulgaria, not on the showing of a Turk or of a foreigner, but on the admission of the Bulgarian Government. These sufferings and losses, of course, are part of the case for an indemnity, but they also constitute a case which shall go to the jury of civilised opinion against this particular war and against war in general. They are made, observe, while Bulgaria is still at war, when on politic grounds its Government must be very reluctant to state anything like the full extent of its losses.

First of all, then, this document draws our attention to the state of Thrace and Macedonia, of which Bulgaria expects to get the lion's share. It is a country to which nature has not been unkind, and some of it is extraordinarily rich, as for instance the neighbourhood of Drama, which grows some of the choicest tobacco in the world. But practically all this territory has been ravaged and desolated. The official statement declares (with perfect truth) that it is in no condition to pay the interest on that part of the Turkish debt with which it is to be saddled. On the contrary, a heavy expenditure, we are assured, will be necessary in order to restore what has been destroyed—to say nothing of improvements and developments. For a long time the new acquisitions will be a source not of income but of expenditure, a drain on the public purse of Bulgaria. Instead of defraying the cost of war, they will increase it. The present inhabitants of Bulgaria would be positively better off if they were suddenly disappointed of the prize for which they have made these enormous acrifices of blood and treasure.

And everything that one hears confirms this view of the case. The conquered territory has been twice burnt, twice sacked and pillaged : first by the retreating Turks, then by the Bulgarian bands of irregulars. Most of the Turkish farmers (probably nearly all) are fled or dead. Sir Edwin Pears of Constantinople tells me that at least a hundred thousand Mohammedan non-combatants—old or invalided men, women and children—have passed over from Turkey in Europe to Turkey in Asia with their farm implements, carts, horses, and removable belongings. I suppose that nearly all the farms in Thrace have been stripped bare. All movables have been taken away—furniture and implements, horses, oxen, sheep, goats, and pigs. I saw Macedonia under the Old Turks. It was not a happy country. Nay, it was as miserable as a country not actually at war could be. It must now be the very abomination of desolation.

That is the state of the new territory. Bulgaria will look larger on the map, but it is a map which has been painted red with human blood. It is a desolate and solitary place, an estate mortgaged up to the hilt, on which the rates will be at least thirty shillings in the pound.

So much for the first argument urged by Bulgarian statesmen. They want Turkey to pay them an indemnity in order that they may not be ruined by the cost of reclaiming this wilderness—this territory wasted by fire and sword, by Creusot and Krupp, by Cross and Crescent, strewn with burnt farms and the mouldering carcases of men and horses and cattle.

What is the second argument?

Bulgaria, as a result of the war, say these official exponents of her financial and economic predicament has lost 25,000 men in the prime of life ; and 25,000 more have been invalided or maimed for the rest of their days—50,000 in all, a very moderate estimate I am afraid.[1] Now apart altogether from the economic value of these men—merchants, manufacturers, shop-keepers, farmers, mechanics, labourers, etc.—the Bulgarian Government estimates that the taxpayers who remain will have to find more than £400,000 a year for a generation to come in pensions to the families of the 25,000 dead and to the other 25,000

[1] This was before the storm of Adrianople.

men who are maimed and rendered incapable of earning a livelihood.

And here let me remind you what these lost workers and future charges mean to Bulgaria. It is not a country like ours which can think in millions. Its population at the last census was only 4,337,000. The loss of 50,000 workers and taxpayers to Bulgaria is as the loss of 500,000 men of all ranks and classes would be to our own dear country—husbands, lovers, sons, fathers, brothers. What infinite pathos! The whole available army of Bulgaria under a most severe system of conscription cannot be more than 400,000 men. So that above twelve per cent (one in eight) of Bulgaria's conscript force has been destroyed on the showing of an official document. Then again the whole Bulgarian revenue in 1911 was only £6,700,000, so that a charge of over £400,000 in pensions means nearly one-sixteenth of her whole revenue—equivalent to some £12,000,000 sterling for the United Kingdom. And taxes in Bulgaria are already very high. The Bulgarians have adopted Tariff Reform as well as conscription, and so the necessaries of life are far more expensive than in England.

So much for the second plea.

What is the Third?

The Bulgarian Government declares—and the powerful ambassadors of Krupp and Creusot are not likely to disagree—that, immediately after the war, Bulgaria will have to rearm its troops with new rifles, buy fresh guns, accoutrements, etc., because most of the weapons used in this war are already worn out ; and it will be necessary to return at once to the old level of efficiency.

So the third argument—the third plea—for an indemnity is that the war has worn out Bulgaria's armaments, and that therefore new armaments must be bought ; and as Bulgaria cannot afford to buy them Turkey must pay for them by contributing an indemnity. This really means that English and French creditors must lend more money to Turkey in order to enable Bulgaria to put herself into immediate condition for another war, possibly against her allies. Yet wars are often recommended as an escape from the intolerable burden of rival armaments !

That is the third argument.

What is the Fourth ?

The fourth argument, or plea, for an idemnity is the appalling misery of the country. Since the beginning of war business and credit have been suspended ; no one has been legally bound to pay his debts. Let me translate what the Bulgarian Government has to say on this head : " The national economy will undergo for two years the evil consequences of the war. Our industry and trade have suffered a cruel and painful stagnation for over four months, and there will inevitably follow [1] a mass of failures among business men, manufactures, and artisans. Nor can the losses of the farmers be neglected. The autumn sowings did not take place in time, and there is a risk that the spring sowings will be spoiled if the troops are retained with the colours much longer. The whole country would then be threatened by famine. And beyond all this, the loss to the livestock of the country is enormous, since over 200,000 horses, oxen, and buffaloes employed in the army transport service are dead or useless." This is the fourth, the last and the strongest plea that could possibly be entered by Bulgaria, I do not say for an indemnity from bankrupt Turkey, but for charity from those who can afford it. We can all admire the efficiency, toughness and courage of a race, so long and so cruelly oppressed by the Turkish conqueror. We can all pity the sufferings and sorrows of the sick, the wounded, and the bereaved. We can all, I hope, learn from this awful lesson the horror and folly of war and the terrible consequences, the ruinous results, of attempting to remedy great evils and great grievances by the greatest of all evils. If it proves anything, the present case of Bulgaria

[1] *I.e.*, when the moratorium declared at the beginning of the war, which made debts irrecoverable, comes to an end.

proves that force is no remedy—that economic and social ruin is the price even of a victorious war of liberation.

Other pens may paint the still more pitiful plight of the Turks and the Montenegrins, or the financial embarrassments of Servia and Greece. A word is due to the diplomats of our most civilised and Christian Powers. This conflict would have been avoided if the Concert of Europe had done its duty any time in the last thirty years. The duty was clear; the claim was urgent. We had only to unite in compelling the Turks to carry out a fair scheme of Macedonian reforms. But the Great Powers and their Foreign Offices were taken up with bickerings and jealousies, with ententes and alliances, with colonial wars and rival armaments. The voice of justice and humanity was addressed to deaf ears.

What are the consequences? For months Russia and Austria-Hungary have been mobilised at enormous cost. Their trade has been prostrated. An immense crop of bankruptcies is recorded, and great sums will have to be borrowed to pay for calling out these hundreds of thousands of conscripts from their homes. And now the trouble has spread to France and Germany. In both countries it is proposed to spend many millions upon defensive armaments. How long is this madness to last and where is it to end?

ENGLISH NEWSPAPERS AND THEIR
AUTHORITY

A GERMAN Professor once said to me that he attributed international troubles mainly to newspapers :—"If only we could have a perfect press we might look for a perfect world." But perhaps nations have the press as well as the Governments they deserve. Anyhow, the imperfections of the world will always be represented in its newspapers, if not over-represented; partly because a morbid and mendacious sensationalism is supposed to attract readers, partly because when any great mischief is on foot the first step usually taken is " to square the press." In some countries this operation presents no difficulties. In England much capital and dexterity are required to secure a fair approach to unanimity, even for Stock Exchange purposes. Newspapers, it must be remembered, are either rich and flourishing, or poor and struggling. The proprietors of the rich ones too often regard their property as a purely commercial venture, and allow more latitude to the advertising manager than is compatible with the purity of their news columns. The unsuccessful newpapers, which are on the margin of cultivation or are worked at a loss, cannot afford to be particular unless their owners have large purses and tender consciences. Some shining examples and many sound arguments might be offered to prove that honesty pays, even in a commercial sense, when applied to capably conducted newspapers. But that would open up too large a field. I am content to affirm from experience that advertisers distinguish between newspapers in which they can only buy space and those in which they can also buy opinions in the shape of editorials and business notes and preliminary puffs.

A newspaper is, or should be, a record of events and a mirror of opinions. To secure the utmost possible accuracy and to present your facts in a brief yet attractive form is almost incredibly difficult. In fact, no one who has not served on a great daily paper can quite understand how hard is the task of editor and sub-editor—what wide knowledge, what insight into character, what skill in selection and rejection go to the making of good news columns. No doubt any industrious and moderately well educated person, who starts with a large stock of health and common sense, should make a good journalist, and in time he will develop a remarkable faculty of distinguishing at sight, or by taste, news of a corrupt or romantic or merely futile description. But a good editor will also remember that his paper is a mirror of opinion. Not only will he give fair and accurate reports of important speeches by public men, but he will also offer free entry to his correspondence columns to all who have something to say and can say that something civilly, concisely, and grammatically. In this, and in many other respects, the provincial press is superior to the London press, as English and American newspapers are superior to those of the Continent, which indeed hardly ever print the opinions of their readers. Ministers are absurdly sensitive to London criticisms and to the gossip of the Clubs. They often misinterpret public opinion because they neglect to look for it in the provincial mirror. I will venture to say that a careful reader of the *Manchester Guardian* (Liberal), and the *Yorkshire Post* (Conservative), will be in a far better position to judge public opinion than if he were to devote his attention to any four London newspapers.

Once it has turned the corner a paper can be maintained with a moderate amount of ability. To establish a new one is a difficult job, requiring a good deal of perseverance and capital and enterprise. Casualties are common in Fleet Street. Some years ago the Liberal *Tribune* failed, and the Con-

servative *St. James's Gazette* was extinguished, or
" absorbed," by the *Evening Standard*. These were
penny papers. The last fatality to throw penmen
and compositors out of work was the amalgamation
in 1912 of two competing halfpenny morning newspapers, the *Morning Leader* and the *Daily News*.
Several other halfpenny papers published in London
have disappeared, and altogether popular belief in
the commercial success of the halfpenny press has
received a shock. Like the weekly entertainment
sheets, with or without prize competitions (such as
Tit-Bits, *Answers*, or *Pearson's Weekly*), from which
a new type of newspaper capitalist learned to make
his fortune, the halfpenny Daily depends for its
prosperity on advertisements, and for its advertisements on the extent, or supposed extent, of its
circulation. The cheap and nasty Weekly appeals
to the baser sort. It tries to give the vulgar
something a little more vulgar than that to which
they are accustomed in daily life. This is apparently
the journalistic secret of amusing the common reader
—to startle him with something a little lower than
the ordinary joke. And papers which supply plenty
of these jokes, coupled with little bits of statistical
information, perhaps, or fragments of society gossip,
will sell by the hundred thousand. Such a paper
costs hardly anything to produce, and it may have a
large advertisement revenue. Mr. Harmsworth, now

L

a peer, a most successful manufacturer of cheap
publications, proved his skill in catering for the
popular taste—as well as his real mastery of tech-
nique—by the invention of the *Daily Mail* and the
Daily Mirror, of which, it is said, the first was
designed for those who cannot think, and the second
for those who cannot read.   His purchase of *The
Times* may no doubt have been dictated by non-
commercial considerations, and perhaps it was a
mistake to attempt threepenny (or twopenny) journalism.   When Prince Von Bülow described *The
Times* as an *edition de luxe* of the *Daily Mail*, he
drew attention to a connection, which damaged
the political influence of *The Times* abroad.   It was
a natural retort to the campaign against Germany,
which *The Times* was then carrying on in concert
with officialdom.

The latest device for curing the evils of a press
that does not pay is to amalgamate properties, so as
to eliminate competition.   From the public point of
view this is unfortunate ; for it directly reduces the
number of independent journalists, and has a
tendency, which deserves more detailed study, to
increase the insidious and apparently growing power
of the advertising and commercial departments.   Of
course, we would all rather have one good paper than
two bad ones ; and where two non-dividend-paying
properties will make one profitable concern, we may

regret the loss of an independent voice, but we cannot complain of the decision. Indeed it may be welcomed if it results in the news columns and the leader columns being divorced from the advertising columns. An honest paper is one in which the news is uncoloured and the opinions are unbought. The introduction of advertisements which look like news into the news columns and the substitution of puffs for opinions are two growing mischiefs. A few years ago the City page was improving. But since then one has observed signs of deterioration, especially where independent criticisms might impair the revenue.

Let us turn from the City side, from questions of price and success to problems of style—from newspapers considered as a business to journalism considered as an art.

When the English newspaper first became cheap enough to be popular and widely read, De Quincey analysed the effects of this new institution upon our phraseology. The healthy and holy horror he felt for " journalese " is expressed in the story of his flight from the newspaper-reading landlady who used the word "anteriorly." The conclusion he reaches is that the newspaper style injures the reader more than the writer—not, however, because the reader reads and reads until he insensibly acquires the watery redundancy of his favourite journal, but because, " shrinking through long experience from the plethoric form of cumulative and periodic writing in which the journalist supports or explains his views, every man who puts a business value upon his time slips naturally into a trick of shorthand reading." Now, with all deference to De Quincey, I should have thought that the trick of shorthand reading is a safeguard against the infection of a longhand style. Certainly shorthand reading has become more common and far more necessary in these later days. There is no more reason why our English should be corrupted by casting the eye over the headlines of newspapers than by a glance at advertisement hoardings. De Quincey himself entertains the objection that where so much is certain to prove " mere iteration and teasing surplusage," little can be lost by this or any other process of abridgement. He seems to admit that no injury is to be apprehended from skipping some verbose article about nothing in particular ; but it is the indirect and not the direct effect of shorthand reading that he fears. The patient, we are told, "suffers as an intellectual being, for he acquires a factitious propensity ; he forms an incorrigible habit of desultory reading." Apart altogether from style, this loose or shorthand reading, it is argued, produces inaccuracy. Even from the standpoint of accumulating information, it were a thousandfold better to "read through a score of books chosen judiciously than to have raced through the library of a Vatican at a newspaper pace." True, but a citizen who skips or skims his newspapers will have time for the careful reading of real literature. There can be no dispute as to the fact that nearly all journalists sin against the golden rule which urges us to be terse, so long as it involves no sacrifice of lucidity. Verbosity and even repetition are not vain in the eyes of the journalistic tribe. How many writers in the Press combine brevity with perspicacity? The origin of the evil may be disputed, and certainly its causes are various. For example, many journalists have worked their way up through the ranks upon the basis of a penny-a-line; and a man who earns his bread and butter on the scale of a penny-a-line is certain to cultivate the vice of tautology. Long words are naturally preferred to short ones, and the art of circumlocution is consciously studied or unconsciously learned. I am inclined to think that since De Quincey's death these temptations have been reduced. Often the pressure of advertisements operates against lengthiness, and the efforts of the sub-editor (who is more valued now than he used to be) are directed to correct the very fault which the penny-a-line system has encouraged. The sub-editor has to prune the long-drawn periods of his colleagues who report, or tell stories, or write impressions.

Probably after the penny-a-line system (the system of paying by the line or by the column) the most potent cause of prolixity is haste—the haste in which journalists have to compose. The necessity for speed produces longhand writing as it produces shorthand reading, while the perilous habit of dictating to a stenographer emphasises and extends the mischief. It is in writing as in speaking. Hurry makes long speeches and long articles. Only by the expenditure of time and care can the discourse of an hour be packed into twenty minutes. And here, perhaps, lies the possibility of a reformed journalism. When once the newspaper proprietor has perceived that circumlocution is the most costly vice of the modern newspaper, he will begin to see the wisdom of paying more for a terse inch than for a distended foot. And he may find—after squeezing out the water—that the public will be sensible enough to pay gladly for a square inch of quality as much as it has paid for a square foot of quantity.

A good test of honesty and competence in everyday journalism is its treatment of telegrams. Whether the invention of telegraphy has done less good than harm to journalism is a vexed question. I hope there is a balance of advantage. But the cost of long-distance cabling tempts to undue compression at the correspondent's end and inexcusable expansion in the sub-editor's room. Hence the value of foreign telegrams and the valuation which should be put upon them vary from newspaper to newspaper. Much skill and insight are required for their interpretation. The telegram is, in fact, our chief stumbling-block. We know as a rule how to discount a leading article. Overcharged invective and monotonous praise fall ineffectual upon the public mind. The editor who declares in leaded type that the Government is a gang of criminals is no more persuasive than his rival who assures us that these same criminals never stray from the path of wisdom and righteousness. Abuse, no doubt, is more interesting than praise. Even journalists innocent of accuracy and logic may possess a talent for "general invective," like the youth who once applied to Mr. Morley for work on the *Pall Mall Gazette*.

The public, I suspect, often reacts too far against the opinions which its newspapers seek to impose. Certainly some statesmen obtain undeserved influence and popularity merely because they are denounced by the gutter press. " There must be some good in ' So-and-so,' after all," says the man in the street after reading a furious attack upon him in the *Daily Menace*. And the silent voter has shown over and over again that he is capable of thinking for himself and of resisting the reiterated opinions of the most popular and influential newspapers. But it is another matter altogether when he reads a foreign telegram, duly dated from some distant place. What is he to say when the man on the spot tells him what is thought on the spot, and assures him from Berlin that the whole German nation intends to invade England, that transports are being prepared and that airships are selecting suitable landing-places? We would ask such a person whether he is aware, or whether the suspicion ever crosses his mind, that a certain proportion of most telegrams are actually written in London, and the more eloquent the telegram the larger the proportion. I know of one " foreign telegram " which was actually concocted in the office for a London newspaper of repute. I have seen telegrams of five lines converted by a fluent and imaginative sub-editor into half a column or more. It is to be remembered, of course, that most messages consist of a row of substantives, with a very occasional verb, and therefore it is absolutely necessary that something should be done to produce grammatical sentences. Every telegram is condensed, because every word costs money. And so a good many " of's " and " the's " and " are's " have to be added. The honest policy and the best policy is to add as little as possible, and never to impart anything new into what the writer has sent. If a word is unintelligible let it be omitted. In this busy age nobody wants to read more than he can help, and " watered " stock is at a discount. But there is a rivalry in the press: a long telegram looks well, and newspaper proprietors like to show that they are receiving an immense amount of information from all parts of the world. In 1911 there appeared in a great anti-German newspaper the following peroration to a message "from our correspondent" at Tangier :—

It would be most lamentable if adverse criticism on the part of a small and ill-informed minority of the British public should in any way menace the continuation of this policy, thereby giving rise to even the vaguest doubts as to the mutual disadvantages of the Entente.

Of course, it is perfectly possible that the correspondent in question did actually take to the telegraph office in Tangier every word of this message, but if so he should, I submit, have received a severe reprimand from his proprietors, for the cost must have been enormous, and these forty-seven words contain no Tangier information whatsoever. They merely tell us that the correspondent agrees with the foreign policy of his editor at home. The message ought really to have been sent from the editor to the correspondent since it merely informed us that Sir Edward Grey's critics at that time were a small and ill-informed minority of the British public.

Judging by my own experience I should say that to convert a good telegram into plain English will require an addition of about two words (verbs, articles, prepositions, etc.) to every word in the despatch. But some editors are so proud of having a Foreign Page (which the proprietor can't afford to pay for) that they employ unfortunate individuals to amplify "our own correspondent," adding perhaps ten times as many words as the original contained. This plan is stupid as well as dishonest ; for if a meaning is added the news is falsified, and if not there is merely dilution of sense with waste of paper, ink, labour, and time. In normal times one has not much fault to find with Reuter's telegrams, which are the same for all. But the small halfpenny papers have to cut them down, and one notices that the best parts are often cut out—not as a rule because the news goes against the editorial policy (though this does happen), but because a sub-editor knowing nothing of foreign politics, underpaid and over-worked, has to slash and slice wildly at the last moment to make his stuff fit into the column. Some foreign correspondents telegraph leading articles from foreign centres. Others are agents for armament firms, who in good times make far more by their trade than by their profession. They are apt to despatch false or exaggerated news of gigantic preparations by foreign powers. They are often to be met with at an Embassy. But in such matters foreign diplomacy is more active, though less successful, than British. These "mixed" corre-spondents are chiefly to be found in the Near and the Far East, in Southern America and in the Colonies.

Upstarts who are trying to buy or brag their way into smart society put a very high value on newspapers. The ante-rooms of the fashionable sheets in which society records its doings are eagerly resorted to by gossips and fops and fine ladies, sometimes even by Naval Heroes—all in search of cheap advertisements. They are waiting for the editor :— Donec Bithyno libeat vigilare tyranno.

This practice, and that of the politicians who lay themselves out to coax and wheedle the press, is founded on an old theory of the art of climbing. They may appeal to the story of Psapho the Libyan, who, desiring to be worshipped, took young birds and taught them to sing "Psapho is a god." When they could repeat this perfectly he let them fly to the woods, where other birds caught the words and repeated them. This chorus of the birds so impressed his countrymen that they concluded Psapho to be a god and began to offer him sacrifices. Several attempts have been made by individuals in this and other countries to use newspapers as Psapho used birds, but with less success. A campaign of adulation arouses suspicion. It is far better to be calumniated by the opposition press than to be over-praised by your own. I am certain that the influence and authority of our newspapers is much exaggerated, though every one admits that for fifty years after the passing of the first Reform Bill *The Times* was regarded by the governing classes as a sort of oracle. And though generally subservient to the Government of the day, it did have some influence upon politics and the course of events.

In 1849—64 years ago—Cornewall Lewis published " An Essay on the Influence of Authority in Matters of Opinion." It will never be very popular—its author was pleased to have sold two hundred copies —but it will always be worth reading along with Mill's much greater treatise on *Liberty* and Morley's companion volume on *Compromise*. Lewis reminds us how hard it is to draw the line between facts and opinions, between an object of sensation and an object of judgment, and how confusion is apt to grow the deeper one digs into the foundations of consciousness. But the distinction between matters of fact and matters of opinion is vital to moral and political science. As a metaphysician, Hume denied that things exist apart from our perceptions of them ; but as a political philosopher and critic of society, he took for granted what everybody took for granted. Hume, said Johnson, would not run his head against a table, even though he denied it an independent existence. The difference between a thought and a stone wall may be "ultimately" fanciful. Mind and matter may be "ultimately" one. But so long as human nature and society last all progress and all happiness depend upon our thinking and acting in terms intelligible to our fellow-creatures.

Nobody can begin to philosophise upon the power of "the Fourth Estate" until he understands that there is a sort of rivalry between editorial opinion and sub-editorial fact. The authority of the editorial "we" is disputed by an innumerable host of mute and apparently submissive "men in the street"; whereas fact, or what passes for fact, often has more influence upon opinion than the most skilful and persuasive arguments, or the most brilliant invective. Lord Morley once said he would not much mind who wrote the leading articles if he could control the headlines.

Every journalist and every intelligent reader of a daily newspaper must have at least a superficial view of the dividing line between opinions and facts. The newspaper professes to give you its facts in telegrams or reports, and its opinions in leading articles. The best newspapers, it will be agreed, are those that give the most faithful accounts of what happens at home and abroad, the most accurate reports of important speeches, the fairest records of events, whether they support or weaken the conclusions of its editor. Many journals, of course, succumb to the temptation

of making their news help their views. This is the
crime of crimes—to "fake" correspondence and
tamper with telegrams. The news columns are supposed to reflect facts. They should resemble the art
of an honest photographer. The editorial represents
opinions—it is a comment and criticism upon facts
in the light perhaps of ideals and principles, perhaps
in the heat of passion and prejudice. "I remember
it was with extreme difficulty," wrote Gulliver, "that
I could bring my master to understand the meaning
of the word *opinion*, or how a point could be disputable; because reason taught us to affirm or deny
only where we are certain, and beyond our knowledge we cannot do either. So that controversies,
wranglings, disputes, and positiveness in false or
dubious propositions are evils unknown among the
Houyhnhnms." Opinion, as Lewis puts it, is concerned with matters about which doubt may reasonably arise. The existence of a tree or a ship before
the eyes of two persons is not as a rule disputable, or
a matter of opinion, any more than the proposition
that two and two make four. A full report of the
same speech by two good shorthand writers will be
practically identical. But opinions about the speech
may, and—if it is on a party question by a party
leader—probably will, vary almost indefinitely. Just
as the judge has to distinguish between questions of
fact and questions of law, so the newspaper reader

has to discriminate between questions of fact and questions of opinion, and also (if he can) between what is written in good faith and what is written to order—at the dictation of a Government, in return for valuable consideration, in lively gratitude for past favours, or in livelier expectation of favours to come. In free countries we have no press censorship, but how many journalists can afford to be independent? And how many of those who can afford to be independent will consistently resist the subtle influences of interest, appearing as it does under so many specious and attractive disguises?

The newspaper reader has so little time to spare for investigation that he might be expected to swallow all that he sees in print, were it not that there are so many conflicting versions of the truth, so many newspapers disputing for his patronage in various accents and with differing voices. Unless he lives the life of a hermit, with only a single favourite newspaper, our reader finds himself driven into intellectual and critical activity by perpetual variations of fact, and a perpetual clash of opinion. Thus the very multiplicity of newspapers deprives editorial decrees of their pontifical authority, and accounts for a very healthy and, perhaps, increasing scepticism. The more we are read the less we are believed, unless by solid argument, proven facts and truthful forecasts we win the confidence of our public.

To illustrate my argument let me take the cases
of 1880, and 1886, and 1906. From 1877 to 1880
Mr. Gladstone had been agitating against Lord
Beaconsfield's foreign policy. He had denounced
him for supporting the Turks, for invading Afghani-
stan, and for annexing the Transvaal. In fact, he
had arraigned Disraeli's "Imperialism" as the very
antithesis of Liberalism. This policy aroused great
enthusiasm in the country, but official Liberals were
undecided. Many of them were at least as im-
perialistic as their opponents. Among the Radical
jingoes of that time, perhaps the ablest and most
influential was Joseph Cowen, editor of the *Newcastle
Daily Chronicle*, a paper read by every one who
counted in Northumberland and Durham. Cowen
felt so strongly about the merits of the Tory foreign
policy that he supported it vigorously at the General
Election of 1880. Here was an able writer with a
daily paper practically monopolising the attention
of two counties. He had transferred his allegiance,
though he was still called a Radical. Yet at the
General Election of 1880, with this powerful newspaper
against them, the Liberals swept the two counties,
only one or two seats being retained by the Conservatives. The case of 1886 is equally instructive.
The Liberal Government of 1880 to 1885 had been,
on the whole, a disappointment. It had mishandled
the Bradlaugh controversy. It had been unlucky

or unskilful in Egypt, and neither its Land Bills nor its Coercion Bills had removed the miserable disaffection of Ireland. Nevertheless, the Radical programme of Mr. Chamberlain was making a powerful appeal to the democracy, while the passing of the Reform Bill, which enfranchised the agricultural labourer, put Mr. Gladstone in so strong a position that Parnell, wishing to hold the balance, gave the Irish vote to the Tories, and so produced the situation out of which a Home Rule Bill might be expected to grow. Everybody knows how, after the General Election of 1885, Mr. Gladstone developed a Home Rule policy; how Lord Salisbury's Government, when it met the new Parliament in January of 1886, was defeated on a Radical amendment by 329 to 250; how Mr. Gladstone formed a new Government, but was unable to carry the Duke of Devonshire, Mr. Chamberlain, and Mr. John Bright with him; how the Home Rule Bill was consequently defeated on the second reading by 30 votes. At the dissolution of 1886 Mr. Gladstone found in his appeal to the country that he had lost not only some of the strongest and most influential of his colleagues, but also some of his most powerful newspapers in the provinces. Mr. Chamberlain carried off Birmingham and district, and the *Birmingham Post* became the oracle of Liberal Unionism in the Midlands. Many other local newspapers left

M

Mr. Gladstone on the same issue, under the influence of the Cavendishes and other great Whig families which then severed their connection with Liberalism. But to all appearance the chief havoc was wrought in Scotland ; for the two great organs of Scottish Liberalism, by far the most important newspapers in Scotland, the *Scotsman* and the *Glasgow Herald*, refused to follow the hero of the Midlothian campaigns into his Irish adventure ; and in the election of 1886 they threw the whole weight of their authority into the Unionist scales. The *Manchester Guardian*, however, the favourite newspaper of Lancashire, which yielded then, as it yields now, to scarcely any other English newspaper in commercial and political authority, devoted itself unsparingly to the cause of Home Rule. The *Leeds Mercury*, too, which still maintained a lead (soon to be lost) as the principal exponent of Yorkshire opinion, remained with the main body of the party. The *Bradford Observer* also stood in with Home Rule. So far, then, as the press was concerned, Mr. Gladstone had lost almost everything in Scotland and nothing in Lancashire and Yorkshire. What was the result of the polls? He held Scotland fairly well, but lost heavily in Lancashire and Yorkshire.

A last illustration may be taken from the General Election of 1906. Nobody could dispute the predominance of the Conservative and Unionist press. The Liberals during the campaign had not a single penny morning newspaper in London. The ill-starred *Tribune* only appeared after the polling began. In the provinces and Scotland most of the penny provincial papers were Conservative, the *Manchester Guardian* being the one great exception. Among the halfpennies the balance was only less unequal. Upon the whole, it may be doubted whether, out of all the political newspapers sold in England and Scotland, one in five supported Sir Henry Campbell-Bannerman. What happened? The Liberal party obtained the most sweeping victory ever recorded in our political annals. Once more the electors had rejected editorial authority.

In the face of these instances it is clear that the authority of the Press is much exaggerated. The number of men who regard their newspaper as their oracle must be comparatively small ; perhaps there are as many in whom its partisanship excites a critical and contradictory spirit. Probably, too, the news columns are scanned more eagerly than the editorials. When a great political contest takes place the elector reads the speeches of the rival leaders, and no " live " newspaper can afford to reject the good copy which the speech of a popular orator on the other side affords. But let us be clear as to what is meant by resting opinion on authority, lest we may be deceived by words. If one is convinced by a legitimate process of reasoning, the opinion so formed does not rest upon authority. Nor does an opinion adopted from motives of interest or fear rest upon authority. A man who entertains an opinion upon authority, like the man who invests on the mere advice of his broker, does so because he believes that the person whose opinion he adopts, or whose advice he follows, is likely to be right. It may be mere laziness, it may be the result of experience. And who shall blame a man, who has found his own judgment time after time worse than another's, trusting to that other, and treating him as a guide, philosopher, and friend? The confidence and trust which some public men and some journals inspire are great national assets. The influence of a fine public character grounded upon the constant holding up of ideals, the constant exposition of principles, the constant application of those ideals and principles to policy, is a plain example of the legitimate influence of authority over opinion. The same may be said of a newspaper which has gradually built up a reputation for intelligence and probity. Its influence is measured by the trust and confidence of its readers.

IS POLITICAL CONSISTENCY A VIRTUE?

ONE afternoon in the autumn of 1912 the House
of Commons enjoyed a duel between Sir
Edward Carson and Mr. Winston Churchill, in the
course of which they mutually reproached one another with inconsistency. Each charged the other
with having been a Home Ruler at one period and
a Unionist at another; and Mr. Austen Chamberlain,
who started life as a sort of Home Ruler, as a
Radical of the deepest die and a Free-trader of
the most orthodox school, defended the consistency
of Sir Edward Carson against the criticisms of Mr.
Churchill. It was urged against the leader of Ulster
Unionism that he joined the National Liberal Club
when Mr. Gladstone hoisted the Green Flag and
left it when the first Home Rule Bill was defeated.
The public will probably smile over the incident.
The political opinions of a young Irish barrister,
taught by the exigencies of a professional career
to watch the political barometer, should not be too
severely examined. It was a long time ago; and

since Sir Edward Carson became a Unionist Government lawyer he has never faltered. Indeed, he has often been more Unionist than his colleagues. His real inconsistency lies in this, that his military progress through Ulster and his incitements to lawlessness do not harmonise with the character of a Privy Councillor who has been the King's Attorney-General. Mr. Austen Chamberlain's change from Radicalism to Conservatism also occurred at a time when the mind is naturally flexible, and his change from Freetrade to Protection was at least a shining example of filial piety. Besides, most of the Conservative leaders went through the formula of calling themselves Tariff Reformers under the stress and strain of the raging, tearing propaganda. During this same debate Mr. Winston Churchill attributed his own conversion from the Tory to the Liberal party to Free-trade, though his father had been regarded as a champion of Fair Trade. But there was no more reason why young Mr. Churchill should not have joined the triumphant Liberals in 1906 than why young Mr. Carson should not have joined the triumphant Unionists in 1887. The real doubts about Mr. Churchill during the last year, raised by the tone and drift of his speeches, are whether he may not be contemplating another change of party; and these doubts have been strengthened by the fact that his last book of speeches (a very Radical

production of the panic year 1909) is no longer
for sale. But in such cases it is dangerous to
prophesy. There is certainly now alive a peer who
has changed his party three or four times. But is
there any precedent for a politician of Cabinet rank
" ratting " twice within a decade?

In its vulgar or popular form consistency is, of
course, party loyalty. It is only a rule of thumb.
You may alter your opinions; in fact, you must
alter your opinions if the party programme changes,
because you are a member of the party, to which
you contribute such political light or heat as you
possess. On the whole, this rough test is good
enough. A politician is a public character. He
joins the party which attracts him most, and having
become a member of the crew, he usually sticks to
it in fair weather and foul. Some men naturally
think of the party solely as a ladder to promotion,
a means of attaining office or title. Others happily
are inspired more by public spirit than by personal
ambition. They associate their party with principles,
projects, and ideals; with a popular hero perhaps,
or a great tradition. They like public work for
its own sake. These men are the salt of a party,
and in the long run they count for far more than
the mere trimmers and time-servers. An excess
of consistency and devotion to principle is often
troublesome to the Whips, whose business it is to

get men at all times and in all circumstances into the party lobby. There is also a false sort of independence. Thus a low-class politician often affects a show of independence when he fails to get what he wants. He pretends that his conscience revolts against something that has been said or done by the leaders, the truth being that he has missed a decoration or a billet. The public cannot always distinguish between these two classes of "disloyalty," and that is one reason why good men are wisely anxious not to leave their party except on the very gravest grounds. Earnest Free-trade Unionists have been heard to say that Sir Robert Peel was not justified in breaking up the Tory party in 1846, even for the sake of repealing the Corn Laws. Earnest Home Rule Liberals have applied the same criticism to Mr. Gladstone's policy in 1886. There was wit and wisdom in Lord Randolph Churchill's irreverent description of "an old man in a hurry." A self-governing party cannot be marched in a new direction at a moment's notice.

But though the public likes constancy, it is tolerant of one conversion. Just as every dog is supposed to be allowed one bite, so every statesman may be allowed to break once with his past. The younger Pitt, who began as a Whig, a Free-trader, and a Parliamentary reformer, ended as the supreme, undisputed and uncompromising chieftain of the stern and unbending Tories. Burke was turned by the French Revolution from the champion of national and religious rights into the hottest of Imperialists. Peel, most correct and official of pre-Reform Bill reactionaries, was converted to Catholic emancipation and Free Trade. Disraeli began life as a sort of Radical-Socialist. Palmerston was a Tory Minister for the first half of his life, when the Tories held undisputed sway, and a Whig for the second, when the Whigs were supreme. He carried the eighteenth-century idea of party politics as a game of Parliamentary tactics down to the year 1865. A favourite of Canning, he served after Canning's death under Lord Grey, Canning's bitterest opponent. He was a colleague of Lord Chancellor Eldon and of Lord Chancellor Brougham. Lord Derby, the Tory Prime Minister, was a Reformer and a Whig up to 1835. He attacked the Irish Church in 1833, and defended it in 1866. Mr. Gladstone was a Tory till 1846, a Peelite or Conservative Free-trader till 1860, and thereafter foremost among Liberal statesmen. Mr. Joseph Chamberlain, who from 1880 to 1885 frightened moderate Liberals out of their lives with his Radical Programme and doctrine of ransom, while he infuriated the jingoes by his Little Englandism and the Fair Traders by his biting attacks on Protection, passed through the Irish gate into the Unionist party, gave it an over-dose of

Imperialism, and finally forced it to swallow Protection. Yet most of these conversions from opposites to opposites were effected slowly, and by decent stages. It is an advantage of our party system that the prodigal son is not too readily welcomed, unless, indeed, he has a large purse and a small head. The more brilliant the emigrant the more difficult he finds it to effect a landing save in very exceptional weather.

A long essay might, indeed, be devoted to the pros and cons of political consistency. But the sum, pith, and substance of it all can be compressed into a few sentences. In public, as in private life, what we all prize most is trust and confidence. Variability and instability are incompatible with these feelings. If we cannot forecast what a person is likely to do if he shifts with every change of circumstance, if he has no moral rules and no political principles, if it be apparent that personal ambition and selfish interest are his only guides, then, of course, brilliancy and ability will never raise him very high in the public estimation. The rigid and unbending consistency of the doctrinaire, who avoids all compromises and neglects to watch the winds and the tides, is so rare that it may be dismissed as a harmless error. For political consistency, though it may sometimes be pushed too far, is a prime virtue of public life; and it is to our credit as a nation that brilliant vacillations attract but a light and transient popularity.

JOHN BRIGHT AND HIS PLACE IN POLITICS [1]

ONE day, in conversation with a high authority, I remarked—and the remark was allowed to pass—that John Bright must certainly count among the first six British Statesmen of the Nineteenth Century. For administration, indeed, he had as little talent as Disraeli; but skill in handling clerks and red tape is no necessary ingredient in high statesmanship. Otherwise, what should we say of Mazzini and Cobden, who never held office at all? When we have paid our tribute to the genius of administration in the persons of Peel and Gladstone, we may contrast, without comparing, the immensely superior influence wielded over public policy in the larger sense by Cobden and Bright. They were the originators, who supplied both light and heat; the others were the skilled engineers and mechanics, who supplied and fitted the appropriate machinery. Those who carried out the ideas of the Manchester school

[1] Written on the centenary of his birth.

were great men, but were they greater than those who formed and propagated the ideas? Is the scholar greater than his master?

John Bright was born at Rochdale on Nov. 16, 1811, when Cobden and Disraeli were little boys of seven, and Gladstone was just beginning to walk. Macaulay, in his twelfth year, was composing heroic verses which some Poets Laureate might envy; John Stuart Mill, at five, was communing with the Greek philosophers in their own tongue; Palmerston was already firmly glued to office as Secretary for War.

It was a year of misery and despair, a year marked by Wordsworth's sonnet as "the worst moment of these evil days." Western Europe lay prostrate at the feet of Napoleon. England, unconquered, was already invaded by those spectres of famine and ruin which clung about her till near the end of the Hungry Forties. And the dark clouds of social discontent went on gathering for a storm, until, in 1832 and 1846, revolution was met and mastered by vast political and economic changes. When John Bright celebrated his twenty-first birthday, the great preliminary victory was won. The Reform of 1832 made possible the Repeal of the Corn Laws. Five years before his death the enfranchisement of the agricultural labourer had converted the oligarchy of his boyhood into a representative democracy.

The Brights came of an old Quaker stock of

Wiltshire farmers. One of them, Abraham, moved to Coventry early in the eighteenth century, and there, in 1775, our hero's father Jacob, was born. In 1802 Jacob Bright settled at Rochdale as book-keeper to a firm of cotton-spinners, and before long started manufacturing on his own account. By his second wife, Martha Wood, Jacob had a large family. The eldest son died young. John was the second, and so became the head of the family. His school-days began unsuccessfully at Ackworth in 1822. He was soon afterwards sent to the Friends' School at York, and in 1825 for one more year's training to Newton-in-Bowland, near Clitheroe, where he learnt the gentle art of angling. At fifteen his education was thought to be complete, and he began to work.

More will be known of Bright's youth, his friends, his pursuits, and the gradual growth of his mind, when Mr. George Trevelyan's biography is on our shelves. It is enough for our purpose that the boy set himself to learn his father's business in the mill and the warehouse, became intimate with the machinery, and familiar with the men. In those days bad times meant wholesale starvation in the manufacturing districts. Riots, destruction of machinery, revolutionary meetings, hangings and deportations produced some sturdy politicians, and the Radicalism which John Bright learned was robust. At the same time, he enjoyed himself. He played

cricket, fished, helped to start a Rochdale literary
and philosophical society, gave addresses on Temper-
ance, and threw himself into a lively agitation against
Church rates, which ended in a hard-won victory
over the rich and powerful vicar of Rochdale. In
1833 Bright travelled through the Low Countries
and Germany, and in 1836 he made an eight months'
tour in the Mediterranean, partly by steamer, partly
in a sailing ship. He saw Turkey, Greece, Italy,
and Portugal, bringing back a store of varied impressions, on which, like Cobden, he was to draw in
many future controversies.

When Cobden and Bright came afterwards into
the front rank of politicians, they put their knowledge
of Europe to good use. Had these two plain men
of business stayed at home, their great doctrines
of foreign policy might never have been formed,
or, having been formed, might have failed, for want
of practical illustration and of those critical comments
which observation alone can supply. A Parliament,
which sat at the feet of Palmerston and hung on
his lips, listened in blank wonder, when commercial
upstarts, unbirched by Eton or Harrow, unpolished
by Oxford or Cambridge, stood up to the here-
ditary caste, and exposed its moth-eaten policies,
not merely as morally wrong, but as pernicious to
British interests. Both had seen the Old Turkish
horse (not so very different from the Young one)

on which Aberdeen and Palmerston and Disraeli put our money. Both had seen the Don Pacifico type of swindler (the Civis Britannicus) in the Levant. Both knew, not merely from the Manchester Market or the Port of Liverpool, but by shrewd observation abroad, how much our mills depended on foreign markets and our shipping on foreign custom, how vastly and overwhelmingly true was Lord Derby's saying : " The greatest of British interests is peace." And so, by degrees, they taught their generation to avoid foreign entanglements and to keep out of foreign quarrels. By their influence the competition in armaments was mitigated and the cause of peace advanced. Their lessons seem to have been forgotten, and we are paying the penalty. A new diplomacy has already given us an income-tax graduated up to 1s. 8d. in time of peace, with a scale of armaments unheard of and unparalleled.

It was a common enthusiasm for the education of the working classes that brought about the life-long alliance between Bright and Cobden, the least selfish and the most fruitful political comradeship in our political history. With occasional differences of temper or tactics, these two dauntless men worked together harmoniously, consistently, and strenuously in prosperity and adversity, nearly always against society, often against the populace, for the good of their fellow men and for the advancement of civilization. Each had a strong will and an independent genius, which acted powerfully on the other. Their friendship began when Bright was in his twenty-sixth year. Cobden had already become prominent in the public life of Manchester as a municipal and social reformer. So, in 1837, young Bright went to see if he could persuade the Manchester lion to speak on Education at Rochdale, a place of some manufacturing importance, and a Parliamentary borough under the Reform Bill. Long afterwards, when unveiling the Cobden statue at Bradford, Bright told how, on this occasion, he found Cobden in his office in Moseley Street. " I introduced myself to him. I told him what I wanted. His countenance lit up with pleasure to find that others were working on the question, and he, without hesitation, agreed to come."

In that same year, 1837, the year of Queen Victoria's accession, the famous Anti-Corn Law League was formed at Manchester, with Cobden and Bright on the first provisional committee. Bright spoke several times in the next two years at Anti-Corn Law meetings. In 1841 Cobden was returned for Stockport, and in September came the great tragedy of Bright's life and the noble compact of public service, which he afterwards described in such moving and beautiful language : " I was at Leamington, and on the day when Mr. Cobden called on me—for he happened to be there at the same time on a visit to some relatives—I was in the depths of grief—I might almost say of despair—for the light and sunshine of my house had been extinguished. All that was left on earth of my young wife, except the memory of a sainted life and of a too brief happiness, was lying still and cold in the chamber above us. Mr. Cobden called upon me as my friend, and addressed me, as you might suppose, with words of condolence. After a time he looked up and said: 'There are thousands of homes in England at this moment where wives, mothers, and children are dying of hunger. Now, when the first paroxysm of your grief is past, I would advise you to come with me, and we will never rest until the Corn Law is repealed.'" Bright accepted his friend's proposal, knowing, as he said, that this description of the country was not exaggerated. "I felt in my conscience that here was a work which somebody must do, and, therefore, I accepted his invitation, and from that time we never ceased to labour hard on behalf of the resolution we had made." The discussion, he added, "whether it was good for a man to have half a loaf or a whole loaf," had begun in earnest two years before their solemn covenant; "but for five years or more (1841–6) we devoted ourselves without stint;

N

every working hour almost was given up to the discussion and to the movement."

When the hour of victory came, Cobden and Bright were popular heroes. The governing classes had to admit that the new men had beaten the old guard. There was still a great work of fiscal emancipation, but there were plenty of official statesmen to do it. The Manchester school now began to preach a wider gospel—Peace, Free Trade, Goodwill among Nations—and, as a corollary, retrenchment in armaments. Partly as philosophical Radicals, partly because they found more sympathy with their views among the working men, they began also to preach the necessity for a wider franchise, in order that "the greatest number" might have a voice in the promotion of its "greatest happiness."

But social and political progress was rudely stopped by the Crimean War. In vain did the two friends row against the stream of Jingo sentiment. In vain did they protest in the name of justice, reason, and humanity. In vain did they proclaim the doctrine of non-intervention. Our Government drifted into war, with the passionate approval of almost the whole nation. Cobden and Bright fell in a moment, as it were, from being the most popular to the most odious of public men. Every sort of abuse was heaped on their heads. In many a town of the North a little band of devoted disciples stood with them, but the mass of war feeling was overwhelming. Bright was burnt in effigy. Cobden's own constituents carried resolutions against him. Probably no modern war has been opposed by so small a minority; certainly there is none which the historian finds more difficult to justify on any rational view of British interests. In fact, within a few years the most cynical statesmen admitted that it had been a mistake—we had put our money on the wrong horse. But the awful suffering of the Crimean War was not all loss. It left a lesson in public morals and practical statesmanship which will outlast the barbarous empire of our Turkish ally. It left us a national heritage in the immortal speeches and letters of Bright and Cobden, with some pages in Morley's " Life of Cobden," that could ill be spared. Even among obscure persons the combination of moral courage and common sense is rare. But when popular heroes, who might aspire to any office in the land, deliberately sacrifice their hard-won popularity—this is indeed a spectacle so rare and elevating that every reader in every generation should gratefully salute and celebrate the names of Cobden and Bright. In the House of Commons, indeed, their influence was felt all through the Crimean War. There were many uneasy consciences, besides some minds free from moral pricks, which secretly admitted the force of their arguments. You have only to read the debates and letters of the day to feel this. The insults of Palmerston, and the *Times*, and of the lesser fry, were tolerated by timidity and applauded by the vulgar insolence which is mistaken for patriotism in war-time. Peace had to be made at last; and when it was made most people saw that there were no assets. Yet Jingoism was not dead. The brutality even of the China War was popular enough to extinguish the Manchester school at the polls in 1857, after they had beaten Palmerston in Parliament in the affair of the Lorcha Arrow. Bright was then abroad resting, and unfit for active work. Cobden, physically unequal to the strain of one contest, let alone two, wore himself out fighting Bright's battle and his own. They were both beaten—Cobden at Huddersfield, Bright at Manchester. Their leading friends were also defeated—Gibson, Fox, and Miall. It was a rout comparable (it has been said) to that of "the Peace Whigs" in 1812. How did John Bright receive the blow? With serene philosophy, undaunted courage, and sublime hope. The more one sees and hears of politics and of the eternal controversies between Ins and Outs, the more refreshing and inspiriting is that admirable letter On the Defeat of the Manchester School, which he wrote to Cobden from Venice.

A little more than two years later Cobden had the satisfaction of refusing the offer of a seat in Palmerston's Cabinet. Eleven years later Bright joined the greatest Peace Ministry of modern times—a Ministry founded upon and guided by the principles and maxims of the Manchester school alike in home and foreign policy. No one will ever begin to understand Bright's political character, or the moral authority which he exercised in later life over the minds and hearts of his countrymen, unless and until he firmly grasps the fact that Bright was neither an office-seeker nor a wirepuller; that he cared nothing for manipulating a caucus, or for dispensing patronage. He was, fortunately, independent of salaries, not because he was very rich, but because his habits and tastes were simple. On the occasion of his death, Mr. Gladstone referred in the House of Commons to "the extraordinary efforts which were required to induce Mr. Bright under any circumstances to become a servant of the Crown." Let me quote a few characteristic words from this generous eulogy :—

"It was in the crisis of 1868, with regard to the Irish question, and when especially the fate of the Irish Church hung in the balance, that it was my duty to propose to Mr. Bright that he should become a Cabinet Minister. I do not know that I can ever undertake so difficult a task, but this I do know—that from eleven o'clock at night until one o'clock in the morning we steadily debated that subject, and it was only at the last moment that it was possible for me to set aside the repugnance he had felt to doing anything which might, in the eyes of any one, even of the more ignorant of his fellow-countrymen, appear to depart in the slightest degree from that lofty independence of character which he had heretofore maintained, and which, I will venture to say, never, to the end of his career, was for a moment lowered." [1]

Had Disraeli been alive, he too would have done justice to Bright's memory. Disraeli had a more penetrating insight into character than Gladstone, and if he lacked the sonorous and majestic eloquence of his rival, yet he could sometimes reveal a great man in true perspective, and in language of almost Tacitean brevity. And here let me say that modern political writers, especially of the Radical school, are apt to forget the services rendered to Great Britain by Disraeli in the middle years of last century. He did nothing either to make or to prolong the Crimean War, which he described as "just, but unnecessary." When scares were being worked up by militarists and Jingoes, and the public was alarmed by the designs attributed to Napoleon the Third, Disraeli, in Opposition—when he might easily have made party capital by another policy—"consistently

[1] Hansard, March 29, 1889.

laboured "—I quote the well-weighed words of Spencer Walpole—"to remain on good terms with France." And when the Invasion Panic led to demands for fortifications and armaments, he struggled "almost more consistently than Gladstone himself" on behalf of economy. He saw that, to increase the strength of a country, you should increase its resources, and declared that the power to raise the income-tax in an emergency is a far more formidable weapon than increased armaments in time of peace. Lastly, during the Slave War, when Society was clamouring for a recognition of the Confederate States, and when both Gladstone and Lord John Russell blundered execrably, " Disraeli never suffered himself to depart from the attitude of strict neutrality which he maintained from the beginning, and preserved to the end, of the great American Civil War." On the last point we have Bright's own testimony (" Hansard," vol. 177, p. 1619), given in the House of Commons to the Tory Party: " Learn from the example set you by the right honourable gentleman. He, with a thoughtfulness and statesmanship which you do not all acknowledge—he did not say a word from that bench likely to create difficulty with the United States." In short, Disraeli had learned much from the Manchester school, and if he afterwards forgot some of it in office, we must not lose sight of his self-restraint and prescience as leader of the Opposition.

This digression upon the relations between John Bright and Benjamin Disraeli—between the "Old" Radical and the "Young" Tory—suggests another upon the relations between the leaders of the Manchester school and the Philosophical Radicals. Originally, if it is permissible to repeat oneself,[1] the difference and the connection between the Manchester Men, or Cobdenites, and the Philosophical Radicals, or Benthamites, was this: The Manchester Men were disciples of Adam Smith and Bentham, while the Philosophical Radicals followed Bentham and Adam Smith. But what really distinguished Cobden and Bright from John Stuart Mill and his school were actuality and simplicity and concentration. Plain men, to whom Mill's "Political Economy" was Greek, were quite at home with Cobden or Bright. Upon one reform —the proposal to exempt peaceful shipping from capture in war-time—the two schools differed, for Mill at first favoured the rule as likely to prevent war. Morley pronounces Mill's argument to be "abstract and unreal when compared with Cobden's." Mill's half-hearted admission of protection for infant industries is another illustration. Bright used to say that

[1] See "Free Trade and the Manchester School" (Harper Bros.), page xi.

the practical mischief caused by this paragraph has out-weighed all the wise things that are inculcated in Mill's "Political Economy." But another and younger philosopher, idealistic in aim, if obscurantist in style, was an enthusiastic admirer of Bright. This was Thomas Hill Green, a moral and political philosopher of no mean order, who stood out at Oxford and Balliol against the glittering materialism of Jowett. A contemporary wrote of Green in 1862: "he is a Philosophical Radical, but of a very particular kind. Almost all his definite opinions might be endorsed by Bright or Cobden." His biographer, Nettleship, has recalled a passage from Green's maiden speech on a political platform, delivered in 1867. Speaking of John Bright, he said: "If he had not kept his light burning through the thick darkness of the Palmerstonian *régime*, I know not whether the nation would have emerged from its political apathy during this generation. For many years he stood virtually alone,

> 'Against example good,
> Against allurement, custom, and a world
> Offended, fearless of reproach and scorn.'

This is the man who, the 'educated Liberals' tell us, is not a statesman. I want to know who shall have most credit for statesmanship, men who 'take upon them the mystery of things, as if they were

God's spies,' and who yet cannot see one inch
beyond their nose—men who, for these years past,
have been writing themselves down as asses in
prophecies which the next week's news refuted—or
the man who throughout his career, whether in
regard to the Crimean War, or India, or America,
has shown a foresight that has been verified by
events.   They call him a demagogue : but whom
does the name best fit?   Men whose trade it is
to prophesy smooth things to any one who has
aught to give, or one who has been a butt for
more insult and contumely than any one in this
generation?   They say he is a revolutionist, when
they themselves advocate a system which empties
the country of its yeoman, the natural support of
true conservatism, and, by treating five-sixths of
the people as political aliens, leads by inexorable
necessity to revolution."

This Oxford stalwart was inclined to regret
Bright's adhesion to the Gladstone Ministry in 1868,
just as some may now regret the rapid inclusion
of independent Liberals in the charmed circle of
officialdom.   It may be interesting to add that
among Bright's speeches Green's favourites were
those on India in the House of Commons, June 24,
1858; those on reform and foreign policy at Birmingham, October 27 and 29, 1858, and at Rochdale, January 28, 1859; and that on the National

Defences in the House of Commons, August 3, 1860, the last being "that of a sober man among drunkards." After meeting Bright at Oxford in 1864, Green wrote: "I can best describe him as a great brick. He is simple as a boy, full of fun, with a very pleasant flow of conversation and lots of good stories. He does not seem to mind what he says to anybody; but though he is sufficiently brusque, his good humour saves him from ever seeming rude. There is nothing declamatory or pretentious about his talk; indeed, though very pleasant, it would not be particularly striking were it not for the strong feeling which it sometimes shows." It was about this time, I think, that my father and some Huddersfield Liberals met Bright as he was passing through the town, and asked him eagerly what he thought of the political outlook. He answered, with concise emphasis: "We shall do no good till that old heathen, Palmerston, is gone." When Bright once reached an opinion on either men or things, it was clear and unambiguous. He was "upright and downright," as his old friend, the late Dr. Spence Watson put it. And though his mind, like most strong minds, had its prejudices and limitations, he was always eager for the truth, and careful to master the case of his opponents.

The twenty-five years of co-operation with Cobden

(only ended by Cobden's all-too-early death in 1865)
were certainly the great period in Bright's public life.
But though the loss was irreparable, his genius as an
orator and his authority over the public mind were
to be again and again displayed.   When, at last, he
broke reluctantly with Gladstone in 1886, he was
returned unopposed by his constituents in Birmingham.   Perhaps the most conspicuous moments in
these later years were his championship of franchise
reform in 1866 and 1867, his support of Irish Church
Disestablishment and of Land Reform, his resignation
on the bombardment of Alexandria in 1882, his
attack on the House of Lords in 1884, with a
remarkable forecast of the Veto Bill, and, finally,
his letters and speeches against Mr. Gladstone's
Home Rule Bill in 1886.   In the earlier period
Cobden, no doubt, deserved, as he has received, the
chief credit for the repeal of the Corn Laws and the
enactment of Free Trade.   But can we be sure that
he could have won the victory without Bright?   And
against Cobden's pre-eminence in economic reasoning, and in a train of persuasive argument, we may
set Bright's intense moral force and the sublime
flights of eloquence which thrill us still, though we,
mere readers, cannot hear the voice, or see the
gestures, or breathe the atmosphere.   Is there anything finer in the history of political morality, or in
the literature of rhetoric, than Bright's speeches

against the Crimean War or those in which he championed the cause of the American Republic against the Slave States of the South? It is just possible that, but for Bright, our Government might have been embroiled. It is certain that Bright's influence and eloquence saved us in the eyes of the North. Bright alone among foreigners is honoured by a bust in the White House. A volume of his speeches on the question was issued at Boston in 1865, and the last of his important public utterances was an earnest plea for eternal friendship with our American kinsmen.

That Bright should by some have been refused the title of statesman is not surprising, when we consider how that word has been debased. It is true, as I have said, that Bright was no administrator. The great administrative statesmen of the nineteenth century were Peel and Gladstone. Cobden was the chief original and constructive mind, the maker of a peaceful revolution. Bright stands to the rising democracy as Burke stood to the old oligarchy—an inspiring moral force. But there were two Burkes and only one Bright. From first to last the great Quaker was all of a piece. His very limitations help to convey a notion of strength and rugged grandeur. Burke's philosophy was rich, varied, and complex, like his scheme of economical reform. Bright's was plain, simple, and intelligible, like the Act for

repealing the Corn Laws. The secret of his greatness is revealed in a single sentence from one of his
speeches : " I most devoutly believe that the moral
law was not written for men alone in their individual
character, but that it was written as well for nations."
It was, I imagine, the association of this devout
belief with a sublime gift for words that made of
Bright the greatest of English orators.   As an
example of his eloquence let me here cite one
entrancing passage from a speech delivered at Edinburgh in 1868 : "It is a long way from Belgrave
Square to Bethnal Green.   It is not pleasant to
contrast the palatial mansions of the rich and the
dismal hovels of the poor, the profuse and costly
luxuries of the wealthy with the squalid and hope-
less misery of some millions of those who are below
them.   But I ask you, as I ask myself a thousand
times, is it not possible that this mass of poverty
and suffering may be reached and be raised, or
taught to raise itself?   What is there that man
cannot do if he tries?   The other day he descended
to the mysterious depths of the ocean, and with an
iron hand sought, and found, and grasped, and
brought up to the surface the lost cable, and with it
made two worlds into one.   I ask, are his conquests
confined to the realms of science?   Is it not possible
that another hand, not of iron, but of Christian
justice and kindness, may be let down to moral

depths even deeper than the cable fathoms, to raise up from thence the sons and daughters of misery and the multitude who are ready to perish? This is the great problem which is now before us. It is one which is not for statesmen only, not for preachers of the Gospel only—it is one which every man in the nation should attempt to solve. The nation is now in power, and if wisdom abide with power, the generation to follow may behold the glorious day of what we, in our time, with our best endeavours, can only hope to see the earliest dawn."

It was in this noble spirit, with this disinterested zeal for raising up the poor and succouring the oppressed, that Bright approached popular grievances.

As a reformer, he was always from five to fifty years ahead of the day. It was so with Free Trade, India, Irish Land Reform, Church Disestablishment, the Limitation of the Lords' Veto. Everything that he proposed was based upon plain moral principles and common sense. As he was not anxious to get into office, and was not troubling from hour to hour about his "career," he did not wait for good things to become popular before he pledged his support. On the contrary, his object throughout life was to make good things popular, to drive the reforms and causes in which he believed into the region of practical politics. When they were there he was quite content that others should draft Bills and conduct them

through the House of Commons, and obtain whatever credit rapid changes of front can secure. A
critic, who was more penetrating than sympathetic,
once declared that Mr. Gladstone was more adhesive
to projects than to principles. Assuredly Mr. Bright
was more adhesive to principles than to projects.
All the same, he had a gift for sketching out a line
of policy with sufficient definiteness to enable homely
people to lay hold of it, and he had a good conceit of
these broad projects, as may be seen in his last two
great speeches—on the House of Lords and Irish
Home Rule. In the last-named, he sketched an
alternative plan, under which Irish legislation would
have been initiated by Irish members sitting in
Grand Committee. He described Mr. Gladstone's
Irish Legislature—the subordinate Parliament sitting
in Dublin—as "a vestry which will be incessantly
beating against the bars of its cage, striving to
become a Parliament"—a picturesque criticism,
applicable however with still greater force to Mr.
Chamberlain's counter-proposal of a still more subordinate body, to be called " a national council."

This picturesque criticism of the Home Rule
Parliament may remind us that Bright was a poet
and a humorist. He had fancy, pathos, fiery indig-
nation, as well as the rhetorical art and a talent for
invective. These qualities will be found abundantly
by those who are wise enough to read extensively in

his speeches and letters. It has been said often
enough that Lucan was an orator rather than a poet.
But you will find in Lucan, as you will find in
Bright, some of the purest gems of poetry, and great
thoughts nobly framed. But Bright had even more
in common with the mighty satirist of the Roman
Empire. He is the Juvenal of British oratory, who
lashed without fear or mercy the vices of a gross,
braggart, bellicose, and ill-informed Imperialism.
The Roman chastisement was only for the dead—
those whose urns were ranged along the Appian
Way. Bright, in a happier age, was free to strike
at the living. But for this freedom of criticism the
British Empire must long ago have sunk into the
degenerate weakness of Imperial Rome. We need
not forget Cobbett, Shelley, Byron, Romilly,
Brougham, and the Philosophical Radicals. They,
in their several ways, exhibited at various times the
same independent courage, the same disregard for
social and political consequences. But Bright carried
the tradition high, and vindicated the grand power of
free speech in a free community. He was the tribune
of the people, and he forced the governing classes to
make concession after concession to the rights and
interests of the masses. If the Corn Law repeal of
1846 can be called a personal triumph for Cobden,
the Reform Bill of 1866 can be called a personal
triumph for Bright. The weak-kneed Liberals, who

o

disliked and eventually destroyed the Bill of '66, only
to make way for the more radical measure passed by
Disraeli, were immortalized by Bright. Who would
ever have remembered their leader Horsman if
Bright had not told us how "he retired into his
political cave of Adullam, into which he invites
every one who is in distress and every one who is dis-
contented"? And what could be more picturesque
than his description of the ill-assorted alliance between Horsman and Lowe?   After telling the House
how Horsman at last succeeded in "hooking" Lowe,
Bright continued: "I know it was the opinion many
years ago of a member of the Cabinet that two men
could not make a party. When a party is formed of
two men so amiable and so disinterested as the two
right honourable gentlemen, we may hope to see for
the first time in Parliament a party perfectly har-
monious, and distinguished by mutual and unbroken
trust. But there is one difficulty which it is impossible to remove. This party of two is like the
Scotch terrier, that was so covered with hair that you
could not tell which was the head and which was the
tail."   In the following year he dubbed a similar cave
(led by Grant Duff and Fawcett) the Tea-room
Party, and likened their efforts to those of a coster-
monger and a donkey trying to upset an express
train. The Bright coinage always rings true.
Whether you like it or not, there is no suspicion

of counterfeit. "A mixture of pomposity and servility," is what he felt and said about a political courtier's speech. "The last refuge of political ignorance and passion," is just what Bright thought about the House of Lords, and he said it in 1872. We may compare his translation of a Latin motto, " Omnia pro tempore nihil pro veritate : "Everything for the *Times*, but nothing for the truth," during the struggle against the Paper Duties. To Mrs. Booth, in reference to assaults on Salvation Army missionaries, he wrote : "The people who mob you would doubtless have mobbed the Apostles." He described the unpopular peace after Majuba as "a course at once magnanimous and just."

Like Macaulay, Bright was absolutely free from the servility of the courtier, and in this respect office made no difference to him. Thus, in November, 1878, when Beaconsfield tried to snub plain men by a grandiloquent observation that the world's affairs are conducted by monarchs and statesmen, Bright retorted that history had not taught him the wisdom of monarchs and statesmen. "On the contrary, almost all the greatest crimes of history have been committed, and all the greatest calamities have been brought upon mankind, through the instrumentality of monarchs and of statesmen. I would rather have the judgment of an intelligent and moral people, informed as to their interest and their duties." He went on to chastize the House of Lords for throwing out Bills introduced to remedy the grievances of Irish farmers, concluding with his ever-memorable dictum, "Force is no remedy." On Lord Carnarvon protesting against this speech as an attack on the Sovereign, the aristocracy, and the landowners, Bright replied :—

"I have defended the monarchy ; the defence is little needed in this country and in this reign, I have warned the aristocracy of danger I wished them to shun. As to land-owners, I have been one of the most prominent supporters of a policy so necessary for the country and so wise for them, that, had it been obstinately resisted, the great landowners of England and Scotland would long ago have been running for their lives, as some Irish landowners are reported to be doing now."

Of a new name for Protection, Bright remarked : "The reciprocity notion is exactly adapted to catch the considerable class of simpletons who have no memory and no logic." Once a low-class politician insinuated that the Brights had supported the repeal of the Corn Laws in the hope of being able to lower factory wages. Bright said : "He may not know that he is ignorant, but he cannot be ignorant that he lies. I think the speaker was named Smith. He is a discredit to the numerous family of that name." A clergyman who had uttered a slander against him on the platform was thus dismissed : " I do not know what Mr Reade is in his pulpit, but I would advise

him to stay there, where he cannot be contradicted.
On the platform he is, what is not uncommon in the
hot partisan priest, ignorant and scurrilous, and a
guide whom no sensible man would wish to follow.
His congregation should pray for him." In 1866 one
Richard Garth, a Queen's Counsel and member of
Parliament, uttered some atrocious libels against
Bright. The letter in reply, perhaps the most con-
clusive and pulverizing document of its kind, ended
as follows :—

"On a review of your speech and your letter, I come to this
conclusion—that you wished to get into Parliament, and were
not particular as to the path which might lead to it. You
threw dirt during your canvass, doubtless knowing that, if
needful, you could eat it afterwards. There are many men
who go 'through dirt to dignities,' and I suspect you have no
objection to be one of them.
    I am, with whatever respect is due to you,
                            Yours, etc.,
                                    JOHN BRIGHT.
Richard Garth, Esq., M.P., Temple, London."

This small attempt to delineate the character of
John Bright at the date of his centenary was born
of a feeling that the country suffered an overwhelming loss by his death, that no one man has filled his
place, and that the only way to repair the loss is to
propagate his doctrines and raise up new men to
apply them to the conditions of our time. That
many politicians should prefer principles to office it

would be unreasonable to expect. That titles and
other decorative rewards of merit should be the
ordinary goal of public spirit in every party is
natural. But the influence and authority which
Cobden and Bright acquired by resolutely preaching
the doctrines they believed, and resolutely refusing
to hold office without substantial guarantees that
their own political characters and opinions would
not be submerged—these are indeed attainments,
achievements, services to our country and to the
world prouder, nobler, and more enduring than all
the titles and honours that might have been showered
upon them.

FRIEDRICH LIST AND THE GERMAN ZOLLVEREIN

BY far the greatest name in the short but rich and fruitful annals of economic science is that of its founder, Adam Smith. Very high among his successors, if our touchstone is to be influence upon national policy, stands Friedrich List [1]—a romantic figure, displaying, through all the disappointments and vicissitudes of a most disappointing and vicissitudinous career, dauntless courage, heroic energy, and unquenchable enthusiasm.

Whether the man of action or the man of thought is the more enviable, admirable, or powerful, is a question of taste which every one must answer for himself. In the art and science of public finance, as well as in the larger sphere of political economy, there is plenty of scope for both —for the pure theorist and for the statesman who is the practical interpreter, perhaps the mere

[1] Born at Reutlingen, August 6, 1789; died by his own hand November 30, 1846, at Kufstein.

instrument, of other men's ideas. Between these two types—between, say, a Ricardo and a Goulburn—there are many intermediates; and it might well be disputed in what order five contemporaries —Bastiat, Mill, Cobden, Gladstone, and List— should be ranked by the discriminating historian of political economy. If Adam Smith illustrates very well the superiority that is usually assigned to the life of philosophic study and discovery, Friedrich List may equally be cited by those who regard an active participation in· public affairs not only as necessary to happiness, but as a positive aid and stimulus to political genius. Both views may be true. Probably there are such differences and distinctions among minds of the highest order that in the very same temperature, soil, and environment, which bring one plant to perfection, another will wither and decay. The sauntering or sedentary life of private tutor, university professor, and customs official suited Adam Smith well enough: it gave him twenty years of golden leisure in which to revolve, and ultimately to revolutionize, economic thought and commercial policy. But such a life would never have satisfied Friedrich List. One man's food is another man's poison.

For reasons which, if not obvious, are discoverable, List—though his influence on commercial

policy and perhaps even on public finance in
general, once approached that of Adam Smith—
is neglected in the universities of Europe and
America. He may perhaps be described as the
Cobbett of Tariff Reform. Reading List for
Cobbett and Adam Smith for Paine, a critic may
be tempted to adapt a famous passage in one of
Hazlitt's sketches. List, with vast industry, an
active imagination and lively pen, never seems to
build upon a perfectly scientific foundation or to
complete any of the work to our full satisfaction ;
whereas Smith seems to clear every problem that
he chooses to handle from all controversy—past,
present, and to come. List provokes us to criticism.
Smith reduces us to silent consent. Smith takes
a bird's-eye view of things, though when occasion
requires he can make good use of the microscope.
List is always eyeing current controversies, fighting
on one side or the other with the acrimony of a
party journalist. The muse of history is his slave
rather than his teacher. Like Cobbett, he sticks
close to whatever business he has in hand, inspects
its component parts, and "keeps fast hold of the
smallest advantages they afford him." Perhaps,
too, we may say that he is a pleasanter writer ;
or at least, that the task of reading him is lighter ;
for he appeals freely to our natural prejudices and
combative instincts, is more desultory, less con-

sistent; and seems to be urged upon his path rather by an urgent opportunism than by the logical necessities of a wide comprehensive and scientific argument. Hazlitt says of Cobbett: "He is therefore tolerated by all parties, though he has made himself by turns obnoxious to all, and even those he abuses read him. The Reformers read him when he was a Tory; the Tories read him now that he is a Reformer. He must, I think, however, be *caviare* to the Whigs."

Similarly almost every type of economist can find something to abuse and something to praise in Friedrich List. He must, I think, be *caviare* to Mr. Balfour. An industrial Protectionist loves him as a protector of manufacturers, if a rural Protectionist loathes him for refusing protection to agriculture. English Tariff Reformers rejoice in his denunciations of Adam Smith; American and German Tariff Reformers like to explain that if List were now alive, he would consider a policy of free trade to be no less wise for the United States or Germany now, than it was in his opinion for England in the forties. Not that List's political career, or his economic opinions, present the almost ludicrous changes and conversions of Cobbett. It is, rather, that the groundwork of argument on which List had to found one part of his brief was difficult to reconcile with what was required for the other part. When he was growing up to manhood, and began to throw himself into politics, Germany was divided into a great number of states, some large like Austria and Prussia; some of moderate size like Saxony, Bavaria, and Württemberg; others mere petty principalities or dukedoms or free towns, but all claiming and exercising the right to surround themselves with customs houses and to tax one another's products and manufactures. It was against this paralysing system of commercial feud that List directed his first energies as an organizer and pamphleteer. In talent, courage, and public spirit he was hardly inferior to Cobden. Constantly distracted, as Cobden was also, by pecuniary anxieties, and exiled, as Cobden happily was not, from his own home by the tyranny of a reactionary Government, he had to live somehow by his own exertions, and by the ceaseless activity of his wits and his pen. If he was at heart a German patriot, his greater Germany embraced not only Austria, but in moments of expansion the Low Countries and even Denmark. And he was a cosmopolitan, a citizen of the world. At one time he seemed likely to settle in England. At another he almost became a Frenchman. The first draft of his principal work was written in French. With a little more encouragement at

Washington he might probably have remained in America to inscribe another distinguished name on the great roll of American citizens. In modern Germany or modern America, he might have made a fortune in some banking house; for his versatile and enterprising mind had a natural bent toward the flotation of financial schemes. He might have been, in fact, a prince of company-promoters; but he lived a little before his time. His ideas were always too large for his age; and instead of laying up wealth, he laid up fame. He did not leave a fortune, but he left a reputation.

Yet List, considering the extraordinary interest that attaches to his writings as well as to his dramatic career, is strangely ignored. To the Free Trader he is a type of reactionary, though he was one of the founders of the great free-trade movement—a movement for the consolidation of Germany, which eventually destroyed more customs houses and more obstacles to trade than had been swept away even by the political whirlwinds of the American and French Revolutions. By the modern bureaucrats and official professors of his native land he is remembered as a rebel against their own class, a rash and dangerous champion of free speech, a believer in democratic institutions, and a Tariff Reformer whose doctrines would be altogether subversive of the so-called "scientific" tariff of modern

Germany. If List had had his way, there would have been free trade from Rotterdam to Memel, and from Kiel to Trieste. This great territory he would indeed have surrounded by a temporary tariff for the purpose of protecting manufactures (but not agriculture) until its "infant" industries were able to resist the competition of their stronger rivals in England. When the time came, and the industries reached the stage at which they could export and compete successfully in neutral countries, the protective tariff would be removed; and the consumers who had been taxed during this period of probation, in order that the productive capacity of the nation might be nursed into life and vigour, would be relieved of their burdens and allowed to enjoy the blessings, not only of cheap food (of which List would never have deprived them), but of cheap clothing and boots and tools, and all the other conveniences of life. This idea of the tariff as a nursery grew upon List during his stay in America. Had he lived another half-century to see the American tariff on worsteds and woollens raised higher and higher until the natural cost of warm clothing was doubled for the whole American people, he might have changed his mind.

The economic contradictions of List are the natural consequence of the part he played as controversialist and propagandist. As controversialist he was eager at all costs to differ from Adam Smith. As propagandist he thought that the manufacturers with whom he worked could be induced to concede internal free trade for the sake of an enlarged home market, only if they were guaranteed against French and English competition. The true answer to this theory is that free trade, by keeping the cost of production at the lowest point, gives all the industries which suit a country best the best chance of success. Moreover, if an industry anywhere is likely to pay, capital will be found; and capital flows most readily to countries where living is cheap and cost of production low. A protective tariff is, on the whole, a danger and an obstacle to investment. Money naturally flows to the places where its purchasing power is highest. Nor can vigorous industries be swamped by the removal of protection; for the imports from abroad have to be paid for, by those things which are most cheaply produced at home. Every reduction of a tariff increases the purchasing power of the home consumer and reduces the cost of production. And every increase of imports has to be paid for, by a corresponding increase of exports. It must often have occurred to List that if free trade between Prussia, Saxony, Holland, and Austria were beneficial, as he stoutly maintained it would be, free trade with Switzerland, Denmark, France, and

England must also be beneficial. In the case of France, he could answer with some appearance of reason that free trade is of no use unless it is mutual and reciprocal. We often hear now that "one-sided" free trade is a great mistake. But when List wrote his principal book, England was already throwing open its ports, so that he had to fall back upon the infant industries argument, an argument that was equally applicable to the case of a Bavarian or Swabian manufacturer, who stood to be ruined by some more powerful Saxon or Bohemian competitor.

Probably, his real reason for desiring a moderate protective tariff for a greater Germany was an idea that this, together with internal free trade and a national system of railways and a national post, would help to consolidate the race. Every patriotic German felt at that time the need for unification. Without political unification Germany would remain what it had been for centuries—weak, poor, and distracted, the seat of domestic jealousies and civil war, an easy prey to the greed and ambition of foreign potentates. If the promise of a protective tariff would help the states of Germany to sink their differences, pull down their customs houses and coalesce, a German economist might easily be induced to acquiesce in a moderate measure of temporary protection. List himself sometimes opened out a larger view, as when he said: "If the whole globe were united by a union like the twenty-four states of North America, free trade would be quite as natural and beneficial as it is now in the union."

The poet Heine, whose friendship List enjoyed during his three years' residence in Paris (1837–40), revisited Germany in the autumn of 1843, and celebrated the journey in a masterpiece of imaginative satire. There is one incident in the piece that may have been suggested by his talks with List. At any rate, it serves to give us a glimpse of Germany in the making. Heine had come to the Prussian frontier—

> "Said a fellow-passenger of mine:
>   The Fatherland goes better;
> See, there is the Prussian Zollverein,
>   The mighty Douanenkette.
>
> The Zollverein's encircling band
>   Will tether the folk together,
> And shield our distracted Fatherland
>   From all political weather.
>
> It gives us an outward visible ark,
>   A bond materialistic;
> The inward grace is the censor's mark,
>   The union idealistic.
>
> The censor makes of our national life
>   A single unanimous whole,
> We need a Germany free from strife,
>   United in tariff and soul."

It is not too much to say that most of the ideas which underlie modern tariffs, both in the old world and in the new, were originated or formulated by List ; and whatever may be our individual opinions of commercial policy, much can be learned from the father of the German Zollverein.

To form a right opinion about tariffs is one of the chief functions of a sound education in political economy. In the heat of fiscal controversy no text-book can be more useful than one which, alike by its virtues and defects, stimulates the mind to further reasoning and research. If List's arguments are sometimes inconsistent, if his logic is sometimes defective, if some of his forecasts have proved wrong, if some of his historical illustrations are false, so much the more reason for consulting with a fresh, active, and critical intelligence the life and writings of one whose influence has helped to mould for more than half a century the commercial policies of two out of the three greatest industrial nations of the world.[1]

[1] Most of the above was first printed as an introduction to the Life of Friedrich List (Smith, Elder, 1909), by my sister, Margaret Hirst.

INSULAR FREE TRADE—MR. BALFOUR'S DOUBTS AND ANXIETIES RESOLVED

IN January 1913, after nine years of costly effort, the Tariff Reform League lost its grip of the Conservative party and the Free Fooders triumphed. The occasion or pretext arose in the previous November. After a series of satisfactory by-elections Lord Lansdowne and Mr. Bonar Law under pressure from the extreme Tariff Reformers—who controlled the party machine—agreed to withdraw the Referendum pledge given by Mr. Balfour just before the last General Election. By that pledge, which was renewed in 1911 by Lord Lansdowne, the leaders of the Opposition had promised not to burden British commerce with a preferential and protectionist tariff until such tariff had been approved by a popular vote. The withdrawal of this pledge in November at the Albert Hall is said to have been authorised by all the members of the front Opposition bench except Mr. Balfour. But a disappointing by-election at Bolton, following a few days after, caused a general revolt among the rank and file of the party, which found first expression in the *Liverpool Courier*, and was then taken up by other provincial newspapers and by the *Daily Telegraph*, as well as by *The Times*, the *Daily Mail*, and other organs controlled by Lord Northcliffe. It seems extraordinary that the party in the House of Commons should not have been consulted in November; but it is explained that the Whips were under Birmingham control, and encouraged Mr. Bonar Law in a course against which he and Lord Lansdowne should have been warned. The fact is that the strict censorship imposed by Mr. Chamberlain, with the aid of the Tariff Reform League, had suppressed freedom of opinion to such an extent that the strength of Free Trade sentiment in the Unionist party was not generally suspected. The suddenness and extent of the revolt was a surprise to everybody. But Tariff Reform had been a "make-believe." A Unionist was not allowed to call himself a Free Trader, but he was allowed to be a Free Trader so long as he called himself a Tariff Reformer and conformed occasionally by listening to one of the paid lecturers.

The lobby men of *The Times* canvassed Unionist members and discovered that almost the whole party disapproved of the new policy. Only twenty wanted the full policy. The rest resented the withdrawal of the pledge, and insisted that if the

Referendum were lost they must be protected by some other device against the "Dear Food Cry" at the next appeal to the country. Mr. Bonar Law manfully declared that this was not the time and he was not the man to haul down the flag; but after some delay and negotiations a memorial was signed and he submitted reluctantly. Food taxes—that is to say the protection of agriculture—were eliminated from the party programme. Thus the key-stone of the arch of protection has been removed, and those who removed it knew what they were about.

The change grew out of the facts. Tariff Reform had been hard hit by statistics. For two years (nay for ten years) the Board of Trade returns had been fighting the battle of Free Trade. Month after month our exports to foreign countries, to the colonies and to India had risen from record to record. The figures for 1912 showed that the reports of the trade boom had not been exaggerated. The defeat of the Tariff Reform League, signalised a few weeks afterwards by the victory of a Unionist Free Trader in Westmoreland, was a natural consequence of commercial prosperity. Perhaps it may be interesting to go back a little, and to illustrate the decline of Tariff Reform by the advance of commerce. This British controversy between Free Trade and Protection has been watched eagerly by the whole civilised world, and it is not a pure accident that the Unionist party is finding it expedient to shelve Tariff Reform just when a large reduction is being effected in the tariff of the United States.

On September 16, 1903, Mr. Balfour wrote a letter accepting the resignation of Mr. Joseph Chamberlain from his Cabinet, on the ground that Mr. Chamberlain's proposal almost certainly involved "taxation, however light, upon foodstuffs," and that "public opinion is not yet ripe for such an arrangement." In the following year Mr. Balfour issued a considered pamphlet upon Tariff Reform, containing "Economic Notes on Insular Free Trade," a speech at Sheffield, and another at Bristol, together with the above-mentioned letter. In his notes on Insular Free Trade Mr. Balfour premised: " I approach the subject from the Free Trade point of view," and "with the desire to promote Free Trade as far as temporary circumstances permit." He believed in the international as well as the national division of labour, and threw no doubt on the Free Trade theory when expressed with due limitations. He admitted that "the fortunes of the Import trade are indissolubly united with those of the Export." Nor was he so despondent as Mr. Chamberlain about the actual conditions of affairs in 1903-4, though they were years of trade depression; for, he observed, "in actual fact, we see Britain hampered indeed by foreign tariffs, yet able, in spite of them, to carry on an export trade, which, if it does not increase as we might wish, yet increases rather than diminishes, and an import trade of unexampled magnitude." But, in order, (he argued) to form an exact estimate of our industrial relations, "we have to consider not merely what is, but what is to be." In other words, "the tendency of trade, not its momentary position, is what chiefly concerns us." He thought the rate of increase in our export trade was unsatisfactory, and that in some branches there were "symptoms of decay." What Mr. Balfour would have liked to do in order to solve his difficult problem in 1903-4—the problem whether the Conservative or Unionist party, under the influence of the ex-Radical member for Birmingham, should commit itself to some new system of protection and Colonial preference, and go back upon the policy of free imports—was to have been able to compare British exports in 1902-3 with British exports in 1906-7 or 1911-12.

It may be dangerous to base a fiscal policy merely upon experience; but there was certainly practical wisdom in Mr. Balfour's plea for a suspension of judgment; and, however fantastical some of the suggestions and hypotheses advanced in the "Notes on Insular Free Trade" may appear, the essay undoubtedly possesses all the subtlety and dialectical charm of its author's best compositions. Few statesmen indeed, at such a moment of party stress,

when the hustlers of Birmingham were busily manipulating the caucus and trying (pretty successfully)
to drive Conservative Free Traders out of the party,
could have produced anything half so well balanced
or half so impartial as this survey. It was quite free
from the frantic jealousy of the foreigner, and from
the wildly impracticable desire to tax him.[1] "No
complaint," wrote Mr. Balfour, "is made of the
relative growth in wealth, population, and prosperity
of other nations. This ought, on the contrary, to be
a matter of rejoicing." Nevertheless, Mr. Balfour
did profess uneasiness about British trade, and "a
closer examination of the details of our export returns," as he confessed towards the end of the essay,
"in no way allays the anxiety which theoretical considerations this suggest." There were warnings, he
thought, not only of a diminution in exports relative
to population, but of a diminution absolute, and he
saw no satisfactory symptoms of a change in fiscal
policy abroad: "Highly developed industrial countries, like Germany, America, and France, give no
sign of any wish to relax their Protectionist system."
In fact, a retrospective study of Mr. Balfour's essay,
the only really elaborate and non-party expression

---

[1] Many simple folk have been persuaded by Tariff Reform
orators that customs duties are a tax on foreign countries, and
that by this means foreigners can be made to pay for the expansion of the British Navy!

of his fiscal opinions, shows that his whole argument for a reconsideration of our fiscal system by the nation, and for a suspension of public judgment, rested, not upon dissatisfaction either with Free Trade or with the volume at that time of British trade, but on a fear that our exports might in the near future diminish both relatively to our population and absolutely in face of the Protectionist policy of foreign countries. " I ask the optimists to study tendencies—the dynamics, not the statics, of trade and manufactures. The ocean we are navigating is smooth enough, but where are we being driven by the tides?" If—he seemed to argue—"the course of trade in the next few years, and especially the course of our manufactured exports, were, unhappily, to confirm my anxieties, and exhibit real symptoms of decay, then it might be right for the Conservative party to adopt the revolutionary changes proposed by Mr. Chamberlain, and embark upon a full-blown policy of Tariff Reform." But if not, and if, on the contrary, the dynamics of British trade were to prove far better even than the statics, then obviously the nation need trouble its head no further, and its leader's anxieties being completely relieved, there could be no object in the Unionist party making itself unpopular, and even ridiculous, by advocating surgical operations or disagreeable medicines for diseases which had proved imaginary. If the British patient, whose pulse Dr. Balfour was then feeling, were to become more and more prosperous and robust Dr. Chamberlain's knife and Dr. Chamberlain's pills would not have to be called into requisition.

The question therefore now is, to what conclusion Mr. Balfour's incursion into dynamics will lead the honest fiscal inquirer, who, taking Mr. Balfour's test, relies upon the exhibit of British exports, and upon the experience of the years succeeding 1902, to which Mr. Balfour appealed. The following is the principal table, appended to "Insular Free Trade," which was supposed to show the stationary condition of British trade during a period (be it remembered) of falling prices :—

TABLE A. (1)

Year.	Value of Exports of British Produce Except Coal, Machinery, and Ships.	Ditto per head of Population.
	Thousand £.	£
1881	215,277,000	6·2
1886	193,186,000	5·3
1891	213,270,000	5·6
1896	208,931,000	5·3
1901	222,726,000	5·4

Mr. Balfour's argument for excepting coal, machinery, and ships has always struck me as the most frivolous part of his method. He might as well have excepted cocoa, cutlery, and cotton goods! Coal is a great employer of labour, and its bulk makes it an invaluable export for the shipping trade. Machinery is, perhaps, the most highly-finished and costly of all our great manufactures. Ships are our special pride, and the more we sell abroad the better for our yards and our trade. Why include jam and omit ships? I shall, therefore, begin with a supplementary table, giving the total exports of British produce, including coal, machinery, and ships, to which, for the sake of our ports and shipping trade should really be added the re-exports of foreign and colonial produce. But these are omitted, in order to show exactly how far Mr. Balfour's own argument should have led a statistician at the time.

TABLE A. (2)

Year.			Total Exports of British Produce. Thousand £.	Ditto per head of Population. £
1881	...	...	234,023 [1]	6·70
1886	...	...	212,433 [1]	5·79
1891	...	...	247,235 [1]	6·54
1896	...	...	240,146 [1]	6·08
1901	...	...	280,022	6·78

To show the real growth of trade during these 20 years an addition of about 15 per cent should be made on account of the fall in prices, i.e., the appreciation of gold.

I now come to the "dynamics" of trade and

[1] Values of ships and boats not included in the Official Returns prior to 1901.

manufactures, which were concealed from Mr. Balfour's vision in the critical years of 1903 and 1904. No doubt the commercial depression which naturally followed the Boer War accounted for much of the pessimism that upset Mr. Chamberlain's balance, and even slightly shook the more reasoned foundations of Mr. Balfour's fiscal faith. First of all, let us continue the total export table, which stopped at 1901. Table B supplies the figures from 1902 to 1912, showing the value of British exports according to the Statistical Abstract of the United Kingdom.

TABLE B.

Year.	Total Export of British Produce. Thousand £.	Ditto per head of Population. £
1902	283,424	6·75
1903	290,800	6·87
1904	300,711	7·00
1905	329,817	7·62
1906	375,575	8·60
1907	426,035	9·66
1908	377,104	8·47
1909	378,180	8·40
1910	430,385	9·58
1911	454,119	10·03
1912	487,434	10·71

Table C sets out the exports to which Mr. Balfour objected, and upon which, presumably, a scientific scheme of Tariff Reform would impose export duties :—

TABLE C.

Year.		Exports of Coal. Thousand £.	Exports of Machinery. Thousand £.	Exports of Ships. Thousand £.
1902	...	26,307	18,755	5,872
1903	...	26,036	20,058	4,284
1904	...	25,491	21,065	4,455
1905	...	24,859	23,260	5,431
1906	...	30,069	26,772	8,644
1907	...	40,170	31,743	10,018
1908	...	39,546	31,000	10,567
1909	...	35,319	28,058	5,927
1910	...	36,100	29,271	8,770
1911	...	36,521	30,961	5,663
1912	...	40,495	33,162	7,032

If these are deducted, Mr. Balfour's table (A (1)) may be continued as follows:—

TABLE D.

Year.			Exports of British Produce except Coal, Machinery, and Ships. Thousand £.	Ditto per head of Population. £
1902	...	...	232,490	5·5
1903	...	...	240,422	5·7
1904	...	...	249,700	5·8
1905	...	...	276,267	6·4
1906	...	...	310,090	7·1
1907	...	...	344,104	7·8
1908	...	...	295,991	6·7
1909	...	...	308,876	6·9
1910	...	...	356,244	7·9
1911	...	...	380,974	8·4
1912	...	...	406,745	8·9

If Mr. Balfour was fairly well satisfied with the "statics" of British trade at the outset of Mr.

Chamberlain's campaign, his anxieties as to its "dynamics" must long since have yielded to joy and pride in the magnificent forward strides which our export trade has taken during the last eight years. Mr. Balfour, in fact, and not Mr. Bonar Law, is the proper person to restore Tariff Reform to the grave where it was buried by Disraeli.

TIME AND SPEED

AS life lengthens its pace seems to increase. Perhaps we think less while we do more. What a German calls the *Mechanisierung* of the universe has both accelerated the rate and enlarged the volume of transactions. " Hustling and hurrying we lay waste our powers"; so another Wordsworth might write if he found himself in the New York subway or a London tube. But let justice be done to the mechanical inventor. Thanks to Arkwright and Watt and Stephenson and the rest of them, machinery is everywhere doing the work of muscle. In return for the same output of energy, labour and skill receive far greater rewards than fell to the handicraftsmen in olden days. If we are busier that is our own fault. Invention has given us leisure if we would have it. But most men prefer to pursue wealth. Business is their most interesting occupation. It is because the majority find leisure so tedious that time-saving appliances generally have only increased the strain upon captains of industry.

Here, however, I shall disregard the general effect of inventions and look merely at improvements in transit and communication.

"Since the mending of roads in England forty or fifty years ago," so Adam Smith told his class at Glasgow in 1762, "its opulence has increased enormously." This may have sounded more like a paradox than a platitude in days when the prosperity of trade was supposed to depend upon tolls and octroi and customs and State regulations of all kinds. But Adam Smith was a wise teacher. He did not say "easy communications make good trade," but "after the improvement of communications in England trade improved and wealth increased." *Post hoc ergo propter hoc.* To make a real argument acceptable one may clothe it in the guise of a fallacy. Learners easily step by analogy from one experience to another. Correct ratiocination appeals only to trained and accurate minds. So the boys at Glasgow received the truth in small doses of common-sense—experience and argument mixed as here in the laying together of two facts causally connected. Most of us can see now that the difference between a good road and a bad one means less strain on the horses, less wear and tear for wagons and carriages, and, above all, an increase in speed. It means, in short, a saving of time and money in both goods and passenger traffic. Smith wanted his north countrymen to take a leaf from the book of English experience. A few miles off, at the old town of Ayr, a younger Scot, John Loudon Macadam, hardly out of his cradle, was destined to give his name to the language by revolutionizing the art of road-making. At the time Smith spoke there was only one stage coach on the road from London to Edinburgh. It ran once a month from each capital, taking from twelve to fourteen days to cover the 400 miles which separate the Edinburgh Rock from the London Stone. The English part of the road was much better. As early as 1706 a stage coach made its way twice a week from London to York in four days, returning in the same time. In 1810 Macadam began to succeed as a road-maker, and twenty years later the first mails were carried by railway. But taking 1730 to 1830 as the period of the great improvement of roads for horse-drawn vehicles, we get an acceleration in passenger traffic of something like 600 per cent.; for in the early years of the nineteenth century the mail coach from Edinburgh to London began to accomplish the journey of 400 miles in less than two days.[1] An inside place cost $11\frac{1}{2}$, an outside $7\frac{1}{2}$ guineas, apart from tips and meals.

The construction and improvement of roads were not universally welcomed. It is related in the

---

[1] $42\frac{1}{2}$ hours seems to have been the final rate. See " The Great North Road," by C. G. Harper, p. 58.

"Wealth of Nations" that early in the eighteenth century some of the Home Counties petitioned Parliament against the extension of turnpike roads, fearing that the remote counties, where labour was cheaper, would be able to undersell their grass and corn in the London market, and so reduce suburban profits and rents. Whatever facilitates transit, whether it be a better road, or a canal, or a railway, multiplies the competition of commerce, and tends to equalize prices, reducing them in large towns, and raising the rewards of labour in distant places where the producer has previously been without a market for his surplus stock.

A stretch of forty years from 1830 to 1870 may be counted as the second period in the modern history of land transit, at least for well-populated, enterprising, and civilized countries like Great Britain. It is the period of railway construction. In that brief period all our towns were connected by a network of lines, and the feverish energy of railway promoters left comparatively little to be done so long as the steam locomotive running upon steel lines provides the cheapest form of long-distance rapid traction. If an express mail coach made the journey from Edinburgh to London a century ago in less than two days, as against twelve days in 1760, the speed has again been accelerated six times; for the distance is now covered by an express train in less than eight hours,

Q

while the fare has been reduced from about £12 to 32 shillings. Even after our main roads had been macadamized and brought to a high state of perfection, the cost and slowness of cartage made long-distance traffic by road impossible for perishable goods and unremunerative for cheap ones. Hence the value of canals and the large amounts of capital which were devoted to the improvement of water transit in the eighteenth century. But what have not railways done for society? Seventy or eighty years ago handloom weavers of flannels at Saddleworth, on the Yorkshire moors, were wont, after finishing a piece of about 50 yards, to carry it on their backs to sell it in Manchester, 12 miles away, where they found their best market. The locomotive has done at least as much as the power loom for the weavers of Lancashire and Yorkshire.

Sea travel has gained in the last century less perhaps in speed, but even more in comfort and security. A first-class liner takes us from Southampton or Liverpool to New York within the week. In 1819 George Ticknor, the historian of Spanish literature, made his way back to America in "a regular New York packet," and the voyage is described as "prosperous and smooth, occupying but thirty-seven days." According to Cobbett "a cabin passage," at that time, for one person from England to the United States cost from thirty to forty-five pounds. The inconveniences for women and children were almost indescribable.

The third period of improvement in land transit—from 1870 to the present time—is conveniently marked by the Tramways Act of 1870. These years saw a great development of electric traction as well as the invention of the bicycle, the motor-car, and the flying machine. When mechanical genius had perfected the railway train in all essentials, the task of enriching and civilizing the world by constructing lines, wherever density of population or natural wealth promised the investor a sufficient profit, was laid upon capital. Where there is no prospect of profit a Government will often build a line for strategic or political ends. So railways are still being constructed in America, Asia, and Africa. But as practical invention ever follows in the wake of discovery, so do the promoters and the capitalists pursue the inventor, multiplying his models and extending his achievements over land and sea in a thousand profitable projects. The inventor, meanwhile, was turning to other fields. The conversion of electricity into a power comparable with steam opened up new possibilities for traction. The clumsy horse and steam tramways were converted into electric tramways, and by the same means the underground railways in great cities were relieved of smoke. How far this process will go no one can say, but it is already an accepted maxim that in populous areas, where frequent services are required, electrification usually pays.

So far, in catering for speed, mechanical invention had done vast good, with few, if any, countervailing disadvantages. The melancholy forebodings of old-fashioned Conservatives like the Duke of Wellington, to whom railways spelt national decadence and ruin, proved almost wholly unfounded. The towns which refused to admit railway stations have bemoaned their mistake ever since. Almost equally wonderful and beneficial was the bicycle, a supplementary boon which has immensely extended the activity and range of active people. At first the bicycle was a fashionable luxury of the rich; now it is a means of innocent and healthy enjoyment for all classes, and an indispensable necessity of daily life to many for whom this time-saving machine provides profitable work at a distance from their homes. The cycle is also a factor in distribution—invaluable to shopkeepers who cannot afford a horse and trap.

Two later inventions have brought no such certain or unmixed gain. The petrol engine applied to loco-motion is superseding the horse, and is competing with tramways and even with railways for short-distance traffic. The old slow horse omnibus has almost disappeared, and the motor-bus, after ruining many investors, has apparently established itself. It

is a cheap and quick means of locomotion in large
towns, and a useful "feeder" to railways. The motor-
car began to be a nuisance soon after the beginning
of this century, and the rapid popularity which it
gained among the rich is responsible for the utter
failure of Parliament to impose reasonable restric-
tions. There is no doubt that if the greatest
happiness of the greatest number were our test, the
pleasure car would stand condemned. Its principle
seems rather to be the smallest happiness of the
smallest number. It gives far more pain than pleasure, far more annoyance than comfort. I once
described it as a device for enabling rich idlers to
save time. It is a snare to men of business who sit
in a car when they ought to be using their legs.
Such pleasures should be seldom used :—*Voluptates
commendat rarior usus.* But when one considers how
much property it injures, how many lives it destroys,
how it smothers pedestrians and gardens with dust,
what enormous damage it has caused to the roads,
there can be no question that the benefits of the few
are obtained at an utterly disproportionate cost to
the many. Where motor-cars are very numerous
cycling and riding have been abandoned as means
of recreation. The revelation of motor-car luxury,
and of the utter disregard which many chauffeurs
entertain for the comfort and safety of others, has
been by general admission one of the incentives to

labour unrest. The Passion for Speed is shared by most magistrates, and homicide when committed by motorists is punished as a trivial offence. Of the flying machine, it may be said that so far it offers all the disadvantages of the motor-car, with none of the advantages. The high flier may commit either suicide or homicide, or both. If he tries his luck often he is sure to come to grief. His only claim so far to consideration is that he has added, like the submarine, to the horrors and terrors of modern warfare.

FOREIGN TRAVEL

THINGS near us are seen life-size, and distance, while it enchants the imagination, destroys the reality. That is a good reason why those who want to know the truth about the world should travel. If it were not for books, telegrams, and letters, Australia or China would look smaller and less important to the average Englishman than his neighbour's field. And even with the aid of books and newspapers it needs a large stock of intelligent sympathy to understand countries and peoples one has never seen. But invention is fast removing the physical obstacles to knowledge of the world. Already railways and steamers have made the journey from London to Chicago quicker and pleasanter by far than was the journey from London to Edinburgh two centuries ago. English comforts and American luxuries, French dinners and German waiters, are everywhere at the service of wealth. Wherever there is plenty of sport, good air for invalids, or good markets for merchandise, good hotels will be found. The watchful eye of capital, which knows no national prejudices in its unceasing search for high interest and adequate security, is always looking for opportunities, and the taste for travel grows with the facilities. Switzerland was the first playground of Europe. The world is now covered with playgrounds, to which active idlers and weary money-makers flock in obedience to the varying fashions of smart society, of sport, or of medical prescription. The African desert, Kashmir, California, Japan, the Canary Isles, Bermuda, the isles of Greece, Uganda, British Columbia, are not too remote for the modern globe-trotter. The commercial traveller is ubiquitous; and "our own correspondent" pursues wars and rumours of wars as keenly as the hunter tracks his quarry. And it is all so new. The stupendous transcontinental railways of North and South America, of Russia, and Siberia, are hardly older than the luxurious steamers that cross the Atlantic and Pacific Oceans. No wonder, then, as the conditions of travelling in all parts of the world, by sea and land, become every year easier, if the number of those who travel for pleasure or profit steadily increases. The cheapness of swift transport has brought also those portentous movements of emigrants who go in search of work and higher wages from the Old to the New World, or wander on the same quest from one European country to another. This constant flowing and ebbing of labour to occupy new farms in new countries and to meet the demands of harvesting or of trade booms is of profound interest. But it belongs to another category altogether. The poor emigrant has little in common with the well-to-do tourist, or commercial traveller. If he is not in search of a new home and a new patriotism, he intends at least to make a little pile before he returns to the land of his birth. English nurses and philanthropists who visited the red cross hospitals at Belgrade, Sofia and Athens during the Balkan war were astonished to find how many wounded men could speak our tongue. That vast political and economic changes may hang from such movements as these no one who has studied the developments in Siberia, Manchuria, Canada, Argentina, or Australia can doubt. And, on the whole, emigration is a mighty factor in raising the rewards of labour as well as in spreading freedom, intelligence and civilization.

But what of the modern tourist? Is he as good a man as his predecessor, who faced so much more risk and discomfort a hundred years ago? Comparisons no doubt are difficult, but there is room to fear that against a great increase in the volume must be set some decrease in the advantages of travel. Sight-seeing, transient pleasures, winter sports, the artificial risks and excitements of mountaineering are

the modern incentives to going abroad. Your modern
traveller may pass with every luxury by day and a
comfortable berth at night to any city in Europe, and
there reside in a luxurious hotel, surrounded by cosmopolitan attendants, who know nothing and care
less of the city or country in which they are accumulating tips. After travelling in this way from one
grand hotel to another, he may return from his trip
in blissful ignorance of the language, the people, the
habits, and prejudices of the country he has visited.
He and his like have seen sights and compared hotels,
but that is the whole story. In short, they are only
tourists conducted or unconducted. Innocent they
went and innocent they return of languages,
institutions and laws other than their own. In the
old days travelling was slow, uncomfortable, and
comparatively dangerous; but it was also comparatively instructive. The German or Italian waiter
with a certain smattering of English or French was
unknown; there were no first-class hotels, no Baedeker,
no Cook. To travel was to learn by personal observation. "There is no map," said one of our old
writers, "like the view of the country. Experience is
the best informer. And one journey will show a man
more than any description can." Claudian in some
charming lines depicted the happiness of the old
countryman who had spent his whole life on his own
farm and thought the neighbouring city of Verona

more remote than the Indies.[1] But the felicity of
rural life is more admired by the poet than relished
by the peasant. We all like what we have not got.
The city man fancies pigs and poultry ; the farmer's
son wants to be a clerk. Feltham, answering Claudian, remarks : " But surely travel fulleth the man ;
he hath lived but locked up in a larger chest, which
hath never seen but one land. A kingdom to the
world is like a corporation to a kingdom; a man may
live in it like an unbred man. He that searcheth
foreign nations is becoming a gentleman of the world."
To which Claudian might have rejoined that where
ignorance is bliss it is folly to toil for knowledge.
And even our own sage did not think it fit that
every man should travel: "it makes a wise man
better, and a fool worse"; for the fool gains nothing
but the gay sights, vices, and "apery" of a country.
He shames his own land by playing the fool abroad,
and he shames foreigners by bringing home their
follies.

Every one has his own ideas of pleasure and must
be his own arbiter.

Velle suum cuique est, nec voto vivitur uno.

"Let me have a companion of my way, were it but
to remark how the shadows lengthen as the sun

[1] Proxima cui nigris Verona remotior Indis,
    Benacumque putat littora rubra lacum.

declines." So wrote Sterne with Sternian pathos.
"One of the pleasantest things in the world is going
a journey" says Hazlitt, "but I like to go by myself.
I can enjoy society in a room; but out of doors
nature is company enough for me." He could not
see the wit of walking and talking at the same time.
"The soul of a journey is liberty, perfect liberty, to
think, feel, do, just as one pleases." But he makes an
exception of going abroad. "I should not feel confident in venturing on a journey in a foreign country
without a companion. I should want at intervals to
hear the sound of my own language. There is an
involuntary antipathy in the mind of an Englishman
to foreign manners and notions that requires the
assistance of social sympathy to carry it off." I give
my vote unhesitatingly for a companion in travel.
Let him be enterprising rather than adventurous,
fond of walking, a diligent student of Baedeker, a
linguist if possible, and, above all, good humoured.
An irritable person should travel alone. So should
those who, having only one language, will talk loud
in a foreign café. Doubtless the solitary traveller
learns most. Lord Bacon's young man who has "to
put his travel into a little room" is enjoined, after
gaining some entrance into the language of a foreign
town, to "sequester himself from the company of his
countrymen, and diet in such places where there is
good company of the nation where he traveleth."

He is to seek acquaintance with secretaries of ambassadors—there were no foreign correspondents then—and visit eminent persons of great name "that he may be able to tell how the life agreeeth with the fame." And on his return let him keep up a correspondence with the best of his foreign acquaintances; and let his travel appear in his conversation rather than in his dress or manners.

What, then, are the higher advantages to be gained by travel? It would be difficult to improve upon the hints given in the old essays, which partly suggested this discourse. We are there told that if a man would better himself by travel he should observe and comment, noting what is bad to avoid it, and taking the good into use. He should register his experiences with the pen lest they slide away unprofitably. He should master the language of the country, not merely to read books but to read men; for to be well read in men is better than any book-learning, and one who is abroad should seek converse with the best, choosing not by the eye but by fame. "For the State, instruction is to be had at the Court; for traffic, among merchants; for religious rights, the clergy; for government, the lawyers; and for the country and rural knowledge, the boors and peasantry can best help you. All rarities are to be seen, especially antiquities; for these show us the ingenuity of elder times in act, and are in one both example and precept. By these, comparing them with modern invention, we may see how the world thrives in ability and brain. But, above all, see rare men. There is no monument like a worthy man alive. We shall be sure to find something in him to kindle our spirits and enlarge our minds with a worthy emulation of his virtues."

To learn something about the manners, opinions and social conditions of foreigners it is well to travel third class and by slow trains. The more you hurry, the less you see. One of the most interesting journeys that I remember was from Agram to a small town in Carniola. I had a three-cornered conversation with a Vienna merchant, a Czech from Bohemia, and a Croatian. Many topics were touched and much ground covered while the train did its forty miles in four short hours, discharging at every station a load of picturesque peasants returning from the Agram market. To travel on the Spanish lines is equally profitable for the same reason ; nor shall I soon forget winding slowly over the melancholy wastes of Macedonia in the Oriental railway, built by Baron Hirsch, from the Servian frontier to Uskub. That was a little before the advent of the Young Turks. A dangerous journey in a tar-boat down the rapids of the Ulea, the great timber river of Finland, walks in Sofia and Belgrade and Salonica and Constantinople, a visit to Washington's home on the

Potomac, the view from Pentelicus of Athens and
Salamis and Aegina, the view of Moscow from
Ivan's Tower, are a few gems in the priceless
collection of a modern traveller.

At least half the pleasure, and more than half the
moral profit, of travel is lost through ignorance of the
language of the country. And this ignorance is often
inexcusable, a consequence of the dull, lazy, and
almost brutish manner in which too many people
consume their leisure. To acquire a language
thoroughly, to master its literature, is no doubt a
difficult if delightful task ; but there is no reason
why any intelligent person with some means and a
little leisure should not gain enough of French,
German, Spanish, Italian, or Scandinavian to enable
him to read the newspapers and "get along" in
conversation with the natives. Russian, indeed, and
the other Slav languages present more formidable
obstacles ; but French and German will smooth the
way through most cities of Eastern and South
Eastern Europe. What, indeed, contributes more to
the magnificent isolation of Englishmen than our indifference to the languages of the Continent ? If we
read more for ourselves we should be a less easy prey
to the panics and jealousies which a malevolent
journalism seeks to promote. If we really knew the
virtues and vices, the aspirations and foibles, the
great qualities and the small failings of other nations

we should be better men and better citizens. The globe-trotter who returns home more boastful and hardly less ignorant than before is a poor advertisement of the tourist agencies. But, happily, there are other and better types, whose sober patriotism is strengthened by broadened sympathies. The study of modern languages is certainly extending. People who travel are beginning to see that a little preliminary study may greatly increase their pleasures and incidentally diminish the expenses of their journeys. Even legislators are watching with more and more interest the social progress of other countries. Invention knows no local boundaries. With all its defects travel remains a civilizing and liberalizing agency, from which the inhabitants of the world are learning to be wiser than their prejudices, braver than their soldiers, and broader than their boundaries.

A PLEA FOR GARDENS

Parvis Epicurus in Hortis

POOR men are inarticulate. It is the main
business of representative institutions, local
and national, to find out the wants of the poor and to
supply them. An obvious, and, I am afraid, in
democracies a popular, plan is to help them at the
expense of those who are better off, on the plea that
"wealth is crime enough to him that's poor." A
better way is to enable them to help themselves, to
give them opportunities at present denied them by
law or by those who own the soil. Now there is, I am
persuaded, a cure for one of our worst economic and
social evils; and it is a cure which will add very
greatly to the national wealth. It will not enrich one
class at the expense of another; but it will increase
the total product and enlarge the national dividend.
It will be a source of health and wealth to tens of
thousands of poor families, and it will teach the children a most valuable kind of knowledge—the knowledge of gardening, which is the beginning and end

of agriculture. But a cure implies an evil. What is
that evil? It is the lack of gardens in many villages
and in the suburbs of towns. What is the cure? It
is to supply this want without impoverishing the
owners, but without enriching them at the expense of
their poorer neighbours. But how and why has this
grievance arisen? Why are there so many cottages
without gardens, or with gardens too small to supply
vegetables, fruit, and potatoes, in the midst of green
fields? Was there not an Act passed in the reign of
Queen Elizabeth providing that every cottage should
have a good piece of land? True, but it became a
dead letter. Yet, even so, natural causes would have
multiplied gardens if social reasons and the land laws
had not stood in the way. The causes are various.
Sometimes it is settled policy. The landlord knows
that farmers often object to their labourers having
large gardens for fear they should work less or become
too independent. Often it is merely "economy" of
space. The builder of cottages uses as little land as
possible in order to extract the greatest possible
amount of house rent from the smallest possible
amount of ground. It is the cruellest and stupidest
and least economical of all imaginable economies.
No builder or architect would attempt such a thing
in the case of domestic animals. Years ago, in some
parts of England, cottages used to be built on roadside
wastes, *i.e.*, on public land, and then as opportunity

served they were generally seized by the lord of the manor or the adjoining owner. In such cases there can practically be no garden unless the owner of the field adjoining the road allows it.

I was disgusted the other day, in a prosperous district of the West Riding, where public-spirited men have erected libraries and institutes for the factory hands, to find that even new cottages are still, as a rule, gardenless or with only a tiny patch. In the South of England many villages could be pointed out where this artificial scarcity of cottage gardens exists. I wish some good-hearted courtier or Minister could see a row of gardenless cottages adjoining a paddock of Richmond Park. For fifty years these poor people have looked wistfully upon the green field and longed for a strip of it at their back-door. If the Ranger had lived in one of these cottages for one week the need would have been seen and recognized. But I am thinking especially of a series of factory villages not very far from Bradford. There is plenty of pasture-land, good and bad, running up from the valleys to the moors, letting at from 10s. to £2 an acre, and selling, perhaps, freehold at from £10 to £50 per acre *unless it is suspected that it may be used for building land*, in which case the price demanded may be multiplied by ten. In this neighbourhood I saw a row of twenty or thirty cottages with tiny gardens of two or three yards square, subtended by a field of one acre which had just yielded a hay crop. I am certain that it would not pay any farmer to give more than £2 an acre rent for the field. Possibly the owner, who lives near, thinks it looks nicer as a field than as gardens. But look at the economy. Let each of those twenty working men have one-twentieth of the field— *i.e.*, let each garden be ten times its present length. Let the subdivided acre be cultivated intensively by the spade. Think of the supply of potatoes and vegetables that would be raised with little or no expense. I have no doubt that each cottage would get a supply of health in the shape of fresh vegetables worth a shilling a week in summer; and what a pride and pleasure to the family—what hours of useful and healthful recreation for the man and his wife and his children! The rich man who owns the field might think of this, for his own grandfather doubtless started life in clogs. Suppose, then, that this field, which now yields, perhaps, a net profit of £1 per year, were converted into twenty gardens, each yielding a net profit of £1 a year—for I will make a conservative estimate. That is a marvellous economic change. A field with a capital value of £20 on its present yield is converted into a field worth £400. Let the owner have £2 a year rent instead of £1 profit from the hay, and let the £18 be divided annually between the twenty cottagers. If Mr. Runciman, who is said to be putting thought and business energy into the Board of Agriculture, would visit the cottages round about Dewsbury, and look for further illustrations, he would probably be inclined to agree that in the West Riding alone fifty thousand cottages might easily be found which could be provided with gardens in this way, if they were allowed to take in a bit of pasture or waste land at their very doors.

All owners of vacant lands that adjoin gardenless cottages should take action on their own initiative. I know one landlord in Hertfordshire who has done so. Every cottage in the country ought to have from an eighth to a quarter of an acre of land, and I am told that a quarter of an acre (less intensively cultivated than a smaller plot) would be worth two shillings a week to any capable labourer with a large family.[1] Probably there are at least a million poor wage-earners who could be provided with one-eighth of an acre apiece if there were universal good sense and goodwill among owners and occupiers of land. A very simple Act of Parliament might be framed to meet those cases where intelligence and goodwill do not exist. It might be provided, for instance, that wherever a cottage or small house abuts on a field the cottager shall be entitled to take in so much of the field adjoining his cottage as will make up his garden to one-eighth (or one-quarter) of an acre on paying a

[1] A quarter of an acre garden for every labourer was part of Cobbett's plan. See his "Cottage Economy."

rent, say, one-quarter more than that which the tenant is paying for the said field, or (where the occupier is the owner) one-quarter more than a hypothetical tenant would give for the field for its existing use. If such an Act were passed it is not fanciful to suppose that the incomes of at least a million poor families would be increased by at least a shilling a week, and the annual income of the country by about $2\frac{1}{2}$ millions a year. But this does not allow for the immense benefits to the health which must accrue from the creation of a multitude of new gardens. The provision of gardens touches the many, and a garden at hand is worth an allotment double the size at a distance. The small holdings movement has done good, but it can never touch one-tenth of the people to whom a large garden makes an immediate appeal.

England after all is the land of gardens as well as of factories. And the fame of the English garden is older than the fame of the English factory. Bacon required not less than thirty acres for one of his "prince-like" gardens. That area would give us at least 120 cottage gardens. If then, as Bacon declares, gardening is "the purest of human pleasures" and "the greatest refreshment to the spirits of man," and if again this economic argument be sound, there can surely be no more noble or profitable pursuit for landowner or states-man than to enlarge the supply of cottage gardens.

PRIVATE LUXURY AND PUBLIC WASTE

ALTHOUGH Thrift still opens with her golden key the palace of independence, this Roman goddess, who forms with Industry and Diligence a Ciceronic triumvirate of economic virtues, is, alas! no longer worshipped even in our schools and universities, much less in Parliament and the public offices. We live in a country and in an age given over to public and private luxury. For Wealth, the child of Thrift, is the mother of Extravagance. Habits of profusion among the rich have created false standards of comfort. Costly pleasures are preferred. We seek the superfluous. A vulgar and insolent ostentation annoys the eye at every turn. To be economical is to be penurious. To save is to be mean. To live within your income is almost a reproach. And those who follow the fashion are soothed by a new doctrine into the comfortable belief that a generous scale of living is good for trade, that it stimulates employment and circulates money.

But Public and Private Waste are no novelties. They are as old as civilization itself; and though they caused the decline and fall of mighty empires and ancient families, I shall not join the croaking company that bemoans the decadence of England, or anticipates a general downfall of Anglo-Saxondom. Our prophets of evil generally have an axe to grind; some conjure up national perils on behalf of tariff reform, others in the hope of promoting an expansion of armaments. It is for the second of these that the German and Japanese bogeys are paraded before the British and American publics. But again I am no pessimist. It would have been rash, perhaps, at the beginning of 1909 to ask any considerable body of well-to-do Englishmen to listen patiently to a lecture on the virtues of naval economy. Dreadnoughts were still the rage. " We want eight, we won't wait," was the refrain—until we got them.   But Mr. Lloyd George's Budget with its complement of taxes and super-taxes has borne into every wealthy household another message. It has interpreted the pleasures of national expenditure in the terms of individual taxation. Dives is in pain. Crœsus is counting his treasures. Rhampsinitus has discovered the leakage. Warnings that fell on deaf ears are now listened to with attention. Once more the tax-gatherer, as Lord Morley said during the South African War, is proving himself the true schoolmaster. *Mox intelligent homines quam magnum vectigal sit parsimonia.*

Public and Private Waste are essentially the same. But their causes and consequences deserve separate analysis; and those who practise the second may be persuaded to combine against the first. By Waste in general one means, of course, useless or destructive expenditure. We must not be too strict or pedantic about our definition. That would only lend aid to cavil and casuistry. Better to hold by the substance and let others play with the shadow. I know that every kind of enjoyment can be represented as waste. The chief object, it may be said, of working for a larger income is that we may raise our standard of comfort, and waste a little more. Mark Pattison's dictum that a man should spend 10 per cent. of his income on books would in many cases clearly involve economic waste. He meant of course a man of taste and intelligence. Neither a State nor an individual could submit to a rule that all expenditure should be upon bare necessities, or upon objects that are directly and in the economic sense productive. Poetry and philosophy, the sciences, literature, and the arts cannot be brought within a narrow formula of this kind. But we need not be turned from our purpose by verbal stumbling-blocks. Waste is a large province, though it has indeterminate and shadowy borders.

Many things which one wise man would consider to be waste, another equally wise would regard as legitimate expenditure. But there is a vast amount of waste about which all men of sense are agreed. This, if we may borrow our terminology from international law, may be described as the province of "absolute waste"; the rest is "conditional waste," depending upon time, circumstance, and opinion. Absolute waste we all know when we see it, as when men overdrink, or women overdress, or nations fight about nothing.

Besides the absolute waste, which consists in spending money on wrong objects, there is another kind, which arises not in the object but in the method of attaining it, not in the end but in the means. Thus the Admiralty or War Office may not only waste money upon a wrong kind (or an excessive number) of guns or ships; they may also adopt wrong methods of construction; they may make an improvident contract. In such cases every one would agree that there is waste, whether the guns and ships are wanted or not. Again, a local authority may waste money not only by laying an unnecessary line of trams, but also by laying a necessary line on a wrong principle, or at an excessive cost. It may build a lunatic asylum, or workhouse, where it is not required, or on too palatial a plan, or with fittings needlessly luxurious. I heard the other day of porcelain baths, with the finest brass fittings, being placed at a cost of £13 a piece into a home for poor children belonging to a great local authority. The official was quite indignant when the committee ventured to remonstrate. And yet he would never have dreamed of embarking on such extravagance in his own home. Almost every one who has to do with the administration of public money seems to treat the public purse as inexhaustible. The pettiest clerk in the Civil Service demands an office worthy of a city magnate.

That public waste exists and tends to grow, as legislation gives more and more work to public bodies, no one denies. But while all recognize the evil and grumble more and more as rates and taxes rise, there is not much sign of an intelligent and concerted search for remedies. What is everybody's business is nobody's business. The noisy clamour of the individuals, who profit by public expenditure, is apt to drown the mild remonstrances of the community, which only has to pay the bill. A sensational Press is glad to ventilate any financial scandal which is likely to injure the other party in national or local politics ; but unhappily there are at present few journalists with the time or the capacity to educate the public in economical reform. By constant criticism and eternal vigilance,

—independent, impartial, and discerning—the great newspapers might help to save millions of public money. Alas! their influence is generally on the wrong side. A very large section of the British Press, including all the Unionist newspapers of London, has been engaged for some years past in endeavouring to promote a further expansion of armaments, including a scheme of conscription, without any reference to financial considerations; and what is called social expenditure is handled in very much the same way by most Radical newspapers. The Minority Report on the Poor Law contained innumerable recommendations, nearly all of which would add to the burdens falling upon the rates and taxes. But the vital question of finance was hardly touched upon either by the members of the Commission or their critics.

Failing the Press, which, after all, is only an indirect force—a stimulus to the prodigality of the prodigal or to the frugality of the frugal—there are the Government and the House of Commons, the Treasury, the Comptroller and Auditor-General, who all are, or might be, checks upon extravagance. It is to the first and the second that we must look for the inauguration of any large scheme of economical reform. In so far as waste depends upon policy it depends with us upon Ministers (collectively or individually) and the

House of Commons, just as in the United States it depends upon the President and Congress. But when the atmosphere of public opinion is favourable, the Treasury, if it has a strong Chancellor and Secretary, may save much by careful pruning of estimates ; and the Comptroller and Auditor-General, if he were a person of the vigour and independence desired by Mr. Gladstone (who begged Mr. Cobden to accept the position) might also do a great deal for economy. When Mr. T. G. Bowles was a member of the Public Accounts Committee of the House of Commons that body exerted some influence and excited some fear. But the mode of selection makes it almost impotent in ordinary times. Probably a standing commission of competent and public-spirited men with wide powers of criticism, acting without fear or favour, could save hundreds of thousands if not millions of tax-payers' money. Something may ultimately be achieved by the new Estimates Committee. A similar service might be rendered to ratepayers by the Local Government Board if its auditors could be instructed, invigorated, and clothed with ampler powers. One hears that a publicity bureau is doing admirable work in examining the municipal budgets of some American cities.

Nothing is more hopeful or admirable in our political life than the growing determination to grapple with hard problems of crime, intemperance, poverty, and unemployment. But just as philanthropy without common sense does more harm than good, so the projects of a sentimental socialism, unless they are worked out with a stern eye to economic facts and financial consequences, are bound to come to grief. To proceed with social reforms regardless of expense, as though the public purse were bottomless and the taxable capacity of the people unlimited, can only lead to grave trouble. In the military and naval sphere a different set of considerations apply. The whole expenditure is economically sterilizing and mischievous. But in the present state of the world enough must be spent to ensure a reasonable margin of security. To this practically every sane man will agree, as well as to the further proposition that the expansion of armaments cannot and should not go on indefinitely. A bankrupt nation is formidable neither in peace nor in war. The mania for war expenditure in time of peace offends not only against common sense but against all the maxims and traditions of British Statesmen from Pitt and Fox to Disraeli and Gladstone. Everything in Europe points to the urgency of an international agreement, with a view to the restriction of armaments. But the path of prudence is barred by two great professions and many powerful trades.

A favourite defence of both public and private

waste is that they give employment; and though often used by clever politicians who know better, the fallacy is superficially so attractive and so engaging at first sight that it deserves exposure. As it arises perhaps most frequently in connection with Government employment in the barracks and the dockyards, let me illustrate its meaning by tracing the consequences of recruiting or disbanding troops. The argument, it must be understood, is purely economic. The question of national security is ruled out. If the taxpayers feel insecure they can have more troops or battleships. But let them understand that they are buying the enjoyment of additional security at a sacrifice of capital or income. This is a strong reason for direct taxation. If our sugar and tea duties were removed, and the sum required were obtained by reducing the limit of exemption from income tax, which is now £160, to £100, or lower still, as in Prussia, very beneficial results would ensue. The pressure of naval and military experts, and of the sensational panic-monger, would be counteracted by a more general determination on the part of the public to resist extravagance. One good example of a practicable saving is that of the troops which we maintain in South Africa. The South African Union has placed South Africa in the same position as Canada and Australia and New Zealand, all of which provide for their own military defence. But a British garrison of 10,000 men has been retained in South Africa at a cost of a million a year to the home taxpayers, and a large number of unnecessary recruits have been bribed to leave useful employment in consequence of this South African drain. Meanwhile the shopkeepers of Pretoria were well satisfied that British soldiers should be supported there by the long purse of the British taxpayer. I am glad to say that at last a beginning is being made, and the garrison will be considerably reduced by the end of 1913. But the War Office has kept the money!

What exactly happens when the War Office induces the Cabinet to sanction a force of regulars larger by 10,000 men than is required for the defence of the country? Each superfluous man so recruited costs the taxpayer about £100 a year, all told, of which a small fraction only is for pay. Thus a million of money is withdrawn from private circulation into public circulation. If the 10,000 men recruited are "employables" doing regular and useful work, the wealth which they would have produced is all lost. The 10,000 would have performed some 3,000,000 days of productive labour every year. Instead of that they are being drilled and marched about at the public expense. They are wearing out public clothes and public arms, travelling in railways and ships with tickets paid for by the War Office, and firing away public ammunition. They were labourers in the field and factory, able to support wives and children and to contribute to the public revenue. Now they are unable to do either. They turn to the right about and the left about; they are soldiers. And when they leave the army they are ill-fitted for civil occupations. In times of peace the way to reduce superfluous establishments is to recruit on a smaller scale. Nor need the disbandment of men cause unemployment, because (as Bastiat made clear) at the very time when you throw the men on to the market you throw into the market, by a release of taxes, an amount of money sufficient to employ in useful and profitable occupations double the number.

When you have men superfluously employed in the service of private luxury, the economic waste is, I think, strictly comparable; and a tax falling upon this sort of wasteful expenditure is perhaps the best that can be devised, assuming of course that it is feasible and not too costly to collect. Let me illustrate the point by an imaginary but not impossible example. We will assume that after inquiry the Chancellor of the Exchequer discovers 500 rich men in the kingdom who keep about ten flunkeys apiece. Each flunkey costs his master on an average £100 a year, just about what a soldier costs *his* master—the State. Thus you have 500 wealthy men keeping an

s

army of 5,000 men-servants at a cost of £500,000
a year. Thereupon the Chancellor of the Exchequer,
being in need of money, includes in his Budget a
special tax of £100 per man-servant on the Five
Hundred. The Five Hundred being unwilling to
pay more out of their incomes for men-servants than
they did before, reduce their staffs from ten to five.
Instead of paying £500,000 for 5,000, they pay
the same sum in two parts, half in wages to 2,500
servants and half in taxes to the national exchequer.
If the State lays out the new revenue on useful
works, employing men to improve roads or canals
or to afforest waste lands, then the nation is better
off than it was before the tax. The money which
employed a corps of 2,500 flunkeys now employs the
same number of useful labourers. If, however, the
Secretary for War rather than the President of the
Board of Trade, or Local Government, or Agriculture
gets the ear of the Cabinet, the money may be used
to add 2,500 men to the army. Then from an
economic point of view things are neither better
nor worse, the soldier like the flunkey being a mere
consumer of wealth. Instead of paying for 2,500
flunkeys, the 500 rich men are paying for 2,500
soldiers. If such a tax were imposed one would like
to see the comments of the *Daily Telegraph*, the
Morning Post, and the *Daily Mail*. Would the pen
of the militarist who demands a larger army, or of

the Conservative who denounces confiscatory taxes, be most likely to be employed? Perhaps it would depend on the all-important question—which Government happened to be in office! There was reason in Mr. Birrell's complaint that the journalist, who might well be, if not indifferent to, at least independent of party, is apt to follow it with undeviating servility.

INDEX

The Gresham Press,
UNWIN BROTHERS, LIMITED,
WOKING AND LONDON.

A SELECTION OF BOOKS
PUBLISHED BY METHUEN
AND CO. LTD., LONDON
36 ESSEX STREET
W.C.

CONTENTS

Celano (Brother Thomas of). THE LIVES OF S. FRANCIS OF ASSISI. Translated by A. G. FERRERS HOWELL. With a Frontispiece. *Cr. 8vo. 5s. net.*

Chambers (Mrs. Lambert). LAWN TENNIS FOR LADIES. Illustrated. *Cr. 8vo. 2s. 6d. net.*

*Chesser, (Elizabeth Sloan). PERFECT HEALTH FOR WOMEN AND CHILDREN. *Cr. 8vo. 3s. 6d. net.*

Chesterfield (Lord). THE LETTERS OF THE EARL OF CHESTERFIELD TO HIS SON. Edited, with an Introduction by C. STRACHEY, and Notes by A. CALTHROP. *Two Volumes. Cr. 8vo. 12s.*

Chesterton (G.K.). CHARLES DICKENS. With two Portraits in Photogravure. *Seventh Edition. Cr. 8vo. 6s.*
ALL THINGS CONSIDERED. *Sixth Edition. Fcap. 8vo. 5s.*
TREMENDOUS TRIFLES. *Fourth Edition. Fcap. 8vo. 5s.*
ALARMS AND DISCURSIONS. *Second Edition. Fcap. 8vo. 5s.*
THE BALLAD OF THE WHITE HORSE. *Third Edition. Fcap. 8vo. 5s.*
*TYPES OF MEN. *Fcap. 8vo. 5s.*

Clausen (George). SIX LECTURES ON PAINTING. Illustrated. *Third Edition. Large Post 8vo. 3s. 6d. net.*
AIMS AND IDEALS IN ART. Eight Lectures delivered to the Students of the Royal Academy of Arts. Illustrated. *Second Edition. Large Post 8vo. 5s. net.*

Clutton-Brock (A.) SHELLEY: THE MAN AND THE POET. Illustrated. *Demy 8vo. 7s. 6d. net.*

Cobb (W.F.). THE BOOK OF PSALMS. With an Introduction and Notes. *Demy 8vo. 10s. 6d. net.*

Conrad (Joseph). THE MIRROR OF THE SEA: Memories and Impressions. *Third Edition. Cr. 8vo. 6s.*

Coolidge (W. A. B.). THE ALPS: IN NATURE AND HISTORY. Illustrated. *Demy 8vo. 7s. 6d. net.*

*Correvon (H.). ALPINE FLORA. Translated and enlarged by E. W. CLAYFORTH. Illustrated. *Square Demy 8vo. 16s. net.*

Coulton (G. G.). CHAUCER AND HIS ENGLAND. Illustrated. *Second Edition. Demy 8vo. 10s. 6d. net.*

Cowper (William). THE POEMS. Edited with an Introduction and Notes by J. C. BAILEY. Illustrated. *Demy 8vo. 10s. 6d. net.*

Cox (J. C.). RAMBLES IN SURREY. *Second Edition. Cr. 8vo. 6s.*

Crowley (Ralph H.). THE HYGIENE OF SCHOOL LIFE. Illustrated. *Cr. 8vo. 3s. 6d. net.*

Davis (H. W. C.). ENGLAND UNDER THE NORMANS AND ANGEVINS: 1066-1272. *Third Edition. Demy 8vo. 10s. 6d. net.*

Dawbarn (Charles). FRANCE AND THE FRENCH. Illustrated. *Demy 8vo. 10s. 6d. net.*

Dearmer (Mabel). A CHILD'S LIFE OF CHRIST. Illustrated. *Large Cr. 8vo. 6s.*

Deffand (Madame du). LETTRES DE MADAME DU DEFFAND À HORACE WALPOLE. Edited, with Introduction, Notes, and Index, by Mrs. PAGET TOYNBEE. *In Three Volumes. Demy 8vo. £3 3s. net.*

Dickinson (G. L.). THE GREEK VIEW OF LIFE. *Seventh Edition. Crown 8vo. 2s. 6d. net.*

Ditchfield (P. H.). THE PARISH CLERK. Illustrated. *Third Edition. Demy 8vo. 7s. 6d. net.*
THE OLD-TIME PARSON. Illustrated. *Second Edition. Demy 8vo. 7s. 6d. net.*
*THE OLD ENGLISH COUNTRY SQUIRE. Illustrated. *Demy 8vo. 10s. 6d. net.*

Ditchfield (P. H.) and Roe (Fred). VANISHING ENGLAND. The Book by P. H. Ditchfield. Illustrated by FRED ROE. *Second Edition. Wide Demy 8vo. 15s. net.*

Douglas (Hugh A.). VENICE ON FOOT. With the Itinerary of the Grand Canal. Illustrated. *Second Edition. Round corners. Fcap. 8vo. 5s. net.*
VENICE AND HER TREASURES. Illustrated. *Round corners. Fcap. 8vo. 5s. net.*

Dowden (J.). FURTHER STUDIES IN THE PRAYER BOOK. *Cr. 8vo. 6s.*

Driver (S. R.). SERMONS ON SUBJECTS CONNECTED WITH THE OLD TESTAMENT. *Cr. 8vo. 6s.*

Dumas (Alexandre). THE CRIMES OF THE BORGIAS AND OTHERS. With an Introduction by R. S. GARNETT. Illustrated. *Second Edition. Cr. 8vo. 6s.*
THE CRIMES OF URBAIN GRANDIER AND OTHERS. Illustrated. *Cr. 8vo. 6s.*
THE CRIMES OF THE MARQUISE DE BRINVILLIERS AND OTHERS. Illustrated. *Cr. 8vo. 6s.*
THE CRIMES OF ALI PACHA AND OTHERS. Illustrated *Cr. 8vo. 6s.*

MY MEMOIRS. Translated by E. M. WALLER. With an Introduction by ANDREW LANG. With Frontispieces in Photogravure. In six Volumes. *Cr. 8vo. 6s. each volume.*
VOL. I. 1802-1821. VOL. IV. 1830-1831.
VOL. II. 1822-1825. VOL. V. 1831-1832.
VOL. III. 1826-1830. VOL. VI 1832-1833.
MY PETS. Newly translated by A. R. ALLINSON. Illustrated. *Cr. 8vo. 6s.*

Duncan (F. M.). OUR INSECT FRIENDS AND FOES. Illustrated. *Cr. 8vo. 6s.*

Dunn-Pattison (R. P.). NAPOLEON'S MARSHALS. Illustrated. *Demy 8vo. Second Edition. 12s. 6d. net.*
THE BLACK PRINCE. Illustrated *Second Edition. Demy 8vo. 7s. 6d. net.*

Durham (The Earl of). THE REPORT ON CANADA. With an Introductory Note. *Demy 8vo. 4s. 6d. net.*

Dutt (W. A.). THE NORFOLK BROADS. Illustrated. *Second Edition. Cr. 8vo. 6s.*

Egerton (H. E.). A SHORT HISTORY OF BRITISH COLONIAL POLICY. *Third Edition. Demy 8vo. 7s. 6d. net.*

Evans (Herbert A.). CASTLES OF ENGLAND AND WALES. Illustrated. *Demy 8vo. 12s. 6d. net.*

Exeter (Bishop of). REGNUM DEI. (The Bampton Lectures of 1901.) *A Cheaper Edition. Demy 8vo. 7s. 6d. net.*

Ewald (Carl). MY LITTLE BOY. Translated by ALEXANDER TEIXEIRA DE MATTOS. Illustrated. *Fcap. 8vo. 5s.*

Fairbrother (W. H.). THE PHILO-SOPHY OF T. H. GREEN. *Second Edition. Cr. 8vo. 3s. 6d.*

*ffoulkes (Charles). THE ARMOURER AND HIS CRAFT. Illustrated. *Royal 4to. £2 2s. net.*

Firth (C. H.). CROMWELL'S ARMY : A History of the English Soldier during the Civil Wars, the Commonwealth, and the Protectorate. Illustrated. *Second Edition. Cr. 8vo. 6s.*

Fisher (H. A. L.). THE REPUBLICAN TRADITION IN EUROPE. *Cr. 8vo. 6s. net.*

FitzGerald (Edward). THE RUBA'IYAT OF OMAR KHAYYÁM. Printed from the Fifth and last Edition. With a Commentary by H. M. BATSON, and a Biographical Introduction by E. D. ROSS. *Cr. 8vo. 6s.*

Flux (A. W.). ECONOMIC PRINCIPLES. *Demy 8vo. 7s. 6d. net.*

Fraser (J. F.). ROUND THE WORLD ON A WHEEL. Illustrated. *Fifth Edition. Cr. 8vo. 6s.*

Galton (Sir Francis). MEMORIES OF MY LIFE. Illustrated. *Third Edition. Demy 8vo. 10s. 6d. net.*

Gibbins (H. de B.). INDUSTRY IN ENGLAND : HISTORICAL OUT-LINES. With Maps and Plans. *Seventh Edition, Revised. Demy 8vo. 10s. 6d.*
THE INDUSTRIAL HISTORY OF ENGLAND. With 5 Maps and a Plan. *Eighteenth and Revised Edition. Cr. 8vo. 3s.*
ENGLISH SOCIAL REFORMERS. *Second Edition. Cr. 8vo. 2s. 6d.*

Gibbon (Edward). THE MEMOIRS OF THE LIFE OF EDWARD GIBBON. Edited by G. BIRKBECK HILL. *Cr. 8vo. 6s.*
THE DECLINE AND FALL OF THE ROMAN EMPIRE. Edited, with Notes, Appendices, and Maps, by J. B. BURY, Illustrated. *In Seven Volumes. Demy 8vo. Each 10s. 6d. net. Also in Seven Volumes. Cr. 8vo. 6s. each.*

Glover (T. R.). THE CONFLICT OF RELIGIONS IN THE EARLY ROMAN EMPIRE. *Fourth Edition. Demy 8vo. 7s. 6d. net.*

Godley (A. D.). LYRA FRIVOLA. *Fourth Edition. Fcap. 8vo. 2s. 6d.*
VERSES TO ORDER. *Second Edition. Fcap. 8vo. 2s. 6d.*
SECOND STRINGS. *Fcap. 8vo. 2s. 6d.*

Gostling (Frances M.). THE BRETONS AT HOME. Illustrated. *Third Edition. Cr. 8vo. 6s.*
AUVERGNE AND ITS PEOPLE. Illustrated. *Demy 8vo. 10s. 6d. net.*

*Gray (Arthur). CAMBRIDGE AND ITS STORY. Illustrated. *Demy 8vo. 7s. 6d. net.*

Grahame (Kenneth). THE WIND IN THE WILLOWS. Illustrated. *Sixth Edition. Cr. 8vo. 6s.*

Granger (Frank). HISTORICAL SOCI-OLOGY : A TEXT-BOOK OF POLITICS. *Cr. 8vo. 3s. 6d. net.*

Grew (Edwin Sharpe). THE GROWTH OF A PLANET. Illustrated. *Cr. 8vo. 6s.*

Griffin (W. Hall) and Minchin (H. C.). THE LIFE OF ROBERT BROWNING. Illustrated. *Second Edition. Demy 8vo. 12s. 6d. net.*

Hale (J. R.). FAMOUS SEA FIGHTS : FROM SALAMIS TO TSU-SHIMA. Illustrated. *Cr. 8vo. 6s. net.*

*Ball (H. R.). THE ANCIENT HISTORY OF THE NEAR EAST FROM THE EARLIEST PERIOD TO THE PERSIAN INVASION OF GREECE. Illustrated. *Demy 8vo.* 15s. net.

Hannay (D.). A SHORT HISTORY OF THE ROYAL NAVY. Vol. I., 1217-1688. Vol. II., 1689-1815. *Demy 8vo.* Each 7s. 6d. net.

Harper (Charles G.). THE AUTOCAR ROAD-BOOK. With Maps. *In Four Volumes. Cr. 8vo.* Each 7s. 6d. net.
 Vol. I.—SOUTH OF THE THAMES.
 Vol. II.—NORTH AND SOUTH WALES AND WEST MIDLANDS.
 Vol. III.—EAST ANGLIA AND EAST MIDLANDS.
 * Vol. IV.—THE NORTH OF ENGLAND AND SOUTH OF SCOTLAND.

Harris (Frank). THE WOMEN OF SHAKESPEARE. *Demy 8vo.* 7s. 6d. net.

Hassall (Arthur). THE LIFE OF NAPOLEON. Illustrated. *Demy 8vo.* 7s. 6d. net.

Headley (F. W.). DARWINISM AND MODERN SOCIALISM. *Second Edition. Cr. 8vo.* 5s. net.

Henderson (M. Sturge). GEORGE MEREDITH: NOVELIST, POET, REFORMER. With a Portrait. *Second Edition. Cr. 8vo.* 6s.

Henley (W. E.). ENGLISH LYRICS: CHAUCER TO POE. *Second Edition. Cr. 8vo.* 2s. 6d. net.

Hill (George Francis). ONE HUNDRED MASTERPIECES OF SCULPTURE. Illustrated. *Demy 8vo.* 10s. 6d. net.

Hind (C. Lewis). DAYS IN CORNWALL. Illustrated. *Third Edition. Cr. 8vo.* 6s.

Hobhouse (L. T.). THE THEORY OF KNOWLEDGE. *Demy 8vo.* 10s. 6d. net.

Hobson (J. A.). INTERNATIONAL TRADE: AN APPLICATION OF ECONOMIC THEORY. *Cr. 8vo.* 2s. 6d. net.
PROBLEMS OF POVERTY: AN INQUIRY INTO THE INDUSTRIAL CONDITION OF THE POOR. *Seventh Edition. Cr. 8vo.* 2s. 6d.
THE PROBLEM OF THE UNEMPLOYED: AN ENQUIRY AND AN ECONOMIC POLICY. *Fifth Edition. Cr. 8vo.* 2s. 6d.

Hodgson (Mrs W.). HOW TO IDENTIFY OLD CHINESE PORCELAIN. Illustrated. *Third Edition. Post 8vo.* 6s.

Holdich (Sir T. H.). THE INDIAN BORDERLAND, 1880-1900. Illustrated. *Second Edition. Demy 8vo.* 10s. 6d. net

Holdsworth (W. S.). A HISTORY OF ENGLISH LAW. *In Four Volumes.* Vols. I., II., III. *Demy 8vo.* Each 10s. 6d. net.

Holland (Clive). TYROL AND ITS PEOPLE. Illustrated. *Demy 8vo.* 10s. 6d. net.
THE BELGIANS AT HOME. Illustrated. *Demy 8vo.* 10s. 6d. net.

Horsburgh (E. L. S.). LORENZO THE MAGNIFICENT: AND FLORENCE IN HER GOLDEN AGE. Illustrated. *Second Edition. Demy 8vo.* 15s. net.
WATERLOO: A NARRATIVE AND A CRITICISM. With Plans. *Second Edition. Cr. 8vo.* 5s.
THE LIFE OF SAVONAROLA. Illustrated. *Cr. 8vo.* 5s. net.

Hosie (Alexander). MANCHURIA. Illustrated. *Second Edition. Demy 8vo.* 7s. 6d. net.

Hudson (W. H.). A SHEPHERD'S LIFE: IMPRESSIONS OF THE SOUTH WILTSHIRE DOWNS. Illustrated. *Third Edition. Demy 8vo.* 7s. 6d. net.

Humphreys (John H.). PROPORTIONAL REPRESENTATION. *Cr. 8vo.* 5s. net.

Hutchinson (Horace G.). THE NEW FOREST. Illustrated. *Fourth Edition. Cr. 8vo.* 6s.

Hutton (Edward). THE CITIES OF SPAIN. Illustrated. *Fourth Edition. Cr. 8vo.* 6s.
THE CITIES OF UMBRIA. Illustrated. *Fourth Edition. Cr. 8vo.* 6s.
*THE CITIES OF LOMBARDY. Illustrated. *Cr. 8vo.* 6s.
FLORENCE AND NORTHERN TUSCANY WITH GENOA. Illustrated. *Second Edition. Cr. 8vo.* 6s.
SIENA AND SOUTHERN TUSCANY. Illustrated. *Second Edition. Cr. 8vo.* 6s.
VENICE AND VENETIA. Illustrated. *Cr. 8vo.* 6s.
ROME. Illustrated. *Third Edition. Cr. 8vo.* 6s.
COUNTRY WALKS ABOUT FLORENCE. Illustrated. *Second Edition. Fcap. 8vo.* 5s. net.
IN UNKNOWN TUSCANY. With Notes by WILLIAM HEYWOOD. Illustrated. *Second Edition. Demy 8vo.* 7s. 6d. net.
A BOOK OF THE WYE. Illustrated. *Demy 8vo.* 7s. 6d. net.

Ibsen (Henrik). BRAND. A Dramatic Poem, Translated by WILLIAM WILSON. *Fourth Edition. Cr. 8vo.* 3s. 6d.

Inge (W. R.). CHRISTIAN MYSTICISM. (The Bampton Lectures of 1899.) *Second and Cheaper Edition. Cr. 8vo.* 5s. net.

Innes (A. D.). A HISTORY OF THE BRITISH IN INDIA. With Maps and Plans. *Cr. 8vo. 6s.*
ENGLAND UNDER THE TUDORS. With Maps. *Third Edition. Demy 8vo. 10s. 6d. net.*

Innes (Mary). SCHOOLS OF PAINTING. Illustrated. *Second Edition. Cr. 8vo. 5s. net.*

Jenks (E.). AN OUTLINE OF ENGLISH LOCAL GOVERNMENT. *Second Edition.* Revised by R. C. K. ENSOR, *Cr. 8vo. 2s. 6d. net.*
A SHORT HISTORY OF ENGLISH LAW: FROM THE EARLIEST TIMES TO THE END OF THE YEAR 1911. *Demy 8vo. 10s. 6d. net.*

Jerningham (Charles Edward). THE MAXIMS OF MARMADUKE. *Second Edition. Cr. 8vo. 5s.*

Johnston (Sir H. H.). BRITISH CENTRAL AFRICA. Illustrated. *Third Edition. Cr. 4to. 18s. net.*
THE NEGRO IN THE NEW WORLD. Illustrated. *Demy 8vo. 21s. net.*

Julian (Lady) of Norwich. REVELATIONS OF DIVINE LOVE. Edited by GRACE WARRACK. *Fourth Edition. Cr. 8vo. 3s. 6d.*

Keats (John). THE POEMS. Edited with Introduction and Notes by E. de SÉLINCOURT. With a Frontispiece in Photogravure. *Third Edition. Demy 8vo. 7s. 6d. net.*

Keble (John). THE CHRISTIAN YEAR. With an Introduction and Notes by W. LOCK. Illustrated. *Third Edition. Fcap. 8vo. 3s. 6d.*

Kempis (Thomas à). THE IMITATION OF CHRIST. From the Latin, with an Introduction by DEAN FARRAR. Illustrated. *Third Edition. Fcap. 8vo. 3s. 6d.*

Kingston (Edward). A GUIDE TO THE BRITISH PICTURES IN THE NATIONAL GALLERY. Illustrated. *Fcap. 8vo. 3s. 6d. net.*

Kipling (Rudyard). BARRACK-ROOM BALLADS. 108th Thousand. *Thirty-first Edition. Cr. 8vo. 6s.* Also *Fcap. 8vo, Leather. 5s. net.*
THE SEVEN SEAS. 89th Thousand. *Nineteenth Edition. Cr. 8vo. 6s.* Also *Fcap. 8vo, Leather. 5s. net.*
THE FIVE NATIONS. 72nd Thousand. *Eighth Edition. Cr. 8vo. 6s.* Also *Fcap. 8vo, Leather. 5s. net.*
DEPARTMENTAL DITTIES. *Twentieth Edition. Cr. 8vo. 6s.* Also *Fcap. 8vo, Leather. 5s. net.*

Lamb (Charles and Mary). THE COMPLETE WORKS. Edited with an Introduction and Notes by E. V. LUCAS. *A New and Revised Edition in Six Volumes.* With Frontispiece. *Fcap. 8vo. 5s. each.* The volumes are :—
I. MISCELLANEOUS PROSE. II. ELIA AND THE LAST ESSAYS OF ELIA. III. BOOKS FOR CHILDREN. IV. PLAYS AND POEMS. V. and VI. LETTERS.

Lankester (Sir Ray). SCIENCE FROM AN EASY CHAIR. Illustrated. *Fifth Edition. Cr. 8vo. 6s.*

Le Braz (Anatole). THE LAND OF PARDONS. Translated by FRANCES M. GOSTLING. Illustrated. *Third Edition. Cr. 8vo. 6s.*

Lock (Walter). ST. PAUL, THE MASTER-BUILDER. *Third Edition. Cr. 8vo. 3s. 6d.*
THE BIBLE AND CHRISTIAN LIFE. *Cr. 8vo. 6s.*

Lodge (Sir Oliver). THE SUBSTANCE OF FAITH, ALLIED WITH SCIENCE: A Catechism for Parents and Teachers. *Eleventh Edition. Cr. 8vo. 2s. net.*
MAN AND THE UNIVERSE: A STUDY OF THE INFLUENCE OF THE ADVANCE IN SCIENTIFIC KNOWLEDGE UPON OUR UNDERSTANDING OF CHRISTIANITY. *Ninth Edition. Demy 8vo. 5s. net.* Also *Fcap. 8vo. 1s. net.*
THE SURVIVAL OF MAN. A STUDY IN UNRECOGNISED HUMAN FACULTY. *Fifth Edition. Wide Crown 8vo. 5s. net.*
REASON AND BELIEF. *Fifth Edition. Cr. 8vo. 3s. 6d. net.*
MODERN PROBLEMS. Cr. 8vo. 5s. net.

Lorimer (George Horace). LETTERS FROM A SELF-MADE MERCHANT TO HIS SON. Illustrated. *Twenty-second Edition. Cr. 8vo. 3s. 6d.* Also *Fcap. 8vo. 1s. net.*
OLD GORGON GRAHAM. Illustrated. *Second Edition. Cr. 8vo. 6s.*

Lucas (E. V.). THE LIFE OF CHARLES LAMB. Illustrated. *Fifth Edition. Demy 8vo. 7s. 6d. net.*
A WANDERER IN HOLLAND. Illustrated. *Thirteenth Edition. Cr. 8vo. 6s.*
A WANDERER IN LONDON. Illustrated. *Twelfth Edition. Cr. 8vo. 6s.*
A WANDERER IN PARIS. Illustrated. *Ninth Edition. Cr. 8vo. 6s.* Also *Fcap. 8vo. 5s.*
A WANDERER IN FLORENCE. Illustrated. Cr. 8vo. 6s.
THE OPEN ROAD: A Little Book for Wayfarers. *Eighteenth Edition. Fcap. 8vo. 5s.* ; *India Paper, 7s. 6d.*
Also Illustrated in colour. Cr. 4to. 15s. net.

THE FRIENDLY TOWN: A Little Book for the Urbane. *Sixth Edition. Fcap. 8vo.* 5s.; *India Paper,* 7s. 6d.
FIRESIDE AND SUNSHINE. *Sixth Edition. Fcap. 8vo.* 5s.
CHARACTER AND COMEDY. *Sixth Edition. Fcap. 8vo.* 5s.
THE GENTLEST ART. A Choice of Letters by Entertaining Hands. *Seventh Edition. Fcap 8vo.* 5s.
THE SECOND POST. *Third Edition. Fcap. 8vo.* 5s.
HER INFINITE VARIETY: A FEMININE PORTRAIT GALLERY. *Sixth Edition. Fcap. 8vo.* 5s.
GOOD COMPANY: A RALLY OF MEN. *Second Edition. Fcap. 8vo.* 5s.
ONE DAY AND ANOTHER. *Fifth Edition. Fcap. 8vo.* 5s.
OLD LAMPS FOR NEW. *Fourth Edition. Fcap. 8vo.* 5s.
LISTENER'S LURE: AN OBLIQUE NARRATION. *Ninth Edition. Fcap. 8vo.* 5s.
OVER BEMERTON'S: AN EASY-GOING CHRONICLE. *Ninth Edition. Fcap. 8vo.* 5s.
MR. INGLESIDE. *Ninth Edition. Fcap. 8vo.* 5s.
   See also Lamb (Charles).

Lydekker (R. and Others). REPTILES, AMPHIBIA, FISHES, AND LOWER CHORDATA. Edited by J. C. CUNNINGHAM. Illustrated. *Demy 8vo.* 10s. 6d. *net.*

Lydekker (R.). THE OX AND ITS KINDRED. Illustrated. *Cr. 8vo.* 6s.

Macaulay (Lord). CRITICAL AND HISTORICAL ESSAYS. Edited by F. C. MONTAGUE. *Three Volumes. Cr. 8vo.* 18s.

McCabe (Joseph). THE DECAY OF THE CHURCH OF ROME. *Third Edition. Demy 8vo.* 7s. 6d. *net.*
THE EMPRESSES OF ROME. Illustrated. *Demy 8vo.* 12s. 6d. *net.*

MacCarthy (Desmond) and Russell (Agatha). LADY JOHN RUSSELL: A MEMOIR. Illustrated. *Fourth Edition. Demy 8vo.* 10s. 6d. *net.*

McCullagh (Francis). THE FALL OF ABD-UL-HAMID. Illustrated. *Demy 8vo.* 10s. 6d. *net.*

McDougall (William). AN INTRODUCTION TO SOCIAL PSYCHOLOGY. *Fourth Edition. Cr. 8vo.* 5s. *net.*
BODY AND MIND: A HISTORY AND A DEFENCE OF ANIMISM. *Demy 8vo.* 10s. 6d. *net.*

'Mdlle. Mori' (Author of). ST. CATHERINE OF SIENA AND HER TIMES. Illustrated. *Second Edition. Demy 8vo.* 7s. 6d. *net.*

Maeterlinck (Maurice). THE BLUE BIRD: A FAIRY PLAY IN SIX ACTS. Translated by ALEXANDER TEIXEIRA DE MATTOS. *Fcap. 8vo. Deckle Edges.* 3s. 6d. *net. Also Fcap. 8vo. Cloth,* 1s. *net.* AN Edition, illustrated in colour by F. CAYLEY ROBINSON, is also published. *Cr. 4to. Gilt top.* 21s. *net.* Of the above book Twenty-nine Editions in all have been issued.
MARY MAGDALENE: A PLAY IN THREE ACTS. Translated by ALEXANDER TEIXEIRA DE MATTOS. *Third Edition. Fcap. 8vo. Deckle Edges.* 3s. 6d. *net. Also Fcap. 8vo.* 1s. *net.*
DEATH. Translated by ALEXANDER TEIXEIRA DE MATTOS. *Fourth Edition. Fcap. 8vo.* 3s. 6d. *net.*

Mahaffy (J. P.). A HISTORY OF EGYPT UNDER THE PTOLEMAIC DYNASTY. Illustrated. *Cr. 8vo.* 6s.

Maitland (F. W.). ROMAN CANON LAW IN THE CHURCH OF ENGLAND. *Royal 8vo.* 7s. 6d.

Marett (R. R.). THE THRESHOLD OF RELIGION. *Cr. 8vo.* 3s. 6d. *net.*

Marriott (Charles). A SPANISH HOLIDAY. Illustrated. *Demy 8vo.* 7s. 6d. *net.*
THE ROMANCE OF THE RHINE. Illustrated. *Demy 8vo.* 10s. 6d. *net.*

Marriott (J. A. R.). THE LIFE AND TIMES OF LUCIUS CARY, VISCOUNT FALKLAND. Illustrated. *Second Edition. Demy 8vo.* 7s. 6d. *net.*

Masefield (John). SEA LIFE IN NELSON'S TIME. Illustrated. *Cr. 8vo.* 3s. 6d. *net.*
A SAILOR'S GARLAND. Selected and Edited. *Second Edition. Cr. 8vo.* 3s. 6d. *net.*

Masterman (C. F. G.). TENNYSON AS A RELIGIOUS TEACHER. *Second Edition. Cr. 8vo.* 6s.
THE CONDITION OF ENGLAND. *Fourth Edition. Cr. 8vo.* 6s. *Also Fcap. 8vo.* 1s. *net.*

Mayne (Ethel Colburn). BYRON. Illustrated. *In two volumes. Demy 8vo.* 21s. *net.*

Medley (D. J.). ORIGINAL ILLUSTRATIONS OF ENGLISH CONSTITUTIONAL HISTORY. *Cr. 8vo.* 7s. 6d. *net.*

Methuen (A. M. S.). ENGLAND'S RUIN: DISCUSSED IN FOURTEEN LETTERS TO A PROTECTIONIST. *Ninth Edition. Cr. 8vo.* 3d. *net.*

Miles (Eustace). LIFE AFTER LIFE: OR, THE THEORY OF REINCARNATION. *Cr. 8vo.* 2s. 6d. *net.*
THE POWER OF CONCENTRATION: How TO ACQUIRE IT. *Fourth Edition. Cr. 8vo.* 3s. 6d. *net.*

Millais (J. G.). THE LIFE AND LETTERS OF SIR JOHN EVERETT MILLAIS. Illustrated. *New Edition*. *Demy 8vo*. 7s. 6d. net.

Milne (J. G.). A HISTORY OF EGYPT UNDER ROMAN RULE. Illustrated. *Cr. 8vo*. 6s.

Moffat (Mary M.). QUEEN LOUISA OF PRUSSIA. Illustrated. *Fourth Edition*. *Cr. 8vo*. 6s.
MARIA THERESA. Illustrated. *Demy 8vo*. 10s. 6d. net.

Money (L. G. Chiozza). RICHES AND POVERTY, 1910. *Tenth and Revised Edition*. *Demy 8vo*. 5s. net.
MONEY'S FISCAL DICTIONARY, 1910. *Second Edition*. *Demy 8vo*. 5s. net.
INSURANCE VERSUS POVERTY. *Cr. 8vo*. 5s. net.
THINGS THAT MATTER: PAPERS ON SUBJECTS WHICH ARE, OR OUGHT TO BE, UNDER DISCUSSION. *Demy 8vo*. 5s. net.

Montague (C. E.). DRAMATIC VALUES. *Second Edition*. *Fcap. 8vo*. 5s.

Moorhouse (E. Hallam). NELSON'S LADY HAMILTON. Illustrated. *Third Edition*. *Demy 8vo*. 7s. 6d. net.

*Morgan (C. Lloyd). INSTINCT AND EXPERIENCE. *Cr. 8vo*. 5s. net.

*Nevill (Lady Dorothy). MY OWN TIMES. Edited by her son. *Demy 8vo*. 15s. net.

Norway (A. H.). NAPLES: PAST AND PRESENT. Illustrated. *Fourth Edition*. *Cr. 8vo*. 6s.

*O'Donnell (Elliott). WEREWOLVES. *Cr. 8vo*. 5s. net.

Oman (C. W. C.), A HISTORY OF THE ART OF WAR IN THE MIDDLE AGES. Illustrated. *Demy 8vo*. 10s. 6d. net.
ENGLAND BEFORE THE NORMAN CONQUEST. With Maps. *Second Edition*. *Demy 8vo*. 10s. 6d. net.

Oxford (M. N.), A HANDBOOK OF NURSING. *Sixth Edition, Revised*. *Cr. 8vo*. 3s. 6d. net.

Pakes (W. C. C.). THE SCIENCE OF HYGIENE. Illustrated. *Second and Cheaper Edition*. Revised by A. T. NANKIVELL. *Cr. 8vo*. 5s. net.

Parker (Eric). THE BOOK OF THE ZOO. Illustrated. *Second Edition*. *Cr. 8vo*. 6s.

Pears (Sir Edwin). TURKEY AND ITS PEOPLE. *Second Edition*. *Demy 8vo*. 12s. 6d. net.

Petrie (W. M. Flinders). A HISTORY OF EGYPT. Illustrated. *In Six Volumes*. *Cr. 8vo*. 6s. each.
VOL. I. FROM THE 1ST TO THE XVITH DYNASTY. *Seventh Edition*.
VOL. II. THE XVIITH AND XVIIITH DYNASTIES. *Fourth Edition*.
VOL. III. XIXTH TO XXXTH DYNASTIES.
VOL. IV. EGYPT UNDER THE PTOLEMAIC DYNASTY. J. P. MAHAFFY.
VOL. V. EGYPT UNDER ROMAN RULE. J. G. MILNE.
VOL. VI. EGYPT IN THE MIDDLE AGES. STANLEY LANE-POOLE.
RELIGION AND CONSCIENCE IN ANCIENT EGYPT. Illustrated. *Cr. 8vo*. 2s. 6d.
SYRIA AND EGYPT, FROM THE TELL EL AMARNA LETTERS. *Cr. 8vo*. 2s. 6d.
EGYPTIAN TALES. Translated from the Papyri. First Series, ivth to xiith Dynasty. Illustrated. *Second Edition*. *Cr. 8vo*. 3s. 6d.
EGYPTIAN TALES. Translated from the Papyri. Second Series, xviiith to xixth Dynasty. Illustrated. *Cr. 8vo*. 3s. 6d.
EGYPTIAN DECORATIVE ART. Illustrated. *Cr. 8vo*. 3s. 6d.

Phelps (Ruth S.). SKIES ITALIAN: A LITTLE BREVIARY FOR TRAVELLERS IN ITALY. *Fcap. 8vo*. *Leather*. 5s. net.

Pollard (Alfred W.). SHAKESPEARE FOLIOS AND QUARTOS. A Study in the Bibliography of Shakespeare's Plays, 1594-1685. Illustrated. *Folio*. 21s. net.

Porter (G. R.). THE PROGRESS OF THE NATION. A New Edition. Edited by F. W. HIRST. *Demy 8vo*. 21s. net.

Power (J. O'Connor). THE MAKING OF AN ORATOR. *Cr. 8vo*. 6s.

Price (Eleanor C.). CARDINAL DE RICHELIEU. Illustrated. *Second Edition*. *Demy 8vo*. 10s. 6d. net.

Price (L. L.), A SHORT HISTORY OF POLITICAL ECONOMY IN ENGLAND FROM ADAM SMITH TO ARNOLD TOYNBEE. *Seventh Edition*. *Cr. 8vo*. 2s. 6d.

Pycraft (W. P.). A HISTORY OF BIRDS. Illustrated. *Demy 8vo*. 10s. 6d. net.

Rawlings (Gertrude B.). COINS AND HOW TO KNOW THEM. Illustrated. *Third Edition*. *Cr. 8vo*. 6s.

Regan (C. Tate). THE FRESHWATER FISHES OF THE BRITISH ISLES. Illustrated. *Cr. 8vo*. 6s.

Reid (Archdall). THE LAWS OF HEREDITY. *Second Edition*. *Demy 8vo*. 21s. net.

Robertson (C. Grant). SELECT STAT-
UTES, CASES, AND DOCUMENTS,
1660-1894. *Demy 8vo.* 10s. 6d. *net.*
ENGLAND UNDER THE HANOVER-
IANS. Illustrated. *Second Edition.* Demy
8vo. 10s. 6d. *net.*

Roe (Fred). OLD OAK FURNITURE.
Illustrated. *Second Edition.* Demy 8vo.
10s. 6d. *net.*

*Ryan (P. F. W.). STUART LIFE AND
MANNERS; A SOCIAL HISTORY. Illustrated. *Demy 8vo.* 10s. 6d. *net.*

St. Francis of Assisi. THE LITTLE
FLOWERS OF THE GLORIOUS
MESSER, AND OF HIS FRIARS.
Done into English, with Notes by WILLIAM
HEYWOOD. Illustrated. *Demy 8vo.* 5s. *net.*

'Saki' (H. H. Munro). REGINALD.
Third Edition. Fcap. 8vo. 2s. 6d. *net.*
REGINALD IN RUSSIA. *Fcap. 8vo.*
2s. 6d. *net.*

Sandeman (G. A. C.). METTERNICH.
Illustrated. *Demy 8vo.* 10s. 6d. *net.*

Schidrowitz (Philip). RUBBER. Illustrated. *Demy 8vo.* 10s. 6d. *net.*

Selous (Edmund). TOMMY SMITH'S
ANIMALS. Illustrated. *Eleventh Edi-
tion. Fcap. 8vo.* 2s 6d.
TOMMY SMITH'S OTHER ANIMALS.
Illustrated. *Fifth Edition.* Fcap. 8vo.
2s. 6d.
JACK'S INSECTS. Illustrated. *Cr. 8vo.* 6s.

Shakespeare (William).
THE FOUR FOLIOS, 1623; 1632; 1664;
1685. Each £4 4s. *net*, or a complete set,
£12 12s. *net.*
THE POEMS OF WILLIAM SHAKE-
SPEARE. With an Introduction and Notes
by GEORGE WYNDHAM. Demy 8vo. Buck-
ram. 10s. 6d.

Shelley (Percy Bysshe). THE POEMS
OF PERCY BYSSHE SHELLEY. With
an Introduction by A. CLUTTON-BROCK and
notes by C. D. Locock. *Two Volumes.*
Demy 8vo. 21s. *net.*

Sladen (Douglas). SICILY: The New
Winter Resort. Illustrated. *Second Edition.*
Cr. 8vo. 5s. *net.*

Smith (Adam). THE WEALTH OF
NATIONS. Edited by EDWIN CANNAN.
Two Volumes. Demy 8vo. 21s. *net.*

Smith (G. Herbert). GEM-STONES
AND THEIR DISTINCTIVE CHARAC-
TERS. Illustrated. *Cr. 8vo.* 6s. *net.*

Snell (F. J.). A BOOK OF EXMOOR.
Illustrated. *Cr. 8vo.* 6s.
THE CUSTOMS OF OLD ENGLAND.
Illustrated. *Cr. 8vo.* 6s.

'Stancliffe.' GOLF DO'S AND DONT'S.
Fourth Edition. Fcap. 8vo. 1s. *net.*

Stevenson (R. L.). THE LETTERS OF
ROBERT LOUIS STEVENSON. Edited
by Sir SIDNEY COLVIN. *A New and Enlarged Edition in four volumes. Third
Edition. Fcap. 8vo. Each* 5s. *Leather,
each* 5s. *net.*

Stevenson (M. I.). FROM SARANAC
TO THE MARQUESAS AND BEYOND.
Being Letters written by Mrs. M. I. STEVEN-
SON during 1887-88. Illustrated. *Cr. 8vo.*
6s. *net.*
LETTERS FROM SAMOA, 1891-95. Edited
and arranged by M. C. BALFOUR. Illus-
trated. *Second Edition. Cr. 8vo.* 6s. *net.*

Storr (Vernon F.). DEVELOPMENT
AND DIVINE PURPOSE. *Cr. 8vo.* 5s.
net.

Streatfeild (R. A.). MODERN MUSIC
AND MUSICIANS. Illustrated. *Second
Edition. Demy 8vo.* 7s. 6d. *net.*

Swanton (E. W.). FUNGI AND HOW
TO KNOW THEM. Illustrated. *Cr. 8vo.*
6s. *net.*

Symes (J. E.). THE FRENCH REVO-
LUTION. *Second Edition. Cr. 8vo.* 2s. 6d.

Tabor (Margaret E.). THE SAINTS IN
ART. Illustrated. *Fcap. 8vo.* 3s. 6d. *net.*

Taylor (A. E.). ELEMENTS OF META-
PHYSICS. *Second Edition. Demy 8vo.*
10s. 6d. *net.*

Taylor (Mrs. Basil) (Harriet Osgood).
JAPANESE GARDENS. Illustrated.
Cr. 4to. 21s. *net.*

Thibaudeau (A. C.). BONAPARTE AND
THE CONSULATE. Translated and
Edited by G. K. FORTESCUE. Illustrated.
Demy 8vo. 10s. 6d. *net.*

Thomas (Edward). MAURICE MAE-
TERLINCK. Illustrated. *Second Edition.*
Cr. 8vo. 5s. *net.*

Thompson (Francis). S E L E C T E D
POEMS OF FRANCIS THOMPSON.
With a Biographical Note by WILFRID
MEYNELL. With a Portrait in Photogravure.
Seventh Edition. Fcap. 8vo. 5s. *net.*

Tileston (Mary W.). DAILY STRENGTH
FOR DAILY NEEDS. *Nineteenth Edition. Medium 16mo.* 2s. 6d. *net. Lamb-
skin* 3s. 6d. *net.* Also an edition in superior
binding, 6s.
THE STRONGHOLD OF HOPE.
Medium 16mo. 2s. 6d. *net.*

Toynbee (Paget). DANTE ALIGHIERI
HIS LIFE AND WORKS. With 16 Illustrations. *Fourth and Enlarged Edition. Cr.
8vo.* 5s. *net.*

Trevelyan (G. M.). ENGLAND UNDER THE STUARTS. With Maps and Plans. *Fifth Edition. Demy 8vo. 10s. 6d. net.*

Triggs (H. Inigo). TOWN PLANNING: PAST, PRESENT, AND POSSIBLE. Illustrated. *Second Edition. Wide Royal 8vo. 15s. net.*

*Turner (Sir Alfred E.). SIXTY YEARS OF A SOLDIER'S LIFE. *Demy 8vo. 12s. 6d. net.*

Underhill (Evelyn). MYSTICISM. A Study in the Nature and Development of Man's Spiritual Consciousness. *Fourth Edition. Demy 8vo. 15s. net.*

*Underwood (F. M.). UNITED ITALY. *Demy 8vo. 10s. 6d. net.*

Urwick (E. J.). A PHILOSOPHY OF SOCIAL PROGRESS. *Cr. 8vo. 6s.*

Vaughan (Herbert M.). THE NAPLES RIVIERA. Illustrated. *Second Edition. Cr. 8vo. 6s.*
FLORENCE AND HER TREASURES. Illustrated. *Fcap. 8vo. Round corners. 5s. net.*

Vernon (Hon. W. Warren). READINGS ON THE INFERNO OF DANTE. With an Introduction by the REV. DR. MOORE. *Two Volumes. Second Edition. Cr. 8vo. 15s. net.*
READINGS ON THE PURGATORIO OF DANTE. With an Introduction by the late DEAN CHURCH. *Two Volumes. Third Edition. Cr. 8vo. 15s. net.*
READINGS ON THE PARADISO OF DANTE. With an Introduction by the BISHOP OF RIPON. *Two Volumes. Second Edition. Cr. 8vo. 15s. net.*

Wade (G. W.), and Wade (J. H.). RAMBLES IN SOMERSET. Illustrated. *Cr. 8vo. 6s.*

Waddell (L. A.). LHASA AND ITS MYSTERIES. With a Record of the Expedition of 1903-1904. Illustrated. *Third and Cheaper Edition. Medium 8vo. 7s. 6d. net.*

Wagner (Richard). RICHARD WAGNER'S MUSIC DRAMAS: Interpretations, embodying Wagner's own explanations. By ALICE LEIGHTON CLEATHER and BASIL CRUMP. *Fcap. 8vo. 2s. 6d. each.*
THE RING OF THE NIBELUNG.
    Fifth Edition.
PARSIFAL, LOHENGRIN, AND THE HOLY GRAIL.
TRISTAN AND ISOLDE.
TANNHÄUSER AND THE MASTERSINGERS OF NUREMBERG.

Waterhouse (Elizabeth). WITH THE SIMPLE-HEARTED: Little Homilies to Women in Country Places. *Third Edition. Small Pott 8vo. 2s. net.*
THE HOUSE BY THE CHERRY TREE. A Second Series of Little Homilies to Women in Country Places. *Small Pott 8vo. 2s. net.*
COMPANIONS OF THE WAY. Being Selections for Morning and Evening Reading. Chosen and arranged by ELIZABETH WATERHOUSE. *Large Cr. 8vo. 5s. net.*
THOUGHTS OF A TERTIARY. *Small Pott 8vo. 1s. net.*

Waters (W. G.). ITALIAN SCULPTORS AND SMITHS. Illustrated. *Cr. 8vo. 7s. 6d. net.*

Watt (Francis). EDINBURGH AND THE LOTHIANS. Illustrated. *Second Edition. Cr. 8vo. 10s. 6d. net.*

*Wedmore (Sir Frederick). MEMORIES. *Demy 8vo. 7s. 6d. net.*

Weigall (Arthur E. P.). A GUIDE TO THE ANTIQUITIES OF UPPER EGYPT: From Abydos to the Sudan Frontier. Illustrated. *Cr. 8vo. 7s. 6d. net.*

Welch (Catharine). THE LITTLE DAUPHIN. Illustrated. *Cr. 8vo. 6s.*

Wells (J.). OXFORD AND OXFORD LIFE. *Third Edition. Cr. 8vo. 3s. 6d.*
A SHORT HISTORY OF ROME. *Eleventh Edition.* With 3 Maps. *Cr. 8vo. 3s. 6d.*

Wilde (Oscar). THE WORKS OF OSCAR WILDE. *In Twelve Volumes. Fcap. 8vo. 5s. net each volume.*
    I. LORD ARTHUR SAVILE'S CRIME AND THE PORTRAIT OF MR. W. H. II. THE DUCHESS OF PADUA. III. POEMS. IV. LADY WINDERMERE'S FAN. V. A WOMAN OF NO IMPORTANCE. VI. AN IDEAL HUSBAND. VII. THE IMPORTANCE OF BEING EARNEST. VIII. A HOUSE OF POMEGRANATES. IX. INTENTIONS. X. DE PROFUNDIS AND PRISON LETTERS. XI. ESSAYS. XII. SALOMÉ, A FLORENTINE TRAGEDY, and LA SAINTE COURTISANE.

Williams (H. Noel). THE WOMEN BONAPARTES. The Mother and three Sisters of Napoleon. Illustrated. *Two Volumes. Demy 8vo. 24s. net.*
A ROSE OF SAVOY: MARIE ADÉLAÏDE OF SAVOY, DUCHESSE DE BOURGOGNE, MOTHER OF LOUIS XV. Illustrated. *Second Edition. Demy 8vo. 15s. net.*
THE FASCINATING DUC DE RICHELIEU: LOUIS FRANÇOIS ARMAND DU PLESSIS (1696-1788). Illustrated. *Demy 8vo. 15s. net.*
A PRINCESS OF ADVENTURE: MARIE CAROLINE, DUCHESSE DE BERRY (1798-1870). Illustrated. *Demy 8vo. 15s. net.*

Wood (Sir Evelyn). FROM MIDSHIP-MAN TO FIELD-MARSHAL. Illustrated. *Fifth Edition. Demy 8vo. 7s. 6d. net. Also Fcap. 8vo. 1s. net.*

THE REVOLT IN HINDUSTAN (1857-59). Illustrated. *Second Edition. Cr. 8vo. 6s.*

Wood (W. Birkbeck), and Edmonds (Col. J. E.). A HISTORY OF THE CIVIL WAR IN THE UNITED STATES (1861-5). With an Introduction by Spenser Wilkinson. With 24 Maps and Plans. *Third Edition. Demy 8vo. 12s. 6d. net.*

Wordsworth (W.). THE POEMS. With an Introduction and Notes by Nowell C. Smith. *In Three Volumes. Demy 8vo. 15s. net.*

Yeats (W. B.). A BOOK OF IRISH VERSE. *Third Edition. Cr. 8vo. 3s. 6d.*

PART II.—A SELECTION OF SERIES.

Ancient Cities.

General Editor, B. C. A. WINDLE.

Cr. 8vo. 4s. 6d. net each volume.

With Illustrations by E. H. New, and other Artists.

Bristol. Alfred Harvey.
Canterbury. J. C. Cox.
Chester. B. C. A. Windle.
Dublin. S. A. O. Fitzpatrick.

Edinburgh. M. G. Williamson.
Lincoln. E. Mansel Sympson.
Shrewsbury T. Auden.
Wells and Glastonbury. T. S. Holmes.

The Antiquary's Books.

General Editor, J. CHARLES COX

Demy 8vo. 7s. 6d. net each volume.

With Numerous Illustrations.

Archæology and False Antiquities. R. Munro.

Bells of England, The. Canon J. J. Raven. *Second Edition.*

Brasses of England, The. Herbert W. Macklin. *Second Edition.*

Celtic Art in Pagan and Christian Times. J. Romilly Allen. *Second Edition.*

Castles and Walled Towns of England, The. A. Harvey.

Domesday Inquest, The. Adolphus Ballard.

English Church Furniture. J. C. Cox and A. Harvey. *Second Edition.*

English Costume. From Prehistoric Times to the End of the Eighteenth Century. George Clinch.

English Monastic Life. Abbot Gasquet. *Fourth Edition.*

English Seals. J. Harvey Bloom.

Folk-Lore as an Historical Science. Sir G. L. Gomme.

Gilds and Companies of London, The. George Unwin.

Manor and Manorial Records, The. Nathaniel J. Hone. *Second Edition.*

Mediæval Hospitals of England, The. Rotha Mary Clay.

Old English Instruments of Music. F. W. Galpin. *Second Edition.*

Old English Libraries. James Hutt.

Old Service Books of the English Church. Christopher Wordsworth, and Henry Littlehales. *Second Edition.*

Parish Life in Mediæval England. Abbot Gasquet. *Third Edition.*

Parish Registers of England, The. J. C. Cox.

Remains of the Prehistoric Age in England. B. C. A. Windle. *Second Edition.*

Roman Era in Britain, The. J. Ward.

Romano-British Buildings and Earthworks. J. Ward.

Royal Forests of England, The. J. C. Cox.

Shrines of British Saints. J. C. Wall.

The Arden Shakespeare.

Demy 8vo. 2s. 6d. net each volume.

An edition of Shakespeare in single Plays; each edited with a full Introduction, Textual Notes, and a Commentary at the foot of the page.

ALL'S WELL THAT ENDS WELL.
ANTONY AND CLEOPATRA.
CYMBELINE.
COMEDY OF ERRORS, THE.
HAMLET. *Third Edition.*
JULIUS CAESAR.
*KING HENRY IV. PT. I.
KING HENRY V.
KING HENRY VI. PT. I.
KING HENRY VI. PT. II.
KING HENRY VI. PT. III.
KING LEAR.
*KING RICHARD II.
KING RICHARD III.
LIFE AND DEATH OF KING JOHN, THE.
LOVE'S LABOUR'S LOST.
MACBETH.

MEASURE FOR MEASURE.
MERCHANT OF VENICE, THE.
MERRY WIVES OF WINDSOR, THE.
MIDSUMMER NIGHT'S DREAM, A.
OTHELLO.
PERICLES.
ROMEO AND JULIET.
TAMING OF THE SHREW, THE.
TEMPEST, THE.
TIMON OF ATHENS.
TITUS ANDRONICUS.
TROILUS AND CRESSIDA.
TWO GENTLEMEN OF VERONA, THE.
TWELFTH NIGHT.
VENUS AND ADONIS.
*WINTER'S TALE, THE.

Classics of Art.

Edited by DR. J. H. W. LAING.

With numerous Illustrations. Wide Royal 8vo.

THE ART OF THE GREEKS. H. B. Walters. 12s. 6d. net.
THE ART OF THE ROMANS. H. B. Walters. 15s. net.
CHARDIN. H. E. A. Furst. 12s. 6d. net.
DONATELLO. Maud Cruttwell. 15s. net.
FLORENTINE SCULPTORS OF THE RENAISSANCE. Wilhelm Bode. Translated by Jessie Haynes. 12s. 6d. net.
GEORGE ROMNEY. Arthur B. Chamberlain. 12s. 6d. net.
GHIRLANDAIO. Gerald S. Davies. *Second Edition.* 10s. 6d.

MICHELANGELO. Gerald S. Davies. 12s. 6d. net.
RUBENS. Edward Dillon. 25s. net.
RAPHAEL. A. P. Oppé. 12s. 6d. net.
REMBRANDT'S ETCHINGS. A. M. Hind.
*SIR THOMAS LAWRENCE. Sir Walter Armstrong. 21s. net.
TITIAN. Charles Ricketts. 15s. net.
TINTORETTO. Evelyn March Phillipps. 15s. net.
TURNER'S SKETCHES AND DRAWINGS. A. J. FINBERG. 12s. 6d. net. *Second Edition.*
VELAZQUEZ. A. de Beruete. 10s. 6d. net.

The "Complete" Series.

Fully Illustrated. Demy 8vo.

THE COMPLETE BILLIARD PLAYER. Charles Roberts. 10s. 6d. net.
THE COMPLETE COOK. Lilian Whitling. 7s. 6d. net.
THE COMPLETE CRICKETER. Albert E. Knight. 7s. 6d. net. *Second Edition.*
THE COMPLETE FOXHUNTER. Charles Richardson. 12s. 6d. net. *Second Edition.*
THE COMPLETE GOLFER. Harry Vardon. 10s. 6d. net. *Twelfth Edition.*
THE COMPLETE HOCKEY-PLAYER. Eustace E. White. 5s. net. *Second Edition.*
THE COMPLETE LAWN TENNIS PLAYER. A. Wallis Myers. 10s. 6d. net. *Third Edition, Revised.*
THE COMPLETE MOTORIST. Filson Young. 12s. 6d. net. *New Edition (Seventh).*

THE COMPLETE MOUNTAINEER. G. D. Abraham. 15s. net. *Second Edition.*
THE COMPLETE OARSMAN. R. C. Lehmann, 10s. 6d. net.
THE COMPLETE PHOTOGRAPHER. R. Child Bayley. 10s. 6d. net. *Fourth Edition.*
THE COMPLETE RUGBY FOOTBALLER, ON THE NEW ZEALAND SYSTEM. D. Gallaher and W. J Stead. 10s. 6d. net. *Second Edition.*
THE COMPLETE SHOT. G. T. Teasdale-Buckell. 12s. 6d. net. *Third Edition.*
THE COMPLETE SWIMMER. F. Sachs. 7s. 6d. net.
*THE COMPLETE YACHTSMAN. B. Heckstall-Smith and E. du Boulay. 15s. net.

The Connoisseur's Library.

With numerous Illustrations.   Wide Royal 8vo.   25s. net each volume.

ENGLISH FURNITURE. F. S. Robinson.
ENGLISH COLOURED BOOKS. Martin Hardie.
ETCHINGS. Sir F. Wedmore. *Second Edition.*
EUROPEAN ENAMELS. Henry H. Cunynghame.
GLASS. Edward Dillon.
GOLDSMITHS' AND SILVERSMITHS' WORK. Nelson Dawson. *Second Edition.*
ILLUMINATED MANUSCRIPTS. J. A. Herbert. *Second Edition.*

IVORIES. Alfred Maskell.
JEWELLERY. H. Clifford Smith. *Second Edition.*
MEZZOTINTS. Cyril Davenport.
MINIATURES. Dudley Heath.
PORCELAIN. Edward Dillon.
*FINE BOOKS. A. W. Pollard.
SEALS. Walter de Gray Birch.
WOOD SCULPTURE. Alfred Maskell. *Second Edition.*

Handbooks of English Church History.

Edited by J. H. BURN.   Crown 8vo.   2s. 6d. net each volume.

THE FOUNDATIONS OF THE ENGLISH CHURCH. J. H. Maude.
THE SAXON CHURCH AND THE NORMAN CONQUEST. C. T. Cruttwell.
THE MEDIÆVAL CHURCH AND THE PAPACY. A. C. Jennings.

THE REFORMATION PERIOD. Henry Gee.
THE STRUGGLE WITH PURITANISM. Bruce Blaxland.
THE CHURCH OF ENGLAND IN THE EIGHTEENTH CENTURY. Alfred Plummer.

Handbooks of Theology.

THE DOCTRINE OF THE INCARNATION. R. L. Ottley. *Fifth Edition, Revised.* Demy 8vo. 12s. 6d.
A HISTORY OF EARLY CHRISTIAN DOCTRINE. J. F. Bethune-Baker. *Demy 8vo.* 10s. 6d.
AN INTRODUCTION TO THE HISTORY OF RELIGION. F. B. Jevons. *Fifth Edition.* Demy 8vo. 10s. 6d.

AN INTRODUCTION TO THE HISTORY OF THE CREEDS. A. E. Burn. *Demy 8vo.* 10s. 6d.
THE PHILOSOPHY OF RELIGION IN ENGLAND AND AMERICA. Alfred Caldecott. *Demy 8vo.* 10s. 6d.
THE XXXIX ARTICLES OF THE CHURCH OF ENGLAND. Edited by E. C. S. Gibson. *Seventh Edition. Demy 8vo.* 12s. 6d.

The "Home Life" Series.

Illustrated.   Demy 8vo.   6s. to 10s. 6d. net.

HOME LIFE IN AMERICA. Katherine G. Bushey. *Second Edition.*
HOME LIFE IN FRANCE. Miss Betham-Edwards. *Fifth Edition.*
HOME LIFE IN GERMANY. Mrs. A. Sidgwick. *Second Edition.*
HOME LIFE IN HOLLAND. D. S. Meldrum. *Second Edition.*

HOME LIFE IN ITALY. Lina Duff Gordon. *Second Edition.*
HOME LIFE IN NORWAY. H. K. Daniels.
HOME LIFE IN RUSSIA. Dr. A. S. Rappoport.
HOME LIFE IN SPAIN. S. L. Bensusan. *Second Edition.*

The Illustrated Pocket Library of Plain and Coloured Books.

Fcap. 8vo. 3s. 6d. net each volume.

WITH COLOURED ILLUSTRATIONS.

OLD COLOURED BOOKS. George Paston. 2s. net.

THE LIFE AND DEATH OF JOHN MYTTON, ESQ. Nimrod. *Fifth Edition.*

THE LIFE OF A SPORTSMAN. Nimrod.

HANDLEY CROSS. R. S. Surtees. *Fourth Edition.*

MR. SPONGE'S SPORTING TOUR. R. S. Surtees. *Second Edition.*

JORROCKS'S JAUNTS AND JOLLITIES. R. S. Surtees. *Third Edition.*

ASK MAMMA. R. S. Surtees.

THE ANALYSIS OF THE HUNTING FIELD. R. S. Surtees.

THE TOUR OF DR. SYNTAX IN SEARCH OF THE PICTURESQUE. William Combe.

THE TOUR OF DR. SYNTAX IN SEARCH OF CONSOLATION. William Combe.

THE THIRD TOUR OF DR. SYNTAX IN SEARCH OF A WIFE. William Combe.

THE HISTORY OF JOHNNY QUAE GENUS. The Author of 'The Three Tours.'

THE ENGLISH DANCE OF DEATH, from the Designs of T. Rowlandson, with Metrical Illustrations by the Author of 'Doctor Syntax.' *Two Volumes.*

THE DANCE OF LIFE: A Poem. The Author of 'Dr. Syntax.'

LIFE IN LONDON. Pierce Egan.

REAL LIFE IN LONDON. An Amateur (Pierce Egan). *Two Volumes.*

THE LIFE OF AN ACTOR. Pierce Egan.

THE VICAR OF WAKEFIELD. Oliver Goldsmith.

THE MILITARY ADVENTURES OF JOHNNY NEWCOME. An Officer.

THE NATIONAL SPORTS OF GREAT BRITAIN. With Descriptions and 50 Coloured Plates by Henry Alken.

THE ADVENTURES OF A POST CAPTAIN. A Naval Officer.

GAMONIA. Lawrence Rawstorne.

AN ACADEMY FOR GROWN HORSEMEN. Geoffrey Gambado.

REAL LIFE IN IRELAND. A Real Paddy.

THE ADVENTURES OF JOHNNY NEWCOME IN THE NAVY. Alfred Burton.

THE OLD ENGLISH SQUIRE. John Careless.

THE ENGLISH SPY. Bernard Blackmantle. *Two Volumes. 7s. net.*

WITH PLAIN ILLUSTRATIONS.

THE GRAVE: A Poem. Robert Blair.

ILLUSTRATIONS OF THE BOOK OF JOB. Invented and engraved by William Blake.

WINDSOR CASTLE. W. Harrison Ainsworth.

THE TOWER OF LONDON. W. Harrison Ainsworth

FRANK FAIRLEGH. F. E. Smedley.

THE COMPLEAT ANGLER. Izaak Walton and Charles Cotton.

THE PICKWICK PAPERS. Charles Dickens.

Leaders of Religion.

Edited by H. C. BEECHING. *With Portraits.*

Crown 8vo. 2s. net each volume.

CARDINAL NEWMAN. R. H. Hutton.

JOHN WESLEY. J. H. Overton.

BISHOP WILBERFORCE. G. W. Daniell.

CARDINAL MANNING. A. W. Hutton.

CHARLES SIMEON. H. C. G. Moule.

JOHN KNOX. F. MacCunn. *Second Edition.*

JOHN HOWE. R. F. Horton.

THOMAS KEN. F. A. Clarke.

GEORGE FOX, THE QUAKER. T. Hodgkin. *Third Edition.*

JOHN KEBLE. Walter Lock

THOMAS CHALMERS. Mrs. Oliphant. *Second Edition.*

LANCELOT ANDREWES. R. L. Ottley. *Second Edition.*

AUGUSTINE OF CANTERBURY. E. L. Cutts.

WILLIAM LAUD. W. H. Hutton. *Third Ed.*

JOHN DONNE. Augustus Jessop.

THOMAS CRANMER. A. J. Mason.

LATIMER. R. M. Carlyle and A. J. Carlyle.

BISHOP BUTLER. W. A. Spooner.

The Library of Devotion.

With Introductions and (where necessary) Notes.

Small Pott 8vo, cloth, 2s. ; leather, 2s. 6d. net each volume.

THE CONFESSIONS OF ST. AUGUSTINE. *Seventh Edition.*

THE IMITATION OF CHRIST. *Sixth Edition.*

THE CHRISTIAN YEAR. *Fifth Edition.*

LYRA INNOCENTIUM. *Third Edition.*

THE TEMPLE. *Second Edition.*

A BOOK OF DEVOTIONS. *Second Edition.*

A SERIOUS CALL TO A DEVOUT AND HOLY LIFE. *Fourth Edition.*

A GUIDE TO ETERNITY.

THE INNER WAY. *Second Edition.*

ON THE LOVE OF GOD.

THE PSALMS OF DAVID.

LYRA APOSTOLICA.

THE SONG OF SONGS.

THE THOUGHTS OF PASCAL. *Second Edition.*

A MANUAL OF CONSOLATION FROM THE SAINTS AND FATHERS.

DEVOTIONS FROM THE APOCRYPHA.

THE SPIRITUAL COMBAT.

THE DEVOTIONS OF ST. ANSELM.

BISHOP WILSON'S SACRA PRIVATA.

GRACE ABOUNDING TO THE CHIEF OF SINNERS.

LYRA SACRA: A Book of Sacred Verse. *Second Edition.*

A DAY BOOK FROM THE SAINTS AND FATHERS.

A LITTLE BOOK OF HEAVENLY WISDOM. A Selection from the English Mystics.

LIGHT, LIFE, and LOVE. A Selection from the German Mystics.

AN INTRODUCTION TO THE DEVOUT LIFE.

THE LITTLE FLOWERS OF THE GLORIOUS MESSER ST. FRANCIS AND OF HIS FRIARS.

DEATH AND IMMORTALITY.

THE SPIRITUAL GUIDE. *Second Edition.*

DEVOTIONS FOR EVERY DAY IN THE WEEK AND THE GREAT FESTIVALS.

PRECES PRIVATAE.

HORAE MYSTICAE: A Day Book from the Writings of Mystics of Many Nations.

Little Books on Art.

With many Illustrations. Demy 16mo. 2s. 6d. net each volume.

Each volume consists of about 200 pages, and contains from 30 to 40 Illustrations, including a Frontispiece in Photogravure.

ALBRECHT DÜRER. L. J. Allen.

ARTS OF JAPAN, THE. E. Dillon. *Third Edition.*

BOOKPLATES. E. Almack.

BOTTICELLI. Mary L. Bonnor.

BURNE-JONES. F. de Lisle.

CELLINI. R. H. H. Cust.

CHRISTIAN SYMBOLISM. Mrs. H. Jenner.

CHRIST IN ART. Mrs. H. Jenner.

CLAUDE. E. Dillon.

CONSTABLE. H. W. Tompkins. *Second Edition.*

COROT. A. Pollard and E. Birnstingl.

ENAMELS. Mrs. N. Dawson. *Second Edition.*

FREDERIC LEIGHTON. A. Corkran.

GEORGE ROMNEY. G. Paston.

GREEK ART. H. B. Walters. *Fourth Edition.*

GREUZE AND BOUCHER. E. F. Pollard.

HOLBEIN. Mrs. G. Fortescue.

ILLUMINATED MANUSCRIPTS. J. W. Bradley.

JEWELLERY. C. Davenport.

JOHN HOPPNER. H. P. K. Skipton.

SIR JOSHUA REYNOLDS. J. Sime. *Second Edition.*

MILLET. N. Peacock.

MINIATURES. C. Davenport.

OUR LADY IN ART. Mrs. H. Jenner.

RAPHAEL. A. R. Dryhurst.

REMBRANDT. Mrs. E. A. Sharp.

*RODIN. Muriel Ciolkowska.

TURNER. F. Tyrrell-Gill.

VANDYCK. M. G. Smallwood.

VELAZQUEZ. W. Wilberforce and A. R. Gilbert.

WATTS. R. E. D. Sketchley. *Second Edition.*

The Little Galleries.

Demy 16mo. 2s. 6d. net each volume.

Each volume contains 20 plates in Photogravure, together with a short outline of the life and work of the master to whom the book is devoted.

A LITTLE GALLERY OF REYNOLDS.
A LITTLE GALLERY OF ROMNEY.
A LITTLE GALLERY OF HOPPNER.

A LITTLE GALLERY OF MILLAIS.
A LITTLE GALLERY OF ENGLISH POETS.

The Little Guides.

With many Illustrations by E. H. NEW and other artists, and from photographs.

Small Pott 8vo, cloth, 2s. 6d. net; leather, 3s. 6d. net, each volume.

The main features of these Guides are (1) a handy and charming form ; (2) illustrations from photographs and by well-known artists ; (3) good plans and maps ; (4) an adequate but compact presentation of everything that is interesting in the natural features, history, archæology, and architecture of the town or district treated.

CAMBRIDGE AND ITS COLLEGES. A. H. Thompson. *Third Edition, Revised.*

CHANNEL ISLANDS, THE. E. E. Bicknell.

ENGLISH LAKES, THE. F. G. Brabant.

ISLE OF WIGHT, THE. G. Clinch.

LONDON. G. Clinch.

MALVERN COUNTRY, THE. B. C. A. Windle.

NORTH WALES. A. T. Story.

OXFORD AND ITS COLLEGES. J. Wells. *Ninth Edition.*

SHAKESPEARE'S COUNTRY. B. C. A. Windle. *Fourth Edition.*

ST. PAUL'S CATHEDRAL. G. Clinch.

WESTMINSTER ABBEY. G. E. Troutbeck. *Second Edition.*

BERKSHIRE. F. G. Brabant.

BUCKINGHAMSHIRE. E. S. Roscoe.

CHESHIRE. W. M. Gallichan.

CORNWALL. A. L. Salmon.

DERBYSHIRE. J. C. Cox.

DEVON. S. Baring-Gould. *Second Edition.*

DORSET. F. R. Heath. *Second Edition.*

ESSEX. J. C. Cox.

HAMPSHIRE. J. C. Cox.

HERTFORDSHIRE. H. W. Tompkins.

KENT. G. Clinch.

KERRY. C. P. Crane.

LEICESTERSHIRE AND RUTLAND. A. Harvey and V. B. Crowther-Beynon.

MIDDLESEX. J. B. Firth.

MONMOUTHSHIRE. G. W. Wade and J. H. Wade.

NORFOLK. W. A. Dutt. *Second Edition, Revised.*

NORTHAMPTONSHIRE. W. Dry. *Second Ed.*

NORTHUMBERLAND. J. E. Morris.

NOTTINGHAMSHIRE. L. Guilford.

OXFORDSHIRE. F. G. Brabant.

SHROPSHIRE. J. E. Auden.

SOMERSET. G. W. and J. H. Wade. *Second Edition.*

STAFFORDSHIRE. C. Masefield.

SUFFOLK. W. A. Dutt.

SURREY. J. C. Cox.

SUSSEX. F. G. Brabant. *Third Edition.*

WILTSHIRE. F. R. Heath.

YORKSHIRE, THE EAST RIDING. J. E. Morris.

YORKSHIRE, THE NORTH RIDING. J. E. Morris.

YORKSHIRE, THE WEST RIDING. J. E. Morris. *Cloth, 3s. 6d. net ; leather, 4s. 6d. net.*

BRITTANY. S. Baring-Gould.

NORMANDY. C. Scudamore.

ROME. C. G. Ellaby.

SICILY. F. H. Jackson.

The Little Library.

With Introductions, Notes, and Photogravure Frontispieces.

Small Pott 8vo. Each Volume, cloth, 1s. 6d. *net.*

Anon. A LITTLE BOOK OF ENGLISH LYRICS. *Second Edition.*

Austen (Jane). PRIDE AND PREJUDICE. *Two Volumes.*
NORTHANGER ABBEY.

Bacon (Francis). THE ESSAYS OF LORD BACON.

Barham (R. H.). THE INGOLDSBY LEGENDS. *Two Volumes.*

Barnett (Annie). A LITTLE BOOK OF ENGLISH PROSE.

Beckford (William). THE HISTORY OF THE CALIPH VATHEK.

Blake (William). SELECTIONS FROM THE WORKS OF WILLIAM BLAKE.

Borrow (George). LAVENGRO. *Two Volumes.*
THE ROMANY RYE.

Browning (Robert). SELECTIONS FROM THE EARLY POEMS OF ROBERT BROWNING.

Canning (George). SELECTIONS FROM THE ANTI-JACOBIN : with some later Poems by George Canning.

Cowley (Abraham). THE ESSAYS OF ABRAHAM COWLEY.

Crabbe (George). SELECTIONS FROM THE POEMS OF GEORGE CRABBE.

Craik (Mrs.). JOHN HALIFAX, GENTLEMAN. *Two Volumes.*

Crashaw (Richard). THE ENGLISH POEMS OF RICHARD CRASHAW.

Dante Alighieri. THE INFERNO OF DANTE. Translated by H. F. Cary.
THE PURGATORIO OF DANTE. Translated by H. F. Cary.
THE PARADISO OF DANTE. Translated by H. F. Cary.

Darley (George). SELECTIONS FROM THE POEMS OF GEORGE DARLEY.

Deane (A. C.). A LITTLE BOOK OF LIGHT VERSE.

Dickens (Charles). CHRISTMAS BOOKS. *Two Volumes.*

Ferrier (Susan). MARRIAGE. *Two Volumes.*
THE INHERITANCE. *Two Volumes.*

Gaskell (Mrs.). CRANFORD. *Second Ed.*

Hawthorne (Nathaniel). THE SCARLET LETTER.

Henderson (T. F.). A LITTLE BOOK OF SCOTTISH VERSE.

Kinglake (A. W.). EOTHEN. *Second Edition.*

Lamb (Charles). ELIA, AND THE LAST ESSAYS OF ELIA.

Locker (F.). LONDON LYRICS.

Marvell (Andrew). THE POEMS OF ANDREW MARVELL.

Milton (John). THE MINOR POEMS OF JOHN MILTON.

Moir (D. M.). MANSIE WAUCH.

Nichols (Bowyer). A LITTLE BOOK OF ENGLISH SONNETS.

Smith (Horace and James). REJECTED ADDRESSES.

Sterne (Laurence). A SENTIMENTAL JOURNEY.

Tennyson (Alfred, Lord). THE EARLY POEMS OF ALFRED, LORD TENNYSON.
IN MEMORIAM.
THE PRINCESS.
MAUD.

Thackeray (W. M.). VANITY FAIR. *Three Volumes.*
PENDENNIS. *Three Volumes.*
HENRY ESMOND.
CHRISTMAS BOOKS.

Vaughan (Henry). THE POEMS OF HENRY VAUGHAN.

Waterhouse (Elizabeth). A LITTLE BOOK OF LIFE AND DEATH. *Thirteenth Edition.*

Wordsworth (W.). SELECTIONS FROM THE POEMS OF WILLIAM WORDSWORTH.

Wordsworth (W.) and Coleridge (S. T.). LYRICAL BALLADS. *Second Edition.*

The Little Quarto Shakespeare.

Edited by W. J. CRAIG. With Introductions and Notes.
Pott 16mo. In 40 Volumes. Leather, price 1s. net each volume.
Mahogany Revolving Book Case. 10s. net.

Miniature Library.

Demy 32mo. Leather, 1s. net each volume.

EUPHRANOR: A Dialogue on Youth. Edward FitzGerald.

THE LIFE OF EDWARD, LORD HERBERT OF CHERBURY. Written by himself.

POLONIUS: or Wise Saws and Modern Instances. Edward FitzGerald.

THE RUBÁIYÁT OF OMAR KHAYYÁM. Edward FitzGerald. *Fourth Edition.*

The New Library of Medicine.

Edited by C. W. SALEEBY. *Demy 8vo.*

CARE OF THE BODY, THE. F. Cavanagh. *Second Edition.* 7s. 6d. net.

CHILDREN OF THE NATION, THE. The Right Hon. Sir John Gorst. *Second Edition.* 7s. 6d. net.

CONTROL OF A SCOURGE; or, How Cancer is Curable, The. Chas. P. Childe. 7s. 6d. net.

DISEASES OF OCCUPATION. Sir Thomas Oliver. 10s. 6d. net. *Second Edition.*

DRINK PROBLEM, in its Medico-Sociological Aspects, The. Edited by T. N. Kelynack. 7s. 6d. net.

DRUGS AND THE DRUG HABIT. H. Sainsbury.

FUNCTIONAL NERVE DISEASES. A. T. Schofield. 7s. 6d. net.

HYGIENE OF MIND, THE. T. S. Clouston. *Fifth Edition.* 7s. 6d. net.

INFANT MORTALITY. Sir George Newman. 7s. 6d. net.

PREVENTION OF TUBERCULOSIS (CONSUMPTION), THE. Arthur Newsholme. 10s. 6d. net. *Second Edition.*

AIR AND HEALTH. Ronald C. Macfie. 7s. 6d. net. *Second Edition.*

The New Library of Music.

Edited by ERNEST NEWMAN. *Illustrated. Demy 8vo. 7s. 6d. net.*

BRAHMS. J. A. Fuller-Maitland. *Second Edition.*

HANDEL. R. A. Streatfeild. *Second Edition.*

HUGO WOLF. Ernest Newman.

Oxford Biographies.

Illustrated. Fcap. 8vo. Each volume, cloth, 2s. 6d. net; leather, 3s. 6d. net.

DANTE ALIGHIERI. Paget Toynbee. *Third Edition.*

GIROLAMO SAVONAROLA. E. L. S. Horsburgh. *Fourth Edition.*

JOHN HOWARD. E. C. S. Gibson.

ALFRED TENNYSON. A. C. Benson. *Second Edition.*

SIR WALTER RALEIGH. I. A. Taylor.

ERASMUS. E. F. H. Capey.

THE YOUNG PRETENDER. C. S. Terry.

ROBERT BURNS. T. F. Henderson.

CHATHAM. A. S. McDowall.

FRANCIS OF ASSISI. Anna M. Stoddart.

CANNING. W. Alison Phillips.

BEACONSFIELD. Walter Sichel.

JOHANN WOLFGANG GOETHE. H. G. Atkins.

FRANÇOIS DE FÉNELON. Viscount St. Cyres.

Three Plays.

Fcap. 8vo. 2s. net.

THE HONEYMOON. A Comedy in Three Acts. Arnold Bennett. *Second Edition.*

KISMET. Edward Knoblauch.

MILESTONES. Arnold Bennett and Edward Knoblauch. *Second Edition.*

The States of Italy.

Edited by E. ARMSTRONG and R. LANGTON DOUGLAS.

Illustrated. Demy 8vo.

A HISTORY OF MILAN UNDER THE SFORZA. Cecilia M. Ady. 10s. 6d. net.

A HISTORY OF PERUGIA. W. Heywood. 12s. 6d. net.

A HISTORY OF VERONA. A. M. Allen. 12s. 6d. net.

The Westminster Commentaries.

General Editor, WALTER LOCK.

Demy 8vo.

THE ACTS OF THE APOSTLES. Edited by R. B. Rackham. *Sixth Edition.* 10s. 6d.

THE FIRST EPISTLE OF PAUL THE APOSTLE TO THE CORINTHIANS. Edited by H. L. Goudge. *Third Edition.* 6s.

THE BOOK OF EXODUS Edited by A. H. M'Neile. With a Map and 3 Plans. 10s. 6d.

THE BOOK OF EZEKIEL. Edited by H. A. Redpath. 10s. 6d.

THE BOOK OF GENESIS. Edited with Introduction and Notes by S. R. Driver. *Eighth Edition.* 10s. 6d.

THE BOOK OF THE PROPHET ISAIAH. Edited by G. W. Wade. 10s. 6d.

ADDITIONS AND CORRECTIONS IN THE SEVENTH AND EIGHTH EDITIONS OF THE BOOK OF GENESIS. S. R. Driver. 1s.

THE BOOK OF JOB. Edited by E. C. S. Gibson. *Second Edition.* 6s.

THE EPISTLE OF ST. JAMES. Edited with Introduction and Notes by R. J. Knowling. *Second Edition.* 6s.

The "Young" Series.

Illustrated. Crown 8vo.

THE YOUNG BOTANIST. W. P. Westell and C. S. Cooper. 3s. 6d. net.

THE YOUNG CARPENTER. Cyril Hall. 5s.

THE YOUNG ELECTRICIAN. Hammond Hall. 5s.

THE YOUNG ENGINEER. Hammond Hall. *Third Edition.* 5s.

THE YOUNG NATURALIST. W. P. Westell. *Second Edition.* 6s.

THE YOUNG ORNITHOLOGIST. W. P. Westell. 5s.

Methuen's Shilling Library.

Fcap. 8vo. 1s. net.

CONDITION OF ENGLAND, THE. G. F. G. Masterman.

DE PROFUNDIS. Oscar Wilde.

FROM MIDSHIPMAN TO FIELD-MARSHAL. Sir Evelyn Wood, F.M., V.C.

*IDEAL HUSBAND, AN. Oscar Wilde.

*JIMMY GLOVER, HIS BOOK. James M. Glover.

*JOHN BOYES, KING OF THE WA-KIKUYU. John Boyes.

LADY WINDERMERE'S FAN. Oscar Wilde.

LETTERS FROM A SELF-MADE MERCHANT TO HIS SON. George Horace Lorimer.

LIFE OF JOHN RUSKIN, THE. W. G. Collingwood.

LIFE OF ROBERT LOUIS STEVENSON, THE. Graham Balfour.

*LIFE OF TENNYSON, THE. A. C. Benson.

*LITTLE OF EVERYTHING, A. E. V. Lucas.

LORD ARTHUR SAVILE'S CRIME. Oscar Wilde.

LORE OF THE HONEY-BEE, THE. Tickner Edwardes.

MAN AND THE UNIVERSE. Sir Oliver Lodge.

MARY MAGDALENE. Maurice Maeterlinck.

SELECTED POEMS. Oscar Wilde.

SEVASTOPOL, AND OTHER STORIES. Leo Tolstoy.

THE BLUE BIRD. Maurice Maeterlinck.

UNDER FIVE REIGNS. Lady Dorothy Nevill.

*VAILIMA LETTERS. Robert Louis Stevenson.

*VICAR OF MORWENSTOW, THE. S. Baring-Gould.

Books for Travellers.

Crown 8vo. 6s. each.

Each volume contains a number of Illustrations in Colour.

*A WANDERER IN FLORENCE. E. V. Lucas.

A WANDERER IN PARIS. E. V. Lucas.

A WANDERER IN HOLLAND. E. V. Lucas.

A WANDERER IN LONDON. E. V. Lucas.

THE NORFOLK BROADS. W. A. Dutt.

THE NEW FOREST. Horace G. Hutchinson.

NAPLES. Arthur H. Norway.

THE CITIES OF UMBRIA. Edward Hutton.

THE CITIES OF SPAIN. Edward Hutton.

*THE CITIES OF LOMBARDY. Edward Hutton.

FLORENCE AND NORTHERN TUSCANY, WITH GENOA. Edward Hutton.

SIENA AND SOUTHERN TUSCANY. Edward Hutton.

ROME. Edward Hutton.

VENICE AND VENETIA. Edward Hutton.

THE BRETONS AT HOME. F. M. Gostling.

THE LAND OF PARDONS (Brittany). Anatole Le Braz.

A BOOK OF THE RHINE. S. Baring-Gould.

THE NAPLES RIVIERA. H. M. Vaughan.

DAYS IN CORNWALL. C. Lewis Hind.

THROUGH EAST ANGLIA IN A MOTOR CAR. J. E. Vincent.

THE SKIRTS OF THE GREAT CITY. Mrs. A. G. Bell.

ROUND ABOUT WILTSHIRE. A. G. Bradley.

SCOTLAND OF TO-DAY. T. F. Henderson and Francis Watt.

NORWAY AND ITS FJORDS. M. A. Wyllie.

Some Books on Art.

ART AND LIFE. T. Sturge Moore. Illustrated. *Cr. 8vo. 5s. net.*

AIMS AND IDEALS IN ART. George Clausen. Illustrated. *Second Edition. Large Post 8vo. 5s. net.*

SIX LECTURES ON PAINTING. George Clausen. Illustrated. *Third Edition. Large Post 8vo. 3s. 6d. net.*

FRANCESCO GUARDI, 1712-1793. G. A. Simonson. Illustrated. *Imperial 4to. £2 2s. net.*

ILLUSTRATIONS OF THE BOOK OF JOB. William Blake. *Quarto. £1 1s. net.*

JOHN LUCAS, PORTRAIT PAINTER, 1828-1874. Arthur Lucas. Illustrated. *Imperial 4to. £3 3s. net.*

ONE HUNDRED MASTERPIECES OF PAINTING. With an Introduction by R. C. Witt. Illustrated. *Second Edition. Demy 8vo. 10s. 6d. net.*

A GUIDE TO THE BRITISH PICTURES IN THE NATIONAL GALLERY. Edward Kingston. Illustrated. *Fcap. 8vo. 3s. 6d. net.*

SOME BOOKS ON ART—*continued.*

ONE HUNDRED MASTERPIECES OF SCULPTURE. With an Introduction by G. F. Hill. Illustrated. *Demy 8vo.* 10s. 6d. net.

A ROMNEY FOLIO. With an Essay by A. B. Chamberlain. *Imperial Folio.* £15 15s. net.

THE SAINTS IN ART. Margaret E. Tabor. Illustrated. *Fcap. 8vo.* 3s. 6d. net.

SCHOOLS OF PAINTING. Mary Innes. Illustrated. *Cr. 8vo.* 5s. net.

THE POST IMPRESSIONISTS. C. Lewis Hind. Illustrated. *Royal 8vo.* 7s. 6d. net.

CELTIC ART IN PAGAN AND CHRISTIAN TIMES. J. R. Allen. Illustrated. *Second Edition. Demy 8vo.* 7s. 6d. net.

"CLASSICS OF ART." See page 13.

"THE CONNOISSEUR'S LIBRARY." See page 14.

"LITTLE BOOKS ON ART." See page 16.

"THE LITTLE GALLERIES." See page 17.

Some Books on Italy.

A HISTORY OF MILAN UNDER THE SFORZA. Cecilia M. Ady. Illustrated. *Demy 8vo.* 10s. 6d. net.

A HISTORY OF VERONA. A. M. Allen. Illustrated. *Demy 8vo.* 12s. 6d. net.

A HISTORY OF PERUGIA. William Heywood. Illustrated. *Demy 8vo.* 12s. 6d. net.

THE LAKES OF NORTHERN ITALY. Richard Bagot. Illustrated. *Fcap. 8vo.* 5s. net.

WOMAN IN ITALY. W. Boulting. Illustrated. *Demy 8vo.* 10s. 6d. net.

OLD ETRURIA AND MODERN TUSCANY. Mary L. Cameron. Illustrated. *Second Edition. Cr. 8vo.* 6s. net.

FLORENCE AND THE CITIES OF NORTHERN TUSCANY, WITH GENOA. Edward Hutton. Illustrated. *Second Edition. Cr. 8vo.* 6s.

SIENA AND SOUTHERN TUSCANY. Edward Hutton. Illustrated. *Second Edition. Cr. 8vo.* 6s.

IN UNKNOWN TUSCANY. Edward Hutton. Illustrated. *Second Edition. Demy 8vo.* 7s. 6d. net.

VENICE AND VENETIA. Edward Hutton. Illustrated. *Cr. 8vo.* 6s.

VENICE ON FOOT. H. A. Douglas. Illustrated. *Fcap. 8vo.* 5s. net.

VENICE AND HER TREASURES. H. A. Douglas. Illustrated. *Fcap. 8vo.* 5s. net.

°THE DOGES OF VENICE. Mrs. Aubrey Richardson. Illustrated. *Demy 8vo.* 10s. 6d. net.

FLORENCE: Her History and Art to the Fall of the Republic. F. A. Hyett. *Demy 8vo.* 7s. 6d. net.

FLORENCE AND HER TREASURES. H. M. Vaughan. Illustrated. *Fcap. 8vo.* 5s. net.

COUNTRY WALKS ABOUT FLORENCE. Edward Hutton. Illustrated. *Fcap. 8vo.* 5s. net.

NAPLES : Past and Present. A. H. Norway. Illustrated. *Third Edition. Cr. 8vo.* 6s.

THE NAPLES RIVIERA. H. M. Vaughan. Illustrated. *Second Edition. Cr. 8vo.* 6s.

SICILY : The New Winter Resort. Douglas Sladen. Illustrated. *Second Edition. Cr. 8vo.* 5s. net.

SICILY. F. H. Jackson. Illustrated. *Small Pott 8vo.* Cloth, 2s. 6d. net; leather, 3s. 6d. net.

ROME. Edward Hutton. Illustrated. *Second Edition. Cr. 8vo.* 6s.

A ROMAN PILGRIMAGE. R. E. Roberts. Illustrated. *Demy 8vo.* 10s. 6d. net.

ROME. C. G. Ellaby. Illustrated. *Small Pott 8vo.* Cloth, 2s. 6d. net; leather, 3s. 6d. net.

THE CITIES OF UMBRIA. Edward Hutton. Illustrated. *Fourth Edition. Cr. 8vo.* 6s.

°THE CITIES OF LOMBARDY. Edward Hutton. Illustrated. *Cr. 8vo.* 6s.

THE LIVES OF S. FRANCIS OF ASSISI. Brother Thomas of Celano. *Cr. 8vo.* 5s. net.

LORENZO THE MAGNIFICENT. E. L. S. Horsburgh. Illustrated. *Second Edition. Demy 8vo.* 15s. net.

GIROLAMO SAVONAROLA. E. L. S. Horsburgh. Illustrated. *Cr. 8vo.* 5s. net.

ST. CATHERINE OF SIENA AND HER TIMES. By the Author of "Mdlle Mori." Illustrated. *Second Edition. Demy 8vo.* 7s. 6d. net.

DANTE AND HIS ITALY. Lonsdale Ragg. Illustrated. *Demy 8vo.* 12s. 6d. net.

DANTE ALIGHIERI : His Life and Works. Paget Toynbee. Illustrated. *Cr. 8vo.* 5s. net.

THE MEDICI POPES. H. M. Vaughan. Illustrated. *Demy 8vo.* 15s. net.

SHELLEY AND HIS FRIENDS IN ITALY. Helen R. Angeli. Illustrated. *Demy 8vo.* 10s. 6d. net.

HOME LIFE IN ITALY. Lina Duff Gordon. Illustrated. *Second Edition. Demy 8vo.* 10s. 6d. net.

SKIES ITALIAN : A Little Breviary for Travellers in Italy. Ruth S. Phelps. *Fcap. 8vo.* 5s. net.

°A WANDERER IN FLORENCE. E. V. Lucas. Illustrated. *Cr. 8vo.* 6s.

°UNITED ITALY. F. M. Underwood. *Demy 8vo.* 10s. 6d. net.

PART III.—A SELECTION OF WORKS OF FICTION

Albanesi (E. Maria). SUSANNAH AND
ONE OTHER. *Fourth Edition.* Cr.
8vo. 6*s.*
LOVE AND LOUISA. *Second Edition.*
Cr. 8vo. 6*s.*
THE BROWN EYES OF MARY. *Third
Edition. Cr. 8vo.* 6*s.*
I KNOW A MAIDEN. *Third Edition.*
Cr. 8vo. 6*s.*
THE INVINCIBLE AMELIA; or, The
Polite Adventuress. *Third Edition.*
Cr. 8vo. 3*s.* 6*d.*
THE GLAD HEART. *Fifth Edition.*
Cr. 8vo. 6*s.*
*OLIVIA MARY. *Cr. 8vo.* 6*s.*

Bagot (Richard). A ROMAN MYSTERY.
Third Edition. Cr. 8vo. 6*s.*
THE PASSPORT. *Fourth Edition.* Cr.
8vo. 6*s.*
ANTHONY CUTHBERT. *Fourth Edition.*
Cr. 8vo. 6*s.*
LOVE'S PROXY. *Cr. 8vo.* 6*s.*
DONNA DIANA. *Second Edition.* Cr.
8vo. 6*s.*
CASTING OF NETS. *Twelfth Edition.*
Cr. 8vo. 6*s.*
THE HOUSE OF SERRAVALLE. *Third
Edition. Cr. 8vo.* 6*s.*

Balley (H. C.). STORM AND TREASURE.
Third Edition. Cr. 8vo. 6*s.*
THE LONELY QUEEN. *Third Edition.*
Cr. 8vo. 6*s.*

Baring-Gould (S.). IN THE ROAR
OF THE SEA. *Eighth Edition. Cr. 8vo.*
6*s.*
MARGERY OF QUETHER. *Second
Edition. Cr. 8vo.* 6*s.*
THE QUEEN OF LOVE. *Fifth Edition.*
Cr. 8vo. 6*s.*
JACQUETTA. *Third Edition. Cr. 8vo.* 6*s.*
KITTY ALONE. *Fifth Edition. Cr. 8vo.* 6*s.*
NOÉMI. Illustrated. *Fourth Edition.* Cr.
8vo. 6*s.*
THE BROOM - SQUIRE. Illustrated.
Fifth Edition. Cr. 8vo. 6*s.*
DARTMOOR IDYLLS. *Cr. 8vo.* 6*s.*
GUAVAS THE TINNER. Illustrated.
Second Edition. Cr. 8vo. 6*s.*
BLADYS OF THE STEWPONEY. Illus-
trated. *Second Edition. Cr. 8vo.* 6*s.*
PABO THE PRIEST. *Cr. 8vo.* 6*s.*
WINEFRED. Illustrated. *Second Edition.*
Cr. 8vo. 6*s.*
ROYAL GEORGIE. Illustrated. *Cr. 8vo.* 6*s.*
CHRIS OF ALL SORTS. *Cr. 8vo.* 6*s.*
IN DEWISLAND. *Second Edition.* Cr.
8vo. 6*s.*
MRS. CURGENVEN OF CURGENVEN.
Fifth Edition. Cr. 8vo. 6*s.*

Barr (Robert). IN THE MIDST OF
ALARMS. *Third Edition. Cr. 8vo.* 6*s.*
THE COUNTESS TEKLA. *Fifth
Edition. Cr. 8vo.* 6*s.*
THE MUTABLE MANY. *Third Edition.*
Cr. 8vo. 6*s.*

Begbie (Harold). THE CURIOUS AND
DIVERTING ADVENTURES OF SIR
JOHN SPARROW, Bart. ; or, The
Progress of an Open Mind. *Second
Edition. Cr. 8vo.* 6*s.*

Belloc (H.). EMMANUEL BURDEN,
MERCHANT. Illustrated. *Second Edition.*
Cr. 8vo. 6*s.*
A CHANGE IN THE CABINET. *Third
Edition. Cr. 8vo.* 6*s.*

Belloc-Lowndes (Mrs.). THE CHINK
IN THE ARMOUR. *Fourth Edition.*
Cr. 8vo. 6*s.*
*MARY PECHELL. *Cr. 8vo.* 6*s.*

Bennett (Arnold). CLAYHANGER.
Tenth Edition. Cr. 8vo. 6*s.*
THE CARD. *Sixth Edition. Cr. 8vo.* 6*s.*
HILDA LESSWAYS. *Seventh Edition.*
Cr. 8vo. 6*s.*
* BURIED ALIVE. *A New Edition.*
Cr. 8vo. 6*s.*
A MAN FROM THE NORTH. *A New
Edition. Cr. 8vo.* 6*s.*
THE MATADOR OF THE FIVE TOWNS.
Second Edition. Cr. 8vo. 6*s.*

Benson (E. F.). DODO: A Detail of the
Day. *Sixteenth Edition. Cr. 8vo.* 6*s.*

Birmingham (George A.). SPANISH
GOLD. *Sixth Edition. Cr. 8vo.* 6*s.*
THE SEARCH PARTY. *Fifth Edition.*
Cr. 8vo. 6*s.*
LALAGE'S LOVERS. *Third Edition.* Cr.
8vo. 6*s.*

Bowen (Marjorie). I WILL MAIN-
TAIN. *Seventh Edition. Cr. 8vo.* 6*s.*
DEFENDER OF THE FAITH. *Fifth
Edition. Cr. 8vo.* 6*s.*
*A KNIGHT OF SPAIN. *Cr. 8vo.* 6*s.*
THE QUEST OF GLORY. *Third Edi-
tion. Cr. 8vo.* 6*s.*
GOD AND THE KING. *Fourth Edition.*
Cr. 8vo. 6*s.*

Clifford (Mrs. W. K.). THE GETTING
WELL OF DOROTHY. Illustrated.
Second Edition. Cr. 8vo. 3*s.* 6*d.*

Conrad (Joseph). THE SECRET AGENT:
A Simple Tale. *Fourth Ed. Cr. 8vo.* 6*s.*
A SET OF SIX. *Fourth Edition. Cr. 8vo.* 6*s.*
UNDER WESTERN EYES. *Second Ed.*
Cr. 8vo. 6*s.*

*Conyers (Dorothea.). THE LONELY MAN. *Cr. 8vo. 6s.*

Corelli (Marie). A ROMANCE OF TWO WORLDS. *Thirty-first Ed. Cr. 8vo. 6s.*
VENDETTA ; or, THE STORY OF ONE FORGOTTEN. *Twenty-ninth Edition. Cr. 8vo. 6s.*
THELMA : A NORWEGIAN PRINCESS. *Forty-second Edition. Cr. 8vo. 6s.*
ARDATH : THE STORY OF A DEAD SELF. *Twentieth Edition. Cr. 8vo. 6s.*
THE SOUL OF LILITH. *Seventeenth Edition. Cr. 8vo. 6s.*
WORMWOOD : A DRAMA OF PARIS. *Eighteenth Edition. Cr. 8vo. 6s.*
BARABBAS : A DREAM OF THE WORLD'S TRAGEDY. *Forty-sixth Edition. Cr. 8vo. 6s.*
THE SORROWS OF SATAN. *Fifty-seventh Edition. Cr. 8vo. 6s.*
THE MASTER-CHRISTIAN. *Thirteenth Edition. 179th Thousand. Cr. 8vo. 6s.*
TEMPORAL POWER : A STUDY IN SUPREMACY. *Second Edition. 150th Thousand. Cr. 8vo. 6s.*
GOD'S GOOD MAN : A SIMPLE LOVE STORY. *Fifteenth Edition. 154th Thousand. Cr. 8vo. 6s.*
HOLY ORDERS: THE TRAGEDY OF A QUIET LIFE. *Second Edition. 120th Thousand. Crown 8vo. 6s.*
THE MIGHTY ATOM. *Twenty-ninth Edition. Cr. 8vo. 6s.*
BOY : a Sketch. *Twelfth Edition. Cr. 8vo. 6s.*
CAMEOS. *Fourteenth Edition. Cr. 8vo. 6s.*
THE LIFE EVERLASTING. *Fifth Ed. Cr. 8vo. 6s.*

Crockett (S. R.). LOCHINVAR. Illustrated. *Third Edition. Cr. 8vo. 6s.*
THE STANDARD BEARER. *Second Edition. Cr. 8vo. 6s.*

Croker (B. M.). THE OLD CANTONMENT. *Second Edition. Cr. 8vo. 6s.*
JOHANNA. *Second Edition. Cr. 8vo. 6s.*
THE HAPPY VALLEY. *Fourth Edition. Cr. 8vo. 6s.*
A NINE DAYS' WONDER. *Fourth Edition. Cr. 8vo. 6s.*
PEGGY OF THE BARTONS. *Seventh Edition. Cr. 8vo. 6s.*
ANGEL. *Fifth Edition. Cr. 8vo. 6s.*
KATHERINE THE ARROGANT. *Sixth Edition. Cr. 8vo. 6s.*
BABES IN THE WOOD. *Fourth Edition. Cr. 8vo. 6s.*

Danby (Frank.). JOSEPH IN JEOPARDY. *Third Edition. Cr. 8vo. 6s.*

Doyle (Sir A. Conan). ROUND THE RED LAMP. *Twelfth Edition. Cr. 8vo. 6s.*

Fenn (G. Manville). SYD BELTON : THE BOY WHO WOULD NOT GO TO SEA. Illustrated. *Second Ed. Cr. 8vo. 3s. 6d.*

Findlater (J H.). THE GREEN GRAVES OF BALGOWRIE. *Fifth Edition. Cr. 8vo. 6s.*
THE LADDER TO THE STARS. *Second Edition. Cr. 8vo. 6s.*

Findlater (Mary). A NARROW WAY. *Third Edition. Cr. 8vo. 6s.*
OVER THE HILLS. *Second Edition. Cr. 8vo. 6s.*
THE ROSE OF JOY. *Third Edition. Cr. 8vo. 6s.*
A BLIND BIRD'S NEST. Illustrated. *Second Edition. Cr. 8vo. 6s.*

Fry (B. and C. B.). A MOTHER'S SON. *Fifth Edition. Cr. 8vo. 6s.*

Harraden (Beatrice). IN VARYING MOODS. *Fourteenth Edition. Cr. 8vo. 6s.*
HILDA STRAFFORD and THE REMITTANCE MAN. *Twelfth Ed. Cr. 8vo. 6s.*
INTERPLAY. *Fifth Edition. Cr. 8vo. 6s.*

Hichens (Robert). THE PROPHET OF BERKELEY SQUARE. *Second Edition. Cr. 8vo. 6s.*
TONGUES OF CONSCIENCE. *Third Edition. Cr. 8vo. 6s.*
THE WOMAN WITH THE FAN. *Eighth Edition. Cr. 8vo. 6s.*
BYEWAYS. *Cr. 8vo. 6s.*
THE GARDEN OF ALLAH. *Twenty-first Edition. Cr. 8vo. 6s.*
THE BLACK SPANIEL. *Cr. 8vo. 6s.*
THE CALL OF THE BLOOD. *Seventh Edition. Cr. 8vo. 6s.*
BARBARY SHEEP. *Second Edition. Cr. 8vo. 3s. 6d.*
THE DWELLER ON THE THRESHOLD. *Cr. 8vo. 6s.*

Hope (Anthony). THE GOD IN THE CAR. *Eleventh Edition. Cr. 8vo. 6s.*
A CHANGE OF AIR. *Sixth Edition. Cr. 8vo. 6s.*
A MAN OF MARK. *Seventh Ed. Cr. 8vo. 6s.*
THE CHRONICLES OF COUNT ANTONIO. *Sixth Edition. Cr. 8vo. 6s.*
PHROSO. Illustrated. *Eighth Edition. Cr. 8vo. 6s.*
SIMON DALE. Illustrated. *Eighth Edition. Cr. 8vo. 6s.*
THE KING'S MIRROR. *Fifth Edition. Cr. 8vo. 6s.*
QUISANTE. *Fourth Edition. Cr. 8vo. 6s.*
THE DOLLY DIALOGUES. *Cr. 8vo. 6s.*
TALES OF TWO PEOPLE. *Third Edition. Cr. 8vo. 6s.*
THE GREAT MISS DRIVER. *Fourth Edition. Cr. 8vo. 6s.*
MRS. MAXON PROTESTS. *Third Edition. Cr. 8vo. 6s.*

Hutten (Baroness von). THE HALO. *Fifth Edition. Cr. 8vo. 6s.*

'Inner Shrine' (Author of the). THE WILD OLIVE. *Third Edition.* Cr. 8vo. 6s.

Jacobs (W. W.). MANY CARGOES. *Thirty-second Edition.* Cr. 8vo. 3s. 6d.
*Also Illustrated in colour. Demy 8vo. 7s. 6d. net.
SEA URCHINS. *Sixteenth Edition.* Cr. 8vo. 3s. 6d.
A MASTER OF CRAFT. Illustrated. *Ninth Edition.* Cr. 8vo. 3s. 6d.
LIGHT FREIGHTS. Illustrated. *Eighth Edition.* Cr. 8vo. 3s. 6d.
THE SKIPPER'S WOOING. *Eleventh Edition.* Cr. 8vo. 3s. 6d.
AT SUNWICH PORT. Illustrated. *Tenth Edition.* Cr. 8vo. 3s. 6d.
DIALSTONE LANE. Illustrated. *Eighth Edition.* Cr. 8vo. 3s. 6d.
ODD CRAFT. Illustrated. *Fifth Edition.* Cr. 8vo. 3s. 6d.
THE LADY OF THE BARGE. Illustrated. *Ninth Edition.* Cr. 8vo. 3s. 6d.
SALTHAVEN. Illustrated. *Third Edition.* Cr. 8vo. 3s. 6d.
SAILORS' KNOTS. Illustrated. *Fifth Edition.* Cr. 8vo. 3s. 6d.
SHORT CRUISES. *Third Edition.* Cr. 8vo. 3s. 6d.

James (Henry). THE GOLDEN BOWL. *Third Edition.* Cr. 8vo. 6s

Le Queux (William). THE HUNCHBACK OF WESTMINSTER. *Third Edition.* Cr. 8vo. 6s.
THE CLOSED BOOK. *Third Edition.* Cr. 8vo. 6s.
THE VALLEY OF THE SHADOW. Illustrated. *Third Edition.* Cr. 8vo. 6s.
BEHIND THE THRONE. *Third Edition.* Cr. 8vo. 6s.

London (Jack). WHITE FANG. *Eighth Edition.* Cr. 8vo. 6s.

Lucas (E. V.). LISTENER'S LURE; AN OBLIQUE NARRATION. *Eighth Edition.* Fcap. 8vo. 5s.
OVER BEMERTON'S: AN EASY-GOING CHRONICLE. *Ninth Edition.* Fcap 8vo. 5s.
MR. INGLESIDE. *Eighth Edition.* Fcap. 8vo. 5s.
LONDON LAVENDER. Cr. 8vo. 6s.

Lyall (Edna). DERRICK VAUGHAN, NOVELIST. 44th Thousand. Cr. 8vo. 3s. 6d.

Macnaughtan (S.). THE FORTUNE OF CHRISTINA M'NAB. *Fifth Edition.* Cr. 8vo. 6s.
PETER AND JANE. *Fourth Edition.* Cr. 8vo. 6s.

Malet (Lucas). A COUNSEL OF PERFECTION. *Second Edition.* Cr. 8vo. 6s.

THE WAGES OF SIN. *Sixteenth Edition.* Cr. 8vo. 6s.
THE CARISSIMA. *Fifth Ed.* Cr. 8vo. 6s.
THE GATELESS BARRIER. *Fifth Edition.* Cr. 8vo. 6s.

Maxwell (W. B.). THE RAGGED MESSENGER. *Third Edition.* Cr. 8vo. 6s.
THE GUARDED FLAME. *Seventh Edition.* Cr. 8vo. 6s.
ODD LENGTHS. *Second Ed.* Cr. 8vo. 6s.
HILL RISE. *Fourth Edition.* Cr. 8vo. 6s.
THE COUNTESS OF MAYBURY: BETWEEN YOU AND I. *Fourth Edition.* Cr. 8vo. 6s.
THE REST CURE. *Fourth Edition.* Cr. 8vo. 6s.

Milne (A. A.). THE DAY'S PLAY. *Third Edition.* Cr. 8vo. 6s.
*THE HOLIDAY ROUND. Cr. 8vo. 6s.

Montague (C. E.). A HIND LET LOOSE. *Third Edition.* Cr. 8vo. 6s.

Morrison (Arthur). TALES OF MEAN STREETS. *Seventh Edition.* Cr. 8vo. 6s.
A CHILD OF THE JAGO. *Sixth Edition.* Cr. 8vo. 6s.
THE HOLE IN THE WALL. *Fourth Edition.* Cr. 8vo. 6s.
DIVERS VANITIES. Cr. 8vo. 6s.

Ollivant (Alfred). OWD BOB, THE GREY DOG OF KENMUIR. With a Frontispiece. *Eleventh Ed.* Cr. 8vo. 6s.
THE TAMING OF JOHN BLUNT. *Second Edition.* Cr. 8vo. 6s.
*THE ROYAL ROAD. Cr. 8vo. 6s.

Onions (Oliver). GOOD BOY SELDOM; A ROMANCE OF ADVERTISEMENT. *Second Edition.* Cr. 8vo. 6s.

Oppenheim (E. Phillips). MASTER OF MEN. *Fifth Edition.* Cr. 8vo. 6s.
THE MISSING DELORA. Illustrated. *Fourth Edition.* Cr. 8vo. 6s.

Orczy (Baroness). FIRE IN STUBBLE. *Fifth Edition.* Cr. 8vo. 6s.

Oxenham (John). A WEAVER OF WEBS. Illustrated. *Fifth Ed.* Cr. 8vo. 6s.
PROFIT AND LOSS. *Fourth Edition.* Cr. 8vo. 6s.
THE LONG ROAD. *Fourth Edition.* Cr. 8vo. 6s.
THE SONG OF HYACINTH, AND OTHER STORIES. *Second Edition.* Cr. 8vo. 6s.
MY LADY OF SHADOWS. *Fourth Edition.* Cr. 8vo. 6s.
LAURISTONS. *Fourth Edition.* Cr. 8vo. 6s.
THE COIL OF CARNE. *Sixth Edition.* Cr. 8vo. 6s.
*THE QUEST OF THE GOLDEN ROSE. Cr. 8vo. 6s.

Parker (Gilbert). PIERRE AND HIS PEOPLE. *Seventh Edition.* Cr. 8vo. 6s.

MRS. FALCHION. *Fifth Edition.* Cr. 8vo. 6s.

THE TRANSLATION OF A SAVAGE. *Fourth Edition.* Cr. 8vo. 6s.

THE TRAIL OF THE SWORD. Illustrated. *Tenth Edition.* Cr. 8vo. 6s.

WHEN VALMOND CAME TO PONTIAC: The Story of a Lost Napoleon. *Seventh Edition.* Cr. 8vo. 6s.

AN ADVENTURER OF THE NORTH. The Last Adventures of 'Pretty Pierre.' *Fifth Edition.* Cr. 8vo. 6s.

THE BATTLE OF THE STRONG: a Romance of Two Kingdoms. Illustrated. *Seventh Edition.* Cr. 8vo. 6s.

THE POMP OF THE LAVILETTES. *Third Edition.* Cr. 8vo. 3s. 6d.

NORTHERN LIGHTS. *Fourth Edition.* Cr. 8vo. 6s.

Pasture (Mrs. Henry de la). THE TYRANT. *Fourth Edition.* Cr. 8vo. 6s.

Pemberton (Max). THE FOOTSTEPS OF A THRONE. Illustrated. *Fourth Edition.* Cr. 8vo. 6s.

I CROWN THEE KING. Illustrated. Cr. 8vo. 6s.

LOVE THE HARVESTER: A STORY OF THE SHIRES. Illustrated. *Third Edition.* Cr. 8vo. 3s. 6d.

THE MYSTERY OF THE GREEN HEART. *Third Edition.* Cr. 8vo. 6s.

Perrin (Alice). THE CHARM. *Fifth Edition.* Cr. 8vo. 6s.

*THE ANGLO-INDIANS. Cr. 8vo. 6s.

Phillpotts (Eden). LYING PROPHETS. *Third Edition.* Cr. 8vo. 6s.

CHILDREN OF THE MIST. *Sixth Edition.* Cr. 8vo. 6s.

THE HUMAN BOY. With a Frontispiece. *Seventh Edition.* Cr. 8vo. 6s.

SONS OF THE MORNING. *Second Edition.* Cr. 8vo. 6s.

THE RIVER. *Fourth Edition.* Cr. 8vo. 6s.

THE AMERICAN PRISONER. *Fourth Edition.* Cr. 8vo. 6s.

KNOCK AT A VENTURE. *Third Edition.* Cr. 8vo. 6s.

THE PORTREEVE. *Fourth Edition.* Cr. 8vo. 6s.

THE POACHER'S WIFE. *Second Edition.* Cr. 8vo. 6s.

THE STRIKING HOURS. *Second Edition.* Cr. 8vo. 6s.

DEMETER'S DAUGHTER. *Third Edition.* Cr. 8vo. 6s.

Pickthall (Marmaduke). SAID THE FISHERMAN. *Eighth Edition.* Cr. 8vo. 6s.

'Q' (A. T. Quiller Couch). THE WHITE WOLF. *Second Edition.* Cr. 8vo. 6s.

THE MAYOR OF TROY. *Fourth Edition.* Cr. 8vo. 6s.

MERRY-GARDEN AND OTHER STORIES. Cr. 8vo. 6s.

MAJOR VIGOUREUX. *Third Edition.* Cr. 8vo. 6s.

Ridge (W. Pett). ERB. *Second Edition.* Cr. 8vo. 6s.

A SON OF THE STATE. *Third Edition.* Cr. 8vo. 3s. 6d.

A BREAKER OF LAWS. Cr. 8vo. 3s. 6d.

MRS. GALER'S BUSINESS. Illustrated. *Second Edition.* Cr. 8vo. 6s.

THE WICKHAMSES. *Fourth Edition.* Cr. 8vo. 6s.

NAME OF GARLAND. *Third Edition.* Cr. 8vo. 6s.

SPLENDID BROTHER. *Fourth Edition.* Cr. 8vo. 6s.

NINE TO SIX-THIRTY. *Third Edition.* Cr. 8vo. 6s.

THANKS TO SANDERSON. *Second Edition.* Cr. 8vo. 6s.

*DEVOTED SPARKES. Cr. 8vo. 6s.

Russell (W. Clark). MASTER ROCKA-FELLAR'S VOYAGE. Illustrated. *Fourth Edition.* Cr. 8vo. 3s. 6d.

Sidgwick (Mrs. Alfred). THE KINSMAN. Illustrated. *Third Edition.* Cr. 8vo. 6s.

THE LANTERN-BEARERS. *Third Edition.* Cr. 8vo. 6s.

ANTHEA'S GUEST. *Fifth Edition.* Cr. 8vo. 6s.

*LAMORNA. Cr. 8vo. 6s.

Somerville (E. Œ.) and Ross (Martin). DAN RUSSEL THE FOX. Illustrated. *Fourth Edition.* Cr. 8vo. 6s.

Thurston (E. Temple). MIRAGE. *Fourth Edition.* Cr. 8vo. 6s.

Watson (H. B. Marriott). THE HIGH TOBY. *Third Edition.* Cr. 8vo. 6s.

THE PRIVATEERS. Illustrated. *Second Edition.* Cr. 8vo. 6s.

ALISE OF ASTRA. *Third Edition.* Cr. 8vo. 6s.

THE BIG FISH. *Second Edition.* Cr. 8vo. 6s.

Webling (Peggy). THE STORY OF VIRGINIA PERFECT. *Third Edition.* Cr. 8vo. 6s.

THE SPIRIT OF MIRTH. *Fifth Edition.* Cr. 8vo. 6s.

FELIX CHRISTIE. *Second Edition.* Cr. 8vo. 6s.

Weyman (Stanley). UNDER THE RED ROBE. Illustrated. *Twenty-third Edition.* Cr. 8vo. 6s.

Whitby (Beatrice). ROSAMUND. *Second Edition.* Cr. 8vo. 6s.

Williamson (C. N. and A. M.). THE LIGHTNING CONDUCTOR: The Strange Adventures of a Motor Car. Illustrated. *Seventeenth Edition. Cr. 8vo. 6s.* Also *Cr. 8vo. 1s. net.*

THE PRINCESS PASSES: A Romance of a Motor. Illustrated. *Ninth Edition. Cr. 8vo. 6s.*

LADY BETTY ACROSS THE WATER. *Eleventh Edition. Cr. 8vo. 6s.*

SCARLET RUNNER. Illustrated. *Third Edition. Cr. 8vo. 6s.*

SET IN SILVER. Illustrated. *Fourth Edition. Cr. 8vo. 6s.*

LORD LOVELAND DISCOVERS AMERICA. *Second Edition. Cr. 8vo. 6s.*

THE GOLDEN SILENCE. *Sixth Edition. Cr. 8vo. 6s.*

THE GUESTS OF HERCULES. *Third Edition. Cr. 8vo. 6s.*

*THE HEATHER MOON. *Cr. 8vo. 6s.*

Wyllarde (Dolf). THE PATHWAY OF THE PIONEER (Nous Autres). *Sixth Edition. Cr. 8vo. 6s.*

THE UNOFFICIAL HONEYMOON. *Seventh Edition. Cr. 8vo. 6s.*

THE CAREER OF BEAUTY DARLING. *Cr. 8vo. 6s.*

Methuen's Two-Shilling Novels.

Crown 8vo. 2s. net.

*BOTOR CHAPERON, THE. C. N. and A. M. Williamson.

*CALL OF THE BLOOD, THE. Robert Hichens.

CAR OF DESTINY AND ITS ERRAND IN SPAIN, THE. C. N. and A. M. Williamson.

CLEMENTINA. A. E. W. Mason.

COLONEL ENDERBY'S WIFE. Lucas Malet.

FELIX. Robert Hichens.

GATE OF THE DESERT, THE. John Oxenham.

MY FRIEND THE CHAUFFEUR. C. N. and A. M. Williamson.

PRINCESS VIRGINIA, THE. C. N. and A. M. Williamson.

SEATS OF THE MIGHTY, THE. Sir Gilbert Parker.

SERVANT OF THE PUBLIC, A. Anthony Hope.

*SET IN SILVER. C. N. and A. M. Williamson.

SEVERINS, THE. Mrs. Alfred Sidgwick.

SIR RICHARD CALMADY. Lucas Malet.

*VIVIEN. W. B. Maxwell.

Books for Boys and Girls.

Illustrated. Crown 8vo. 3s. 6d.

CROSS AND DAGGER. The Crusade of the Children, 1212. W. Scott Durrant.

GETTING WELL OF DOROTHY, THE. Mrs. W. K. Clifford.

GIRL OF THE PEOPLE, A. L. T. Meade.

HEPSY GIPSY. L. T. Meade. 2s. 6d.

HONOURABLE MISS, THE. L. T. Meade.

MASTER ROCKAFELLAR'S VOYAGE. W. Clark Russell.

ONLY A GUARD-ROOM DOG. Edith E. Cuthell.

RED GRANGE, THE. Mrs. Molesworth.

SYD BELTON: The Boy who would not go to Sea. G. Manville Fenn.

THERE WAS ONCE A PRINCE. Mrs. M. E. Mann.

Methuen's Shilling Novels.

*ANNA OF THE FIVE TOWNS. Arnold Bennett.
BARBARY SHEEP. Robert Hichens.
CHARM, THE. Alice Perrin.
*DEMON, THE. C. N. and A. M. Williamson
GUARDED FLAME, THE. W. B. Maxwell.
JANE. Marie Corelli.
LADY BETTY ACROSS THE WATER. C. N
 & A. M. Williamson.
*LONG ROAD, THE. John Oxenham.
MIGHTY ATOM, THE. Marie Corelli.
MIRAGE. E. Temple Thurston.
MISSING DELORA, THE. E Phillips Oppen-
 heim.

ROUND THE RED LAMP. Sir A. Conan Doyle.
*SECRET WOMAN, THE. Eden Phillpotts.
*SEVERINS, THE. Mrs. Alfred Sidgwick.
SPANISH GOLD. G. A. Birmingham.
TALES OF MEAN STREETS. Arthur Morrison.
THE HALO. The Baroness von Hutten.
*TYRANT, THE. Mrs. Henry de la Pasture.
UNDER THE RED ROBE. Stanley J. Weyman.
VIRGINIA PERFECT. Peggy Webling.
WOMAN WITH THE FAN, THE. Robert
 Hichens.

The Novels of Alexandre Dumas.

Medium 8vo. Price 6d. Double Volumes, 1s.

ACTÉ.
ADVENTURES OF CAPTAIN PAMPHILE, THE.
AMAURY.
BIRD OF FATE, THE.
BLACK TULIP, THE.
BLACK : the Story of a Dog.
CASTLE OF EPPSTEIN, THE.
CATHERINE BLUM.
CÉCILE.
CHÂTELET, THE.
CHEVALIER D'HARMENTAL, THE. (Double
 volume.)
CHICOT THE JESTER.
CHICOT REDIVIVUS.
COMTE DE MONTGOMMERY, THE.
CONSCIENCE.
CONVICT'S SON, THE.
CORSICAN BROTHERS, THE; and OTHO THE
 ARCHER.
CROP-EARED JACQUOT.
DOM GORENFLOT.
DUC D'ANJOU, THE.
FATAL COMBAT, THE.
FENCING MASTER, THE.
FERNANDE.
GABRIEL LAMBERT.
GEORGES.
GREAT MASSACRE, THE.
HENRI DE NAVARRE.
HÉLÈNE DE CHAVERNY.

HOROSCOPE, THE.
LEONE-LEONA.
LOUISE DE LA VALLIÈRE. (Double volume.)
MAN IN THE IRON MASK, THE. (Double
 volume.)
MAÎTRE ADAM.
MOUTH OF HELL, THE.
NANON. (Double volume.)
OLYMPIA.
PAULINE; PASCAL BRUNO; and BONTEKOE.
PÈRE LA RUINE.
PORTE SAINT-ANTOINE, THE.
PRINCE OF THIEVES, THE.
REMINISCENCES OF ANTONY, THE.
ST. QUENTIN.
ROBIN HOOD.
SAMUEL GELB.
SNOWBALL AND THE SULTANETTA, THE.
SYLVANDIRE.
TAKING OF CALAIS, THE.
TALES OF THE SUPERNATURAL.
TALES OF STRANGE ADVENTURE.
TALES OF TERROR.
THREE MUSKETEERS, THE. (Double volume.)
TOURNEY OF THE RUE ST. ANTOINE.
TRAGEDY OF NANTES, THE.
TWENTY YEARS AFTER. (Double volume.)
WILD-DUCK SHOOTER, THE.
WOLF-LEADER, THE.

Methuen's Sixpenny Books.

Medium 8vo.

Albanesi (E. Maria). LOVE AND LOUISA.
I KNOW A MAIDEN.
THE BLUNDER OF AN INNOCENT.
PETER A PARASITE.
*THE INVINCIBLE AMELIA.

Anstey (F.). A BAYARD OF BENGAL.

Austen (J.). PRIDE AND PREJUDICE.

Bagot (Richard). A ROMAN MYSTERY.
CASTING OF NETS.
DONNA DIANA.

Balfour (Andrew). BY STROKE OF SWORD.

Baring-Gould (S.). FURZE BLOOM.
CHEAP JACK ZITA.
KITTY ALONE.
URITH.
THE BROOM SQUIRE.
IN THE ROAR OF THE SEA.
NOÉMI.
A BOOK OF FAIRY TALES. Illustrated.
LITTLE TU'PENNY.
WINEFRED.
THE FROBISHERS.
THE QUEEN OF LOVE.
ARMINELL.
BLADYS OF THE STEWPONEY.
CHRIS OF ALL SORTS.

Barr (Robert). JENNIE BAXTER.
IN THE MIDST OF ALARMS.
THE COUNTESS TEKLA.
THE MUTABLE MANY.

Benson (E. F.). DODO.
THE VINTAGE.

Brontë (Charlotte). SHIRLEY.

Brownell (C. L.). THE HEART OF JAPAN.

Burton (J. Bloundelle). ACROSS THE SALT SEAS.

Caffyn (Mrs.). ANNE MAULEVERER.

Capes (Bernard). THE GREAT SKENE MYSTERY.

Clifford (Mrs. W. K.). A FLASH OF SUMMER.
MRS. KEITH'S CRIME.

Corbett (Julian). A BUSINESS IN GREAT WATERS.

Croker (Mrs. B. M.). ANGEL.
A STATE SECRET.
PEGGY OF THE BARTONS.
JOHANNA.

Dante (Alighieri). THE DIVINE COMEDY (Cary).

Doyle (Sir A. Conan). ROUND THE RED LAMP.

Duncan (Sara Jeannette). THOSE DELIGHTFUL AMERICANS.

Eliot (George). THE MILL ON THE FLOSS.

Findlater (Jane H.). THE GREEN GRAVES OF BALGOWRIE.

Gallon (Tom). RICKERBY'S FOLLY.

Gaskell (Mrs.). CRANFORD.
MARY BARTON.
NORTH AND SOUTH.

Gerard (Dorothea). HOLY MATRIMONY.
THE CONQUEST OF LONDON.
MADE OF MONEY.

Gissing (G.). THE TOWN TRAVELLER.
THE CROWN OF LIFE.

Glanville (Ernest). THE INCA'S TREASURE.
THE KLOOF BRIDE.

Gleig (Charles). BUNTER'S CRUISE.

Grimm (The Brothers). GRIMM'S FAIRY TALES.

Hope (Anthony). A MAN OF MARK.
A CHANGE OF AIR.
THE CHRONICLES OF COUNT ANTONIO.
PHROSO.
THE DOLLY DIALOGUES.

Hornung (E. W.). DEAD MEN TELL NO TALES.

Hyne (C. J. C.). PRINCE RUPERT THE BUCCANEER.

Ingraham (J. H.). THE THRONE OF DAVID.

Le Queux (W.). THE HUNCHBACK OF WESTMINSTER.
THE CROOKED WAY.
THE VALLEY OF THE SHADOW.

Levett-Yeats (S. K.). THE TRAITOR'S WAY.
ORRAIN.

Linton (E. Lynn). THE TRUE HISTORY OF JOSHUA DAVIDSON.

Lyall (Edna). DERRICK VAUGHAN.

Malet (Lucas). THE CARISSIMA.
A COUNSEL OF PERFECTION.

Mann (Mrs. M. E.). MRS. PETER HOWARD.
A LOST ESTATE.
THE CEDAR STAR.
THE PATTEN EXPERIMENT.
A WINTER'S TALE.

Marchmont (A. W.). MISER HOADLEY'S SECRET.
A MOMENT'S ERROR.

Marryat (Captain). PETER SIMPLE.
JACOB FAITHFUL.

March (Richard). A METAMORPHOSIS.
THE TWICKENHAM PEERAGE.
THE GODDESS.
THE JOSS.

Mason (A. E. W.). CLEMENTINA

Mathers (Helen). HONEY.
GRIFF OF GRIFFITHSCOURT
SAM'S SWEETHEART.
THE FERRYMAN.

Meade (Mrs. L. T.). DRIFT.

Miller (Esther). LIVING LIES.

Mitford (Bertram). THE SIGN OF THE SPIDER.

Montrésor (F. F.). THE ALIEN.

Morrison (Arthur). THE HOLE IN THE WALL.

Nesbit (E.). THE RED HOUSE.

Norris (W. E.). HIS GRACE.
GILES INGILBY.
THE CREDIT OF THE COUNTY.
LORD LEONARD THE LUCKLESS.
MATTHEW AUSTEN.
CLARISSA FURIOSA.

Oliphant (Mrs.). THE LADY'S WALK
SIR ROBERT'S FORTUNE.

THE PRODIGALS.
THE TWO MARYS.

Oppenheim (E. P.). MASTER OF MEN.

Parker (Sir Gilbert). THE POMP OF THE LAVILETTES.
WHEN VALMOND CAME TO PONTIAC.
THE TRAIL OF THE SWORD.

Pemberton (Max). THE FOOTSTEPS OF A THRONE.
I CROWN THEE KING.

Phillpotts (Eden). THE HUMAN BOY.
CHILDREN OF THE MIST.
THE POACHER'S WIFE.
THE RIVER.

'Q' (A. T. Quiller Couch). THE WHITE WOLF.

Ridge (W. Pett). A SON OF THE STATE.
LOST PROPERTY.
GEORGE and THE GENERAL.
A BREAKER OF LAWS.
ERB.

Russell (W. Clark). ABANDONED.
A MARRIAGE AT SEA.
MY DANISH SWEETHEART.
HIS ISLAND PRINCESS.

Sergeant (Adeline). THE MASTER OF BEECHWOOD.
BALBARA'S MONEY.
THE YELLOW DIAMOND.
THE LOVE THAT OVERCAME.

Sidgwick (Mrs. Alfred). THE KINSMAN.

Surtees (R. S.). HANDLEY CROSS.
MR. SPONGE'S SPORTING TOUR.
ASK MAMMA.

Walford (Mrs. L. B.). MR. SMITH.
COUSINS.
THE BABY'S GRANDMOTHER.
TROUBLESOME DAUGHTERS.

Wallace (General Lew). BEN-HUR.
THE FAIR GOD.

Watson (H. B. Marriott). THE ADVENTURERS.
CAPTAIN FORTUNE.

Weekes (A. B.). PRISONERS OF WAR.

Wells (H. G.). THE SEA LADY.

Whitby (Beatrice). THE RESULT OF AN ACIDENT.

White (Percy). A PASSIONATE PILGRIM.

Williamson (Mrs. C. N.). PAPA.

CPSIA information can be obtained at www.ICGtesting.com
Printed in the USA
BVOW040320081112

305022BV00003B/7/P